Better Homes and Gardens®

Gardening in the Shade

Anne Halpin

Better Homes and Gardens® Books
Des Moines

BETTER HOMES AND GARDENS® Books
An Imprint of Meredith® Books

GARDENING IN THE SHADE

Senior Editor: Marsha Jahns
Associate Art Director: Lynda Haupert
Designer: Linda Vermie
Illustrator: Gary Palmer
Copy Editor: Mary Helen Schiltz
Proofreaders: Terry Frederickson,
 Sharon Novotne O'Keefe
Indexer: Kathleen Poole
Production Manager: Douglas Johnston
Special thanks: Tom Pellett, garden designer

Director, New Product Development:
 Ray Wolf
Managing Editor: Christopher Cavanaugh

MEREDITH PUBLISHING GROUP

President, Publishing Group:
 Christopher Little
Vice President and Publishing Director:
 John P. Loughlin

MEREDITH CORPORATION

Chairman of the Board and Chief Executive
 Officer: Jack D. Rehm
President and Chief Operating Officer:
 William T. Kerr

Chairman of the Executive Committee:
 E. T. Meredith III

© Copyright 1996 by Meredith Corporation,
 Des Moines, Iowa.
All rights reserved. Printed in the United
 States of America.
First Edition. Printing Number and Year:
 5 4 3 2 1   00 99 98 97 96
Library of Congress Catalog Card Number:
 95-81772
ISBN: 0-696-04652-0

*All of us at Better Homes and Gardens® Books are
dedicated to providing you with the information and
ideas you need to garden successfully. We guarantee
your satisfaction with this book for as long as you own
it. If you have any questions, comments, or
suggestions, please write to us at:*

MEREDITH® BOOKS
Gardening Books
Editorial Department   RW 240
1716 Locust St.
Des Moines, IA 50309-3023

PHOTOGRAPHERS:
Ernest Braun: 85 (center), 87 (bottom), 140 (top)
Kim Brun: 31 (top)
Guy Burgess: 141 (bottom right)
David Cavagnaro: 64 (left), 177 (center right)
Crandall & Crandall: back cover, 59 (left), 91 (right), 119 (right inset), 125 (bottom left and top right), 126 (top right), 129 (bottom left and bottom right), 130 (bottom right)
Stephen Cridland: 31 (bottom)
R. Todd Davis: back cover, 16 (right inset), 36 (inset), 68 (right), 72 (bottom), 74 (left), 75, 76, 80 (top), 94 (top right), 109 (bottom right), 118 (top right), 119 (right), 120 (bottom right), 127 (bottom left), 128 (top right), 151 (bottom left), 157 (top) 161, 163, 169, 174 (top), 183 (top right), 184, 186 (top left)
Mike Dieter: 116 (top right)
Derek Fell: 65, 90 (center and bottom), 91 (left), 92 (center), 99 (right), 113 (top right), 119 (left), 124 (top), 154, 157 (bottom), 158–160, 165, 168 (bottom left), 170 (inset), 172 (top), 173, 174 (bottom), 175 (top right), 176 (left), 177 (top), 178, 180 (bottom), 181, 183 (left), 185 (top right and bottom right)
Randy Foulds: 22–23, 57 (top),
George deGennaro: 48–49, 147 (bottom)
Susan Gilmore: 23 (inset), 50
Karlis Grants: 9 (top), 17 (bottom), 78 (bottom)
Bob Hawks: 13, 21 (bottom)
Hedrick Blessing: 101 (right)
Bill Helms: 94 (top left), 140 (bottom)
Saxon Holt: 26, 27, 36, 57 (bottom), 58 (right), 62, 63 (right), 81, 108 (left), 146 (bottom), 148 (top), 156, 179, 187 (top left)
William Hopkins: 105 (top)
Jon Jensen: 12 (bottom), 33 (bottom right), 97 (top left), 134 (bottom left)
Mike Jensen: 17 (top), 22
Dency Kane: back cover, 6–7, 28–29, 34–35, 37, 42–43, 44 (top), 45, 64 (bottom right), 72 (top), 78 (top), 79, 83, 94 (bottom), 97 (top right and bottom right), 98 (left), 100 (top left and top center), 101 (left), 103 (bottom right), 107 (top right), 108 (bottom right), 109 (top right), 111, 113 (bottom right), 115 (bottom), 117 (left and inset left), 118 (left), 120 (center right), 122 (bottom right), 130 (left and top right), 137 (top), 139 (bottom), 141 (left), 146 (center), 149 (bottom right), 152–153, 155, 164 (bottom), 170 (top), 171 (top), 175 (bottom left),185 (center top)
Peter Krumhardt: 91 (inset), 92 (left), 104 (top right), 131 (right), 133 (top right), 135 (left and top)
Barbara Martin: 85 (bottom), 86
Maris/Semel: 11, 32, 33 (top and bottom left), 58 (left), 95 (top left and left inset), 109 (left), 124 (center), 126 (top left), 132 (bottom), 133 (top left), 134 (top left), 142 (right), 143 (bottom right), 144 (center), 185 (top left, center left, and bottom left)
Jerry Pavia: back cover, 8, 10, 13 (bottom), 14, 15, 16 (left), 20, 24–25, 28, 29, 30, 35, 46, 47, 49 (top), 50–51, 55, 59 (right), 60–61, 63 (top right), 66 (top right), 69 (bottom right), 70 (right), 71 (right), 73, 74 (right), 77 (top), 80 (bottom), 84, 85 (top), 87 (top), 90 (top), 93 (top left), 95 (top right and top right inset), 96, 98 (top right and bottom right), 99 (bottom left), 100 (top right and bottom right), 103 (top left and top right), 104 (left and bottom right), 105 (left), 106 (right), 107 (top left and bottom), 110 (top right), 112 (top left), 121 (top right and bottom right), 123 (bottom left), 126 (bottom right), 127 (top left), 128 (top left), 129 (top right), 131 (left), 137 (center and bottom), 138 (top and center), 141 (top right), 143 (left and right), 144 (top right), 145 (bottom right), 147 (top), 148 (bottom), 149 (top left), 164 (top), 171 (bottom), 172 (bottom), 176 (bottom right), 180 (top)
Joanne Pavia: 125 (bottom right), 139 (top), 142 (left), 151 (top right)
PHOTO NATS: 39 (top), 56, 63 (left), 66 (left and bottom right), 67, 69 (top left and top right), 71 (left), 93 (top right and bottom), 114 (top right and bottom right), 115 (top), 116 (bottom right), 118 (bottom right), 120 (top right), 122 (top left and top right), 123 (right), 128 (bottom), 134 (right), 135 (bottom right), 136, 138 (bottom inset), 144 (bottom right), 145 (top right and bottom left), 150 (bottom), 151 (bottom right), 182 (inset)
Mary Carolyn Pindar: 68 (left)
Susan Roth: front cover, back cover, 4–5, 11 (inset), 12 (top), 13 (top), 18 (bottom), 19, 21 (top), 38, 39 (bottom), 44 (bottom), 48, 54, 70 (left), 77 (inset), 82, 88–89, 106 (bottom), 108 (top right), 110 (bottom), 112 (bottom left), 113 (top left), 114 (bottom left), 120 (left), 123 (top), 124 (bottom), 127 (top right), 132 (top right), 150 (top), 166–167, 168 (top), 177 (bottom right), 186 (bottom left)
Bill Stites: 9 (bottom), 18 (top), 99 (top left), 134 (center left)
M. Stouffer: 31 (inset)
Rick Taylor: 128 (top inset), 187 (top right)

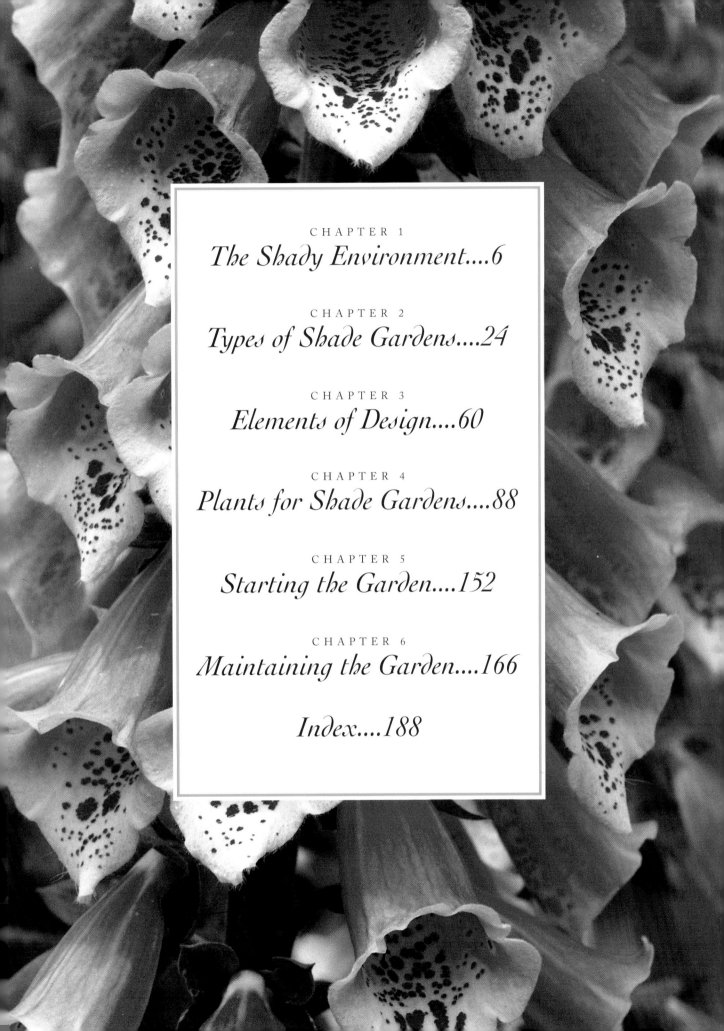

Introduction

The shady garden is a garden of many delights. Shade is often considered a drawback where gardens are concerned, because it limits the gardener's choice of plants to an extent. But shade can be an asset rather than a liability. A shady garden is a much more comfortable place to be on a hot summer day than a garden in full sun. It feels good to get outdoors to weed, water, and deadhead if you can do it in the shade. And shade is more hospitable for plants as well as people. In fact, in warm climates where the summer sun is fierce, afternoon shade is necessary for the survival of many plants. If you live in the South, shade can actually extend the range of plants you can grow, rather than limit it.

Shade brings a touch of mystery to the garden, which can make for a more intimate experience. The dim light allows for surprises. Imagine strolling along a winding path through a woodland garden—there's always something new to discover around the next bend. Woodland and the other natural garden styles that work so well in shady settings also bring the bonus of wildlife. If you plant some shrubs and trees to provide berries and cover for birds and small animals, and add a source of water, you will be able to share your backyard oasis with a host of other creatures.

Shady gardens are full of a special, quiet beauty. The subtle colors and interesting shapes of shade plants can be quite sophisticated and wonderfully soothing. Instead of blazing red and brassy yellows, you will work mostly with luminous whites and soft pastels. Instead of hulking sunflowers and blowsy dahlias, the garden is filled with smaller, more delicate flowers—gracefully spurred columbines, fluffy astilbes, the cheerful dangling lockets of bleeding heart. Shade offers opportunities to feature foliage plants as well as flowers. There are ferns of many textures, ground covers with variegated leaves, and the diverse, colorful range of hostas, coleus, and caladiums.

Finally, shady gardens are often easier to maintain than sunny ones. They don't need to be watered or fertilized as often as sunny gardens. Fewer weeds grow, and there are generally fewer pests to contend with.

So welcome to the shady garden. This book will help you transform your shady site into a lush oasis full of flourishing plants.

CHAPTER ONE

The Shady Environment

Shade is not the same in every shady garden. There are different kinds and degrees of shade, and understanding which type you are dealing with makes it easier to choose plants that will thrive in your garden. Although horticulturalists and gardeners define shade in different ways, most would agree on five categories of shade: partial shade, light shade, medium shade, full shade, and dense shade.

Types of Shade

Partial shade, which sometimes is called **open shade** or **semishade,** is the lightest, most open type of shade and the easiest kind to work with. Partial shade is found in locations that receive three to six hours of sun a day, either in the morning or in the afternoon. Partial shade also describes locations that are in lightly dappled sunlight all day. A garden located to the east or west of a tall hedge, wall, building, or other solid object will be in partial shade because it's in shadow for part of the day and sun for part of the day. You can find the dappled kind of partial shade under an arbor, lath house, or lattice that is not covered with dense, leafy vines such as grapes or wisteria. Many plants grow well in partial shade, and you'll have plenty of choices for your garden.

Light shade, or **thin shade,** is the next degree of shadiness. You'll find light shade under the branches of slender, young trees, or under more mature trees with a high, lacy canopy.

Trees whose leaves are small and whose lowest branches are high above the ground cast light shade. On the ground underneath, shifting patterns of light and shadow change throughout the day, as some of the sun's rays penetrate spaces between the leaves.

Trees or buildings located some distance from the garden also can cast light shade. The garden is outside the deepest shadows but still receives some shade from these objects.

A garden in light shade may receive full, unobstructed sun for just an hour or two during the day, but it's bright enough the rest of the time to support the growth of a variety of

ABOVE: Conditions of light shade can be found under trees with a light, high canopy of foliage that allows bright light and an occasional shaft of sunlight to reach the ground.
RIGHT: A garden that receives full shade for a few hours and partial shade the rest of the day also can be considered lightly shaded.

The Shady Environment

ABOVE: Many gardens have more than one type of shade. Here, the area on the left receives medium to full shade, while the area on the right is in light to medium shade.

LEFT: Shade changes throughout the day and from season to season. The azaleas in front of this house receive some sun in the morning but are shaded in the afternoon.

plants. Light shade also can be defined as full shade for two to three hours a day and partial shade the rest of the day.

Medium shade, or **half shade,** is the kind of shade that's comfortable on a hot day. You'll find medium shade under trees with branches 20 feet or more off the ground and a fairly open canopy. Some people call this high shade.

Medium shade also occurs where there is reflected sunlight or where shade is cast by a north-facing wall but no other barrier blocks the light. In addition, medium shade may be defined as an area that is shady for four or five of the brightest daylight hours, but receives sun at other times.

Many plants grow well in medium shade. Examples include daylilies (*Hemerocallis* species and hybrids), wax begonias (*Begonia* x *semperflorens-cultorum*), fuchsias, impatiens, wood anemone (*Anemone nemorosa*), oak-leaf hydrangea (*Hydrangea quercifolia*), and some rhododendrons.

Plants not naturally found in medium shade adapt to it in different ways. For example, flowers native to woodlands with heavier dappled shade respond to the hours of brighter sun they receive in a garden with light or half shade by producing more flowers, smaller leaves, and shorter stems.

TOP LEFT: A garden on the east side of a lattice fence still receives plenty of morning light, and the lattice filters the hot afternoon sun.
BOTTOM LEFT: To let in more light for plants growing under tall trees, prune lower branches to raise the canopy.

The Shady Environment

ABOVE: The versatile impatiens grows in either sun or shade, and its shallow roots allow planting around the base of a tree.
INSET: Daylilies, too, thrive in sun or partial to light shade. Here, 'Mary Todd' grows near the front of a shady border.

ABOVE: The white foamflowers in the front of this garden flourish even though they receive more sun than in the woodland environments to which they are native.

RIGHT: Trilliums and other woodland wildflowers will adapt to lighter shade in the garden.

Wood anemone (*Anemone nemorosa*) and trilliums (*Trillium* species) behave this way.

Not all plants, however, respond favorably to increased light. Blood-root (*Sanguinaria canadensis*) and shooting star (*Dodecatheon* species) go into dormancy earlier than usual when they're grown in brighter conditions, and the plants may die out after a few years.

The Shady Environment

The garden palette begins to narrow seriously in conditions of **full shade.** Full shade exists beneath the branches of mature trees with dense foliage, usually large leaves, and a spreading canopy. Maples and oaks, unless they're pruned to raise and lighten the canopy, cast full shade during the growing season when they're in leaf. Full shade also is found under trees with low but fairly open branches, such as redbud, hemlock, and dogwood, and near the base of a tall, north-facing wall or hedge.

The best plants for fully shaded conditions are those found in the woods in their native habitats. Hellebores (*Helleborus* species) can stand full shade, as can trailing arbutus (*Epigaea repens*), wild ginger (*Asarum* species), wintergreen (*Gaultheria procumbens*), ivy (*Hedera* species), pachysandra, hostas, most ferns, and violets (*Viola* species).

The worst shade for plants is **dense** or **heavy shade.** Dense shade is the deep, cool shadow cast year-round by mature evergreen trees or by a nearby building. A location on the north side of a tall building is the worst place to garden. Not only is a location in heavy shade cold and dark, but it also is likely to be dry, because the building and trees keep much of the rainfall from reaching the ground.

Probably the best way to deal with dense shade is to put in a deck, patio, or area of hardscape (pavement), and grow shade-tolerant flowers and ferns in containers that you rotate into and out of the area. Don't try to create a permanent garden there. After a few weeks in the shade, move the plants to a brighter location to let them regain their strength.

In the full shade found beneath mature deciduous trees, woodland plants such as foamflower and blue phlox are a good source of color.

The quality of shade is determined by a variety of factors, not just the daily duration. You need to consider all these influences if you want to understand the environment of a potential garden spot.

English ivy and ferns will grow in even the heavy shade of a city courtyard.

ABOVE: One way to garden on a shady
site is to locate the garden some distance
away from the densest trees, to make the best
use of available light.

RIGHT: The open construction of this wall
allows the homeowner to have the formal
look of brick while admitting additional light
for these hostas, begonias, and saxifrage.

The Shady Environment

Shade and Time of Day

The time of day your garden is shaded is important; shade in the afternoon is different from shade in the morning. As a rule, afternoon shade is easier on plants than morning shade.

A location that is shaded in the morning stays cooler longer after the drop in temperature that occurs overnight. If that area is suddenly thrown into sunlight at noon or early in the afternoon, when the sun is most intense, the temperature rises sharply. Plants are exposed to a lot of heat all at once and can become stressed. If the area remains sunny throughout the afternoon, the plants may bake.

The problem is especially acute for plants growing immediately to the west of a brick or masonry wall. The location will catch the hot afternoon sun, and the wall will absorb and retain heat, making the garden even hotter.

Morning and Afternoon Sun

Consider how different the environment is in a garden that is sunny in the morning and shady in the afternoon. Morning sun doesn't reach its full intensity for several hours, allowing plant tissues, the soil, and the air in the garden, to warm up gradually after the cool night. By the time the sun becomes hot, the plants already are partially warm. Before air and soil temperatures hit their daily peak, the garden is in the shade. Conditions are altogether more moderate where there is morning sun and afternoon shade than where there is morning shade and afternoon sun.

If you have a choice between morning sun and afternoon sun when selecting a spot for a shady garden, opt for morning sun. A location to the east of a hedge, fence, trees, tall shrubs, or even a building often is a good place for plants. The garden receives sun all morning and cooling shade from early to midafternoon. It isn't exposed to the worst heat of the day. If your location is next to a building or wall made of brick, stone, concrete, or stucco, however, the masonry will store heat when exposed to the sun and radiate the heat back into the air during the afternoon when the garden is shaded. The environment in this garden will be extremely warm in the afternoon, so choose plants that can tolerate heat.

A location on the east side of a fence, wall, hedge, or trees often is a congenial spot for a shady garden.

A west-facing brick patio or wall can become very hot when exposed to afternoon sun, making it a difficult location for all but the toughest plants, such as English ivy.

Tree Shade vs. Building Shade

The object casting the shade also affects the quality of the shade. Very simply, shade cast by deciduous trees is better than shade cast by evergreens. Both types of tree shade generally are preferable to shade cast by a building or solid wall.

The shadow of a solid object is uniformly dark. Evergreens—especially old, heavy ones—cast their dense shade year-round. The leaves of deciduous trees, however, are gone for half the year. When present, the leaves allow some sunlight through, making their shade less deep. A gardener can work with the shade of deciduous trees, as will be explained later.

Trees with small leaves and a fairly light, high, open canopy are the best kind under which to garden. Honey locust, Lombardy poplar, and birches can support gardens in their shade. Oaks often have their branches relatively high above the ground, and willow oaks have slender leaves, making them good choices for shade gardening. Sweet gum, too, has high branches and open leaves.

Don't plant under good shade trees—trees with large leaves and heavy canopies—and under trees with shallow, wide-spreading roots. Any plant growing within a tree's root zone must compete with the tree for moisture and nutrients, and trees with especially greedy root systems will outcompete the smaller, less aggressive roots of garden plants.

Consequently, avoid planting Norway maple, sugar maple, box elder, silver maple, horse chestnut, sycamore, tulip tree, black walnut, and white pine. Elms are lovely shade trees, and resistant varieties are becoming available, but their shallow roots make gardening nearby difficult. Black walnut is especially bad because its roots and fallen leaves produce an allelopathic chemical called juglone, which is toxic to some plants.

ABOVE: There's enough light at the edge of this shady garden for hostas, astilbe, and even a hydrangea.
LEFT: If you can choose between shade cast by trees or shade cast by a building when selecting a site for your garden, choose tree shade.

Northern Exposures

A location on the north side of a hill or high wall receives little or no direct sun at ground level and can be a problematic—but not impossible—place for a garden. If the area is open to the sky and unobstructed except for the wall or hill, or if additional light can be reflected into the garden as described later in this chapter, a garden should be possible. Choosing shade-tolerant plants and employing a few specialized strategies will allow your north-facing garden to thrive.

A north-facing garden will receive the most light in spring and summer, when the sun is highest in the sky. By autumn, light levels will be substantially reduced. It makes sense, then, to plan a garden for maximum interest in spring and summer. If you include flowering plants, choose spring and summer bloomers.

Spring Mulching

North-facing gardens are shady in the morning and likely to be briefly thrust into sunlight around midday, when the sun is hottest. To moderate the sudden, severe temperature swings possible in this kind of situation, mulch the garden in spring when the soil has warmed.

Note how plants grow on a north-facing slope or next to a north wall, and plan accordingly. In low light, plants grow taller and leggier than normal. Plants next to a wall will tend to lean away from the wall as they grow in search of more light. Be ready to stake tall plants to hold them upright. Training vines to climb trellises and building terraced beds on a hillside are two ways to get more light for plants. Create a spot to view the garden next to the wall from a position farther north of the wall, where the plants will appear to be growing toward the viewer.

Extending the Season

Finally, frost is likely to occur in a northern exposure a week or two later in spring and a week or two earlier in autumn than in other gardens in the same locality. Starting seeds indoors will help you get a headstart on the growing season in spring. You can use cloches, which are "floating" covers of spunbonded polyester, or other frost-protection devices to extend the season at both ends. Have these materials ready to protect sensitive plants during a late or early frost.

Sometimes the best option for a shady site is to eliminate some of the shade. Removing a large tree opened up this hillside to the summer sun.

In this sloping garden, a variety of plants grow in a bright clearing surrounded by trees.

A garden that is shady in summer may be sunny enough to grow bulbs like these narcissus (sharing space here with wild sweet William) before the trees leaf out in spring.

Seasonal Shade

Some parts of your garden may be shady part of the year and sunny part of the year, and you can take advantage of seasonal changes. The angle of the sun changes from summer to winter, and deciduous trees lose their leaves in winter. This combination of factors changes sun and shade patterns in the garden.

To understand where the sun falls on your property at different times of year, make a rough map based on your own observations. Work patterns and busy lifestyles make it difficult for most of us to find time every day to map sun and shade patterns, but you should be able to piece together a reasonable seasonal record on weekends and holidays.

An area that is shaded by deciduous trees in summer may have plenty of sun in spring. Use this location to grow different kinds of hardy bulbs. Daffodils, narcissus, tulips, and hyacinths will flower happily provided they receive sun when they send up buds and come into bloom and shade later when their foliage dies back. Crocuses, however, will not thrive on this sort of regimen. They do best when their dormant bulbs bake in sun-drenched soil after the leaves die back.

A garden that receives spring sun also is a good place for early-blooming perennials such as primroses (*Primula* species) and basket-of-gold (*Aurinia saxatilis*) and for spring wildflowers such as forget-me-nots (*Myosotis* species), trout lily (*Erythronium*

species), and Dutchman's breeches (*Dicentra cucullaria*). In summer, when the garden is shady, shade-tolerant hostas, columbines (*Aquilegia* species and hybrids), astilbes, ferns, and lobelia can take over.

In summer, shade-lovers such as hostas and cinnamon ferns thrive under deep-rooted trees.

Regional Differences in Shade

For some plants, the temperature is as important as the kind and quality of light in determining where they will thrive. Some plants adapt to a wide range of climates and locations; others have more particular needs.

Because of the stronger sun, a shady garden in the South will be warmer, and often brighter, than a shady garden in the North. Many plants that need the warmth of full sun in northern gardens grow better when they receive some shade—especially during the afternoon—in hot climates.

Humidity and cloud cover make a difference, too. Where the weather is often cloudy and damp, such as in the Pacific Northwest, plants can take less shade than in locations where the sun is bright and the air is dry. In fact, in the arid Southwest, even many sun-loving plants can do with a bit of shade in the heat of afternoon.

Dry Shade

Some plants are even more region-specific. Gardeners in the Northwest can grow many shade plants found in English gardens. These plants seldom flourish for long in shade gardens in the eastern part of the United States, however, where summer weather generally is hotter and drier. Dry shade usually is a more difficult location than moist shade. To garden successfully in dry shade, seek out plants that are both shade- and drought-tolerant.

In winter, shade gardens in the subtropical regions of South Florida, southern California, and the arid Southwest are warm enough to support a host of tender plants. Northern gardeners must concentrate on houseplants and evergreens in winter, unless they have access to an atrium or sheltered courtyard.

If you're relatively new to gardening, select plants that are likely to do well in the conditions present in your garden. Purchase plants grown at nurseries in your part of the country, whether you buy locally or by mail. A plant grown outdoors in Connecticut will be hardier than the same species grown in a nursery in South Carolina.

If a plant is on the edge of its hardiness range in your garden, its origin could make the difference between survival and death. Another good tactic is to choose plants that are native to a climate similar to yours, even if they come from somewhere else.

How to Work with Shade

The most sensible way to create a flourishing shade garden is to develop a good understanding of the kind and quality of the shade present in your garden and to grow plants that naturally thrive in the sort of growing conditions you have available. By matching plant needs to existing conditions, you're working with nature, making it possible for the plants in your garden to follow their natural inclinations. Be conservative at first. As you gain experience, you can experiment a bit and push the limits.

Plants are never entirely predictable, and they can surprise you. That primrose or gentian may be on the borderline of its shade tolerance or hardiness in your garden, but with luck, it might survive. You might find a pocket with enough extra light, or enough shelter from a nearby shrub, to allow a few unexpected plants to grow.

Wall Plantings

If you have a solid wall on your property, careful plant choices can allow you to garden close to it. If your garden is on the west side of the wall, where it's shady in the morning and sunny in the afternoon, try growing sun-loving plants that tolerate hot, dry conditions. Although the garden

The light-colored wall of this house reflects additional light into the shady garden.

is shady in the morning, heat-tolerant plants will have a better chance here than shade-lovers. Shade plants would be less able to withstand the sudden, severe temperature changes that occur when the cool, shady garden is plunged into hot afternoon sun.

The east side of a wall can be an especially good location for a garden. Because this spot is shady in the afternoon it stays cooler than other area gardens in summer. The gentler morning sun allows the garden to warm up slowly in the morning, which is preferable for many plants. Because this garden will warm slowly in spring, choose summer-blooming plants for the best display. Gardeners in warm climates may find they can grow plants that do better a zone farther north if they can site the plants on the east side of a wall.

You also can modify shade to make the garden more hospitable to plants.

If your garden receives medium to full shade, for example, you may be able to lighten the shade or get more light into the garden in other ways to expand the list of plants likely to succeed for you.

Lighting Shady Spots

As young trees mature, they cast more shade. By pruning selectively, however, you usually can lighten a dense deciduous canopy, at least somewhat. To let more light into a shady garden, begin by limbing up the trees that cast the most shade. Remove the lower branches to raise the canopy higher off the ground. If you can remove the branches to a height of 20 to 40 feet, you can brighten your garden from a condition of full shade to high or medium shade. If the foliage texture is delicate rather than heavy, you may find yourself with light shade in the garden.

If the garden is still shadier than you'd like, call in a professional arborist to thin the canopy by removing some of the higher branches. Unless you're an experienced tree pruner, this job is best left in the hands of a professional. An arborist will have the equipment and training to safely work high off the ground. He'll be able to choose which branches to remove to let in more light without ruining the form of the tree.

As a last resort, consider removing a tree entirely. It's a shame to take down a tree, especially one that is mature, but if no part of your property is bright enough for a garden, it might be the only solution.

With the addition of some chairs, a shady garden becomes an inviting place to take a break from weeding on a hot summer day.

The Shady Environment

Reflected Light

Another way to get more light into dim beds and borders is by reflection. A garden border next to a path or driveway will benefit from reflected light if the pavement or path is surfaced with light-colored pebbles or concrete rather than with dark asphalt, bluestone, or bark chips.

Your house, garage, outbuildings, and walls also will reflect light into nearby gardens if they're painted white or a light color. In a small garden, you may be able to bounce in more light with judiciously placed mirrors or white-painted lattice panels. You can use these techniques to reflect more light into a garden on the north side of a wall or slope as well.

ABOVE: For maximum light in a shady border, paint nearby fences or walls white and use light-colored paving materials for paths.
BELOW: This shady garden is bright enough that a formal flagstone path is perfectly appropriate.

Getting Plants Out of the Shade

If you can't lighten the shade, move your plants out of the darkest areas. In addition to using seasonally sunny spots, as described earlier, take advantage of sunny locations where you find them, even if you might not have considered gardening there before.

You might find a bright place for a small bed or border in the strip between your front sidewalk and the street, alongside the driveway, in the middle of the front yard, along a property line, or in a clearing between trees in the backyard. Could you carve out a garden—even an unusually shaped garden—in one of these locations? Sometimes the most rewarding gardens are those that begin as imaginative solutions to problems inherent in a particular site. Think creatively as you assess sun and shade patterns on your property. A garden can take shape wherever the best growing conditions are found.

Following the Sun

Experienced gardeners who are well-acquainted with the path traveled by the sun across their garden from season to season may be able to plan for seasonal interest in different locations to follow the sun. Planting spring bloomers farther from the source of shade may give them enough light at the most critical time of year. Positioning summer bloomers closer to the shade source may provide sufficient light because the shadows are shorter when they are in flower. (Shadows are shortest around the summer solstice because the sun is nearly overhead.)

If you believe seasonal succession might work in your garden, try to achieve it by featuring a few special accent plants in each part of the season. Present them against a background of foliage plants of varied tones and textures that will be attractive throughout the growing season, from spring to fall.

Finally, if you simply must grow some plants that need more light than your garden offers, get the plants out of the shade. Trellised vines and well-staked tall plants may grow up far enough to break out of shade cast by a low wall or a shrub that's not too tall. Look for sunny spots in which you could mount window boxes or set

If you can't modify shade in your garden, try moving plants out of the shade with hanging baskets or by growing climbing vines.

pots, tubs, or planters, and grow your heart's desire in containers. Container plants also can be moved to follow the sun from season to season. Mounting a large tub or planter box on casters or a wheeled platform makes it easy to push across a deck or patio to follow the bright spots as they shift over the course of the summer.

Most of the shade problems you face as a gardener can be solved in one way or another. You simply need to find the solutions that work best for you and your landscape.

Integrate shade plants into your living space by building a patio around them (inset)
and by grouping containers by the door for a cheerful welcome (above).

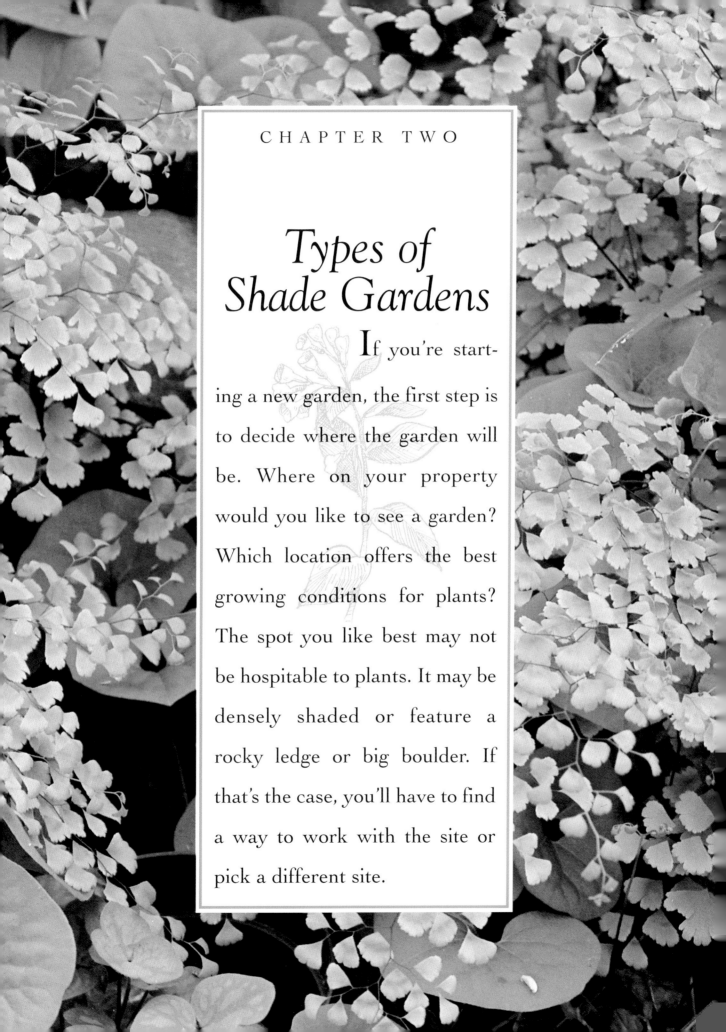

CHAPTER TWO

Types of Shade Gardens

If you're starting a new garden, the first step is to decide where the garden will be. Where on your property would you like to see a garden? Which location offers the best growing conditions for plants? The spot you like best may not be hospitable to plants. It may be densely shaded or feature a rocky ledge or big boulder. If that's the case, you'll have to find a way to work with the site or pick a different site.

Choosing a Site

To make your shade gardening experience less complicated and more enjoyable, choose a garden spot that offers the best environment for plants. The best location for a garden is not necessarily the most obvious one. There are many factors to consider when selecting a site for the garden.

Walking around your property with notebook in hand is the best way to familiarize yourself with its features. Ideally, you should wait an entire year after moving into a house before starting a garden, so you can observe potential locations in every season to assess the environment and how it changes throughout the year. Waiting a year is almost impossible for most of us, but you can partially satisfy your yen to garden by growing plants in containers or by putting a tiny bed in the ground that first year.

This lightly shaded location is a good garden site. Existing rocks at left were incorporated into the garden.

Evaluating a Site

To assess the qualities of your site, first consider the topography of the property itself—the lay of the land. Are you on the side of a hill, or on top of a rise, where strong winds may be a problem? If so, you'll probably need to plant or build some sort of windbreak to protect the garden.

Gardeners near the sea or in other exposed locations also will need to plan for windbreaks. What is the direction of the prevailing wind in winter and summer? If the property is hilly, will it be readily accessible for gardening activities? Would terraced beds running across the slope make it easier to till the soil, plant, and maintain the garden?

Are there low spots where water tends to collect in puddles after it rains, and where snow is slow to melt in winter? For such a location, you'll need to select plants that tolerate soggy, poorly drained soil and a late spring frost. This might be a perfect spot for a small water garden. Pre-formed pond liners are available in kit form and can be installed in a weekend. A low spot that warms slowly in spring also is best suited to a garden designed for maximum interest in summer and fall. Spring bulbs and wildflowers might get started too slowly at the beginning of the season to bloom before deciduous trees overhead get their leaves.

It's also important to evaluate the kind and quantity of shade present in different areas. How does the sun travel across your property over the course of the outdoor growing season? Which locations are sunny in spring? In summer? In autumn? If you live in a warm climate, which areas afford the afternoon shade that is so necessary for so many plants in summer? Consider the type of shade you have, and whether you could modify that shade as described in Chapter 1.

Soil Quality

Soil is another important factor in a garden site, and you need to evaluate the type of soil present in your potential garden spot. Soil quality can vary over a property.

Scoop up a handful of soil in each location you are considering and examine it closely. If the soil is dark colored, dense, moist, and even sticky, if it stays together in a clump after you squeeze it in your hand, or if you can easily roll it into a ball or a rope, the soil probably contains a lot of clay. If the soil is light colored and

Types of Shade Gardens

coarse textured, dries out quickly after it rains, and doesn't hold together when you squeeze a moist handful, it's basically sandy.

Understanding Your Soil

The ideal soil for gardening is a loam that contains a balanced mixture of sand, silt, and clay particles, is crumbly and rich brown in color, and contains lots of organic matter. Few of us are blessed with ideal soil. Nearly any soil can be improved, but you first have to understand the type of soil you have.

You might find clues to your soil in the kinds of plants that grow wild on your property. Some wild plants are found in wet soil, others where it's dry. Some grow in acid conditions, others in alkaline. Some gravitate to fertile soils, others to poor ones.

The best way to learn about your soil is to have the soil tested for pH, nutrient values, and organic matter content. You can purchase a home test kit from a local garden center or mail-order supplier (spend the money to get a good one—they're more reliable) or have a test done through the nearest U. S. Department of Agriculture Cooperative Extension Service office. Most counties have a Cooperative Extension office. They're usually listed in the telephone book with other federal agencies. A third option is to have a private laboratory that performs soil tests analyze your soil.

Mapping Your Yard

As you walk your property to evaluate growing conditions, start making a map that you can use when you're ready to design the garden. The map doesn't need to be an architectural rendering, but it does help to note the dimensions of the lot, and of specific areas where you want to put gardens.

Begin with a copy of the property survey that was done when you bought your house. If you don't have a copy of the survey, take a tape measure (100 feet is best) and an assistant to hold the tape, and make your own measurements. Draw the outline of the property on a large sheet of paper, noting the dimensions. If your property is large, just map the section in which you want to start the garden.

Mark the location of your house, any outbuildings, and notable features such as mature trees, large boulders, and a stream or pond. It's a good idea to make several copies of the map so you can experiment with different designs.

Next, draw in existing gardens, noting their dimensions. Somewhere, you should note compass directions on your map. Make notes of areas that are overgrown and neglected and of trees that are damaged or diseased and need pruning or removing.

Eventually, you'll develop a good picture of your landscape through the growing season. You'll have identified factors that would influence a garden. Finally, you'll choose the location for your new garden. Then you can start planning the garden.

Have the soil tested before planting a new garden so you can add necessary amendments and choose plants that will flourish in your soil type.

Making Shade

Sometimes before you can plant a shade garden, you first have to make shade. Gardeners who want to start a new garden on a cleared lot or in a warm climate should think about creating some shade. The long-term solution to making shade is to plant trees, but you also can build an arbor or pergola and plant vines to cover the structure to create shade underneath. Fences, lattice panels, or trellises supporting vines also will create shade for part of the day—which part depends on the orientation of the screen and the garden. A good shade-maker for warm-climate gardens is a lath house, which creates a pleasant environment for plants and people.

Planting Trees and Shrubs

Shade trees are an investment in the future. It can take 20 years or more for a shade tree to mature, but when you plant trees, you're making an investment in the health of the planet and securing future benefits for your family.

Trees provide shelter that softens the force of wind blowing across the property and shade that reduces summer cooling bills. They also provide deep root systems that anchor soil and pump water up from deep in the subsoil, flushing it out into the upper layer of soil where it is available to other plants as well. Like other green plants, trees conduct the photosynthesis that is one of the main engines driving the ecosystem of the earth. They also provide homes and food for wildlife and shade for us to enjoy.

Plant trees on your property if there aren't any now. Because you're a gardener, plant trees that will supply

INSET: Willow oaks and flowering dogwoods cast dappled shade in which many smaller shade-loving plants perform well.

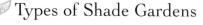

Types of Shade Gardens

shade so you can grow other plants underneath. Good choices include willow and other oaks, Siberian crab apple, hawthorns, honey locust, dogwoods, Japanese pagoda tree (*Sophora japonica*), callery or Bradford pear (*Pyrus calleryana* 'Bradford'), Japanese zelkova, and golden-rain tree (*Koelreuteria paniculata*).

When you plant trees, don't scatter them over the property. Think about what you want the trees to do, and place them accordingly. If you want summer shade for the house or for a lawn area, deck, or patio, for example, plant trees to the south side of the area you want shaded. If you want shade in a large lawn, group the trees into islands with mulch or a ground cover in between to make mowing easier. You might want to group trees into an orchard, a grove, a formal allée along a drive, or a mini-woodland. As the trees mature, you can add the other elements of the woodland, as described later in this chapter under Woodland Gardens.

ABOVE: Groups of trees and shrubs can anchor island beds of perennials and ground covers surrounded by lawn.
INSET: This mixed border combines a golden-chain tree with mock orange, false cypress, hostas, and other plants.

Building Shade

To get some relief from the sun while you wait for young trees to grow, put up an arbor, pergola, or screen covered with fast-growing vines. An arbor is a freestanding structure that consists of an open-framework roof supported at each corner by an upright post. You can cover it by planting vines around the uprights and training the plants up the posts and over the top of the arbor.

A pergola is similar to an arbor. In fact, the two types of structures are often confused. A pergola, however, usually is longer than it is wide. Pergolas often are attached to a house or other building along one side to create a shady patio. They're also used to cover pathways to create sheltered galleries in which to stroll.

Two classic vines for arbors and pergolas are wisteria and grape. Both will create more or less permanent shade, at least during the growing season, but they take time to grow large enough to cover the structure. If you need more immediate but less long-lasting shade, plant large-leaved annual vines such as Dutchman's-pipe (*Aristolochia durior*) or morning glories (*Ipomoea* species).

Lath Houses

A lath house is a shedlike structure made of narrow strips of wood called lath with space left between them. Instead of building a freestanding house of lath strips, some gardeners prefer rooflike panels made of lath over the top of the garden. Lath structures create an evenly filtered shade beneath them that's ideal for many plants in the summer.

OPPOSITE: A romantic wisteria arbor creates a cool, shady spot for hostas underneath.

INSET: A lath house allows gardeners in hot, sunny climates to grow a greater variety of plants.
ABOVE: Inside a lath house, plants grow in filtered shade. Cool-climate gardeners can place houseplants in the lath house in summer.
BELOW: A vine-covered arbor or pergola can create a shady oasis in a sunny garden.

For warm-climate gardeners, a lath house or lath roof can become an indispensable addition to the garden. It creates the perfect amount of shade for growing ferns, alpines, and other plants that could not survive summer in the sun. For gardeners in most parts of the country, a lath house provides a sheltered environment for summering orchids and houseplants outdoors, and for growing tuberous begonias and other shade-loving annuals. A lath shelter is an agreeable place to put a chaise longue, too, when it's time to sit back and enjoy the garden for a while.

You can make planting beds in the ground under a freestanding lath house, as long as it's not too close to a shallow-rooted tree. Another option

is to make raised beds. Under a lath roof sheltering a patio, grow plants in pots, tubs, or planters.

Garden Styles

Shade gardens can take many forms and styles. There are naturalistic options such as woodland gardens and shady meadows, more traditional island beds or informal mixed borders, and formal herbaceous borders. You can plant a shady garden along a small stream or pool, or even grow vegetables and herbs in the shade. You might want a garden of cool white flowers, of colorful spring perennials

LEFT: This spring garden sparkles with fragrant white *Narcissus* 'Thalia,' pink bleeding heart, and white arabis.

and wildflowers, or of tropical-looking foliage plants whose bold leaves are splashed with color. You have many options from which to choose.

When deciding what kind of garden you want to create, you need to consider many factors in addition to growing conditions on the site you've chosen. The overall layout and shape of your property is important, as is its location. If you have a quarter-acre lot in the middle of town, for example, would a shady meadow be appropriate in front of the house. If you live in a coastal area, a rock garden of alpine plants would be difficult. If you live in the desert, don't plan a woodland gar-

Plants are massed in informal drifts along a stream in this woodland garden.

Types of Shade Gardens

den. Think about the architectural style of your house, too. A formal garden with neatly clipped topiaries and parterres outlined with boxwood hedges would be fine next to a formal home but out of place next to a country cottage.

Finally, think about who you are. What kind of garden would suit your personality and your lifestyle? Would your kids and pets trample a bed of delicate ferns and wildflowers? If so, maybe shrubs are a better choice. If baseballs and basketballs are likely to end up in a flower bed, think about planting durable ground covers instead of rare flower species.

ABOVE: Consider the architecture of your house when planning a garden. An informal garden complements a wood shingle or clapboard dwelling, but a brick house looks better with a more formal design.

LEFT: Durable ground covers such as the pachysandra and ajuga shown here are good choices where children and pets may stray into the garden.

ABOVE: A rock-lined stream can be landscaped with a variety of moisture-loving shade plants.

Naturalistic Gardens

Many shade plants are most at home in naturalistic settings that evoke the way plant communities grow in the wild. A natural garden doesn't have to be wild-looking and uncontrolled, although it can be. Three of the best ways to create naturalistic shade plantings are in woodland gardens, informal beds and borders of wildflowers and ferns, and shady meadow-style gardens. You also can plant in the damp ground next to a stream or pool. If your soil is sandy, as in seashore locations, you'll need to find plants that can tolerate dry shade.

Designing a natural-looking garden is similar in many ways to designing a traditional bed or border, except that the plants are placed in a particular environmental context. You'll achieve the most natural, and most effective, look by arranging plants in clumps or flowing drifts.

Don't line up plants in neat rows, dribble them out in long strings, or dot them about the garden. Instead, group them together, allowing the clumps and drifts to meander among the trees and shrubs in the garden. (See Chapter 3 for more information on planting patterns.)

If you're short of funds, start with just a few drifts of a dozen or more plants in a couple of places, rather than scattering plants in ones and twos throughout the garden. Nature plants in broad sweeps of color, and you can, too. Plan on adding more drifts and expanding existing drifts later, as you're able to purchase or propagate more plants.

Consider seasonal changes in the garden, too, and try to plan something of interest in all seasons.

Woodland Gardens

Woodland gardens re-create or suggest the look of a natural forest. Much of the eastern half of the United States was once covered by forests, primarily dominated by deciduous hardwood trees. Along coastal areas and in much of the South, pines, and in some places oaks, predominate. In the mild Pacific Northwest, lush rainforests of Douglas firs, rhododendrons, and mosses flourish in the abundant rainfall. In the Rocky Mountains, the coniferous alpine forests are full of fir, spruce, poplar, and aspen. These are the parts of the country where woodland gardens are most appropriate and fit most naturally into the terrain.

In a woodland garden, plant life exists on several levels. Tall trees with leafy branches form the overhead canopy that shades the ground below. Smaller understory trees and shrubs form the next level of vegetation. In some open woodlands, vines can be found climbing on trees and shrubs. On the forest floor, wildflowers, ferns, and creeping ground covers complete the plant community.

The soil in forest environments usually is acid, the degree of acidity influenced primarily by the underlying bedrock and the dominant trees. In the oak and pine woodlands along the Mid-Atlantic coast, the soil is strongly acid. Many of the pine forests of the South, however, are underlaid with limestone, which is alkaline.

RIGHT AND INSET: For a naturalistic effect in a woodland garden, you need plants on several levels—trees, shrubs, perennials, ferns, and ground covers.

Types of Shade Gardens

ABOVE: When allowed to naturalize, spreading perennials form a carpet of color in a woodland.
INSET: Wild sweet William (*Phlox divaricata*) is excellent for naturalizing. Some primroses also will naturalize in congenial conditions.

Types of Shade Gardens

In deciduous forests, especially, the soil generally is rich in humus from decaying vegetation and is covered with a layer of fallen leaf litter, as autumn leaves remain where they drop and gradually decay. Most of the wildflowers native to this forest environment need that layer of fallen leaves to protect their roots and young shoots.

In the garden, you'll want to re-create these conditions with a thick layer of loose mulch, ideally of shredded leaves. Some woodland plants have special needs for soil that must be met if they are to thrive. Trailing arbutus, for example, must have very acidic soil, and many wild orchids demand sandy soils such as those in the coastal woodlands to which they are native.

Spring Bloomers

Spring is the most colorful season in woodland gardens. Many woodland wildflowers bloom in spring, before the trees overhead send out their leaves. The colors of spring woodland wildflowers tend to be soft; white and yellow are seen in abundance.

Sparkling white bloodroot (*Sanguinaria canadensis*), trilliums, alumroot (*Heuchera americana*), foamflower (*Tiarella cordifolia*), and Dutchman's breeches (*Dicentra cucullaria*) bloom in spring. Primroses, trout lily (*Erythronium americanum*), and, a bit later, goldenstar (*Chrysogonum virginianum*) bring bursts of glowing golden yellow. You can add touches of blue with forget-me-nots (*Myosotis scorpioides*), and soft lavender-blue with wild sweet William (*Phlox divaricata*).

Wildflowers will be most appropriate in your woodland garden. Flamboyant tuberous begonias and tropical-looking caladiums would

Foamflower (*Tiarella cordifolia*)

Goldenstar (*Chrysogonum virginianum*)

look out of place among ferns and forget-me-nots in a woodsy setting.

To create an authentic woodland garden, use species native to your region of the country. The debate rages among botanists and horticulturists over how purely native environmentally based gardens such as woodland gardens should be. You'll have to make up your own mind about whether you want to create a native woodland garden, but here are some points to consider.

Natives or Imports

The argument in favor of native plants has come about as a way to preserve wild plants whose habitat is disappearing from the wild as a result of development, pollution, and other factors, and as a way to avoid problems caused by imported plants that get out of control. Many foreign plants have been introduced into the United States, for practical or purely ornamental purposes, and occasionally they cause problems.

In the Upper Midwest (and elsewhere, too), for example, purple loosestrife (*Lythrum salicaria*) has escaped from gardens and spread rapidly across wetlands, crowding out less aggressive native plant species. In the South, the infamous kudzu vine

covers trees and shrubs, and water hyacinths clog waterways in Florida. Other notorious foreign invaders include Japanese honeysuckle (*Lonicera japonica* 'Halliana'), oriental bittersweet (*Celastrus orbiculatus*), and the melaleuca tree introduced to drain marshy areas in California.

Imported plants that cause problems are a serious issue, but many exotics are well-behaved and wonderful additions to gardens. Should you deny your garden the beauty of Japanese primroses, or azaleas, or chrysanthemums? After all, some native American plants also can be invasive. Mayapple (*Podophyllum peltatum*), bishop's-weed (*Aegopodium podagraria*), and the common violet (*Viola sororia*) are just a few examples.

If you limit your plant choices to those from similar climates elsewhere in the world, which have long been grown in gardens here and are known to be well-behaved, it would seem safe to include nonnatives as well as natives in your woodland garden.

In fact, it's not a simple proposition to have an entirely native garden even if you want to. Many natives are hard to find in nurseries, and those that are available often are time-consuming and difficult to propagate and, thus, expensive.

The other issue to consider regarding native plants is whether it's legitimate to include improved forms of wildflowers in a natural garden. True woodland wildflowers are species plants. Plant breeders have improved on many of these, giving us such beauties as white-flowered bleeding heart, double-flowered trilliums, and oakleaf foamflower.

To be absolutely authentic, your woodland garden should contain only unimproved species wildflowers. If you feel they look out of place and unnatural, don't plant them in your woodland. Perhaps you would like them better in a more traditional bed or border.

Using Existing Trees

It makes sense to create a woodland garden where the necessary trees are already in place. Before adding any new plants, take stock of what's there. Prune damaged and dead branches from trees, and remove any old, weak trees that are in bad shape.

You may need to thin an especially dense stand of trees to let in more light so plants can grow on the ground beneath their branches. Thin conservatively, removing just a few branches from the top and sides of the trees. Remove a few low branches, too, if necessary, to allow for a path under the trees. Try for an irregular, natural look when pruning.

After removing a branch, step back and look at the results. It's important not to overprune. Removing too many branches will ruin the appearance of the trees, and can let in too much light for a woodland garden. If the environment is too bright, some woodland plants, such as male fern (*Dryopteris filix-mas*) and bloodroot (*Sanguinara canadensis*) won't thrive,

Before planting a new woodland garden, prune trees to let in more light and clear out brushy undergrowth to open planting areas.

and grasses may invade and crowd out the more desirable ground covers. It's always better to err on the side of caution when pruning. You can always remove more branches later.

Clearing Out Shrubs

You may need to remove some of the undergrowth and understory shrubs before planting your woodland, too. Keep the most desirable, healthy shrubs and get rid of messy, weedy ones that aren't particularly ornamental. You'll probably want to retain decorative shrubs such as rhododendrons, mountain laurel, and yaupon, perhaps just pruning overgrown specimens to improve their form.

When you want to eliminate shrubs, don't just cut them off at

ground level. Dig out the roots as well, even though it's a lot of work, to open up new planting areas. Leave fallen logs alone. Plants will grow around a hollow log as it decays. In the meantime, it can provide shelter for wildlife and contribute to the natural look of the garden.

When the woodland is cleared out, make paths through the garden-to-be so you can get into the garden to plant and maintain it, and so you and visitors can stroll through the plantings to admire your handiwork. Methods for laying out and surfacing paths are discussed in Chapter 3.

If your woodland is on a slope, you may find it helpful to create terraced beds running across the hillside to provide planting areas for wildflowers

Types of Shade Gardens

and ferns. Use logs to create the terraces, and fill in behind them with well-drained, humusy, fertile soil containing leaf mold.

If you think you'll use the garden at night—perhaps placing a gazebo or picnic table somewhere in a clearing—you'll want to install some type of lighting. Install lights before you plant.

If your woodland has trees but few shrubs, you'll probably want to add some new ones. The list of Plants for Woodland Gardens on page 40 offers some possibilities to consider.

Laying Out the Garden

When shrubs, paths, and lights are in place, begin laying out plantings of herbaceous plants and ground covers. You might want to experiment with different placements for clumps and drifts of plants by sketching planting areas on your garden map. Use colored pencils corresponding to flower or foliage colors to outline and shade in the planting areas. Make sure you like the combination of colors that will dominate drifts and clumps of plants that are next to one another.

Working with color usually is simple in a woodland garden because most of the flowers are whites or pastels and few clash with one another. To keep the occasional clumps of stronger-colored flowers, such as orange-yellow Canada lily (*Lilium canadense*), from standing out and drawing too much attention, surround them with drifts of white flowers to soften the impact.

Multiseason Interest

Plan more than one season in your woodland. If most of the flowers will bloom in spring, plan interesting foliage combinations to catch the eye

Blueberries (*Vaccinium* species)

in summer, and extend the blooming season with late-flowering plants such as black snakeroot (*Cimicifuga racemosa*). Choosing understory shrubs with good autumn color, such as blueberries (*Vaccinium* species) adds interest in fall. For winter, there are evergreens, and deciduous trees and shrubs with attractive texture or colored bark.

Finally, to allow your woodland garden to blend naturally into the surrounding landscape, give some consideration to the edge of the woods,

the transitional zone where the woodland meets the more open area next to it. In nature, woodlands often are edged with a mixture of shrubs that provide a transition to a sunny meadow beyond. On a smaller scale, you might connect a woodland garden to sunnier beds and borders closer to the house by planting an area of meadow grasses and wildflowers, or informal ornamental grasses.

On a small property, you could simply soften the edges of the woodland garden instead of chopping it off abruptly with the kind of neatly defined edge you'd give a traditional herbaceous border or bed. Allow some of the woodland wildflowers and ground covers to flow out from under the trees and shrubs along the woods, and maybe even scatter a few clumps or islands of the more light-tolerant plants farther out into the lawn.

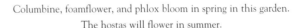

Columbine, foamflower, and phlox bloom in spring in this garden.
The hostas will flower in summer.

Plants for Woodland Gardens

Trees and Shrubs

American holly (*Ilex opaca*)

Arrowwood (*Viburnum dentatum*)

Azaleas (*Rhododendron* species)

Bayberry (*Myrica pensylvanica*)

Blueberries (*Vaccinium* species)

Bristly sarsaparilla (*Aralia hispida*)

Drooping leucothoe (*Leucothoe fontanesiana*)

Dwarf fothergilla (*Fothergilla gardenii*)

Fetterbush (*Pieris floribunda*)

Fringe tree (*Chionanthus virginicus*)

Hemlocks (*Tsuga* species)

Hobblebush (*Viburnum alnifolium*)

Huckleberry (*Gaylussacia baccata*)

Hybrid dogwood (*Cornus x rutgersensis*)

Inkberry (*Ilex glabra*)

Kousa dogwood (*Cornus kousa*)

Maple-leaf viburnum (*Viburnum acerifolia*)

Mountain cranberry (*Vaccinium vitis-idea*)

Mountain laurel (*Kalmia latifolia*)

Oakleaf hydrangea (*Hydrangea quercifolia*)

Oaks (*Quercus* species)

Oregon holly grape (*Mahonia* species)

Pacific dogwood (*Cornus nuttallii*)

Red bay (*Persia borbonia*)

Rhododendron species

Serviceberry (*Amelanchier* species)

Sheep laurel (*Kalmia angustifolia*)

Striped maple (*Acer pensylvanicum*)

Snowberry (*Symphoricarpos albus*)

Sourwood (*Oxydendrum arboreum*)

Sweet fern (*Comptonia peregrina*)

Sweet pepperbush (*Clethra alnifolia*)

Wild raisin (*Viburnum cassinoides*)

Wild sarsaparilla (*Aralia nudicaulis*)

Winterberry (*Ilex verticillata*)

Witch hazel (*Hamamelis virginiana*)

Yews (*Taxus* species)

Woodland Wildflowers and Bulbs

Alumroot (*Heuchera americana*)

American columbine (*Aquilegia canadensis*)

Baby blue-eyes (*Nemophila* species)

Baneberry (*Actaea* species)

Bellwort (*Uvularia perfoliata*)

Big-leaf aster (*Aster cordifolius*)

Black snakeroot (*Cimicifuga racemosa*)

Bloodroot (*Sanguinaria canadensis*)

Bluebells (*Hyacinthoides* species, *Endymion* species)

Bluets (*Houstonia caerulea*)

Canada lily (*Lilium canadense*)

Creeping phlox (*Phlox stolonifera*)

Crested iris (*Iris cristata*)

Dutchman's breeches (*Dicentra cucullaria*)

Fairy bells (*Diosporum* species)

False Solomon's-seal (*Smilacina racemosa*)

Foamflower (*Tiarella cordifolia*)

Fringed bleeding heart (*Dicentra eximia*)

Gentians (*Gentiana* species)

Glory-of-the-snow (*Chionodoxa luciliae*)

Hardy cyclamen (*Cyclamen* species)

Heartleaf (*Hexastylis arifolia*)

Hepatica species

Jack-in-the-pulpit (*Arisaema triphylla*)

Lady's-slipper (*Cypripedium* species)

Lily-of-the-valley (*Convallaria majalis*)

Mayapple (*Podophyllum peltatum*)

Meadow-rue (*Thalictrum polygamum*)

Oconee bells (*Shortia galacifolia*)

Primroses (*Primula* species)

Shooting star (*Dodecatheon meadia*)

Snowdrop (*Galanthus nivalis*)

Squills (*Scilla* species)

Starflower (*Trientalis borealis*)

Toothwort (*Dentaria laciniata*)

Trillium species

Trout lily (*Erythronium* species)

Turkeybeard (*Xerophyllum asphodeloides*)

Turk's-cap lily (*Lilium superbum*)

Twinleaf (*Jeffersonia diphylla*)

Violets (*Viola* species)

Virginia saxifrage (*Saxifraga virginiensis*)

Wandflower (*Galax urceolata*)

White snakeroot (*Eupatorium rugosum*)

Wild geranium (*Geranium maculatum*)

Wild lily-of-the-valley (*Maianthemum canadense*)

Wild sweet William (*Phlox divaricata*)

Wood anemone (*Anemone nemorosa*)

Wood lily (*Lilium philadelphicum*)

Wood sorrel (*Oxalis* species)

Ferns and Ground Covers

Allegheny spurge (*Pachysandra procumbens*)

Bearberry (*Arctostaphylos uva-ursi*)

Bunchberry (*Cornus canadensis*)

Christmas fern (*Polystichum acrostichoides*)

Cinnamon fern (*Osmunda cinnamomea*)

Common polypody (*Polypodium vulgare*)

Haircap moss (*Polytrichum commune*)

Hay-scented fern (*Dennstaedtia punctilobula*)

Lady fern (*Athyrium filix-femina*)

Male fern (*Dryopteris filix-mas*)

Rock fern (*Polypodium virginianum*)

Royal fern (*Osmunda regalis*)

Spotted wintergreen, pipsissewa (*Chimaphila maculata*)

Wild ginger (*Asarum canadense*)

Wintergreen (*Gaultheria procumbens*)

Beds of Wildflowers

Many plants that we think of as wild-flowers are as ornamental as more cultivated garden flowers. The showier wildflowers are as lovely and appropriate in informally designed beds and borders as they are in woodland gardens or other naturalistic settings. A bed or border also is a perfect place to grow improved forms of wildflowers, such as double trilliums.

Create mixed beds of wildflowers and shrubs, or combine wildflowers with the shade plants recommended on pages 52–53 for traditional beds and borders. Wildflowers blend beautifully with ferns, and a bed or border is an ideal place to mix the quiet charm of wildflowers with the lacy foliage of ferns.

To reduce weeding and watering chores, mulch with cocoa bean hulls or other loose material after planting.

Wildflowers for Beds and Borders

The wildflowers listed here are at home in informal beds and borders, as well as in more naturalistic gardens. Combine them with shrubs, ferns, bulbs, or plants recommended for traditional beds and borders on pages 52–53.

Alumroot (*Heuchera americana*)

American columbine (*Aquilegia canadensis*)

Black snakeroot (*Cimicifuga racemosa*)

Bloodroot (*Sanguisorba canadensis*)

Canada anemone (*Anemone canadensis*)

Cardinal flower (*Lobelia cardinalis*)

Catchfly (*Silene* species)

Chinese houses (*Collinsia heterophylla*)

Clarkia species

Creeping phlox (*Phlox stolonifera*)

Crested iris (*Iris cristata*)

False Solomon's-seal (*Smilacina racemosa*)

Foamflower (*Tiarella cordifolia*)

Forget-me-not (*Myosotis* species)

Fringed bleeding heart (*Dicentra eximia*)

Goat's beard (*Aruncus dioicus*)

Goldenrod (*Solidago* species)

Goldenstar (*Chrysogonum virginianum*)

Hepatica species

Jacob's ladder (*Polemonium caeruleum*)

Lupine (*Lupinus* species)

Mealy-cup sage (*Salvia farinacea*)

Merrybells (*Uvularia* species)

Oconee bells (*Shortia galacifolia*)

Purple coneflower (*Echinacea purpurea*)

Rose vervain (*Verbena canadensis*)

Rue anemone (*Anemonella thalictroides*)

Shooting star (*Dodecatheon meadia*)

Spiderwort (*Tradescantia virginiana*)

Trout lily (*Erythronium* species)

Trillium species

Turtle-head (*Chelone* species)

Virginia bluebells (*Mertensia virginica*)

Wild geranium (*Geranium maculatum*)

Wild petunia (*Ruellia makoyana*)

Wild sweet William (*Phlox divaricata*)

Ferns

Blunt-lobed woodsia (*Woodsia obtusa*)

Christmas fern (*Polystichum acrostichoides*)

Cinnamon fern (*Osmunda cinnamomea*)

Common polypody (*Polypodium vulgare*)

Deer fern (*Blechnum spicant*)

Fragile fern (*Cystopteris fragilis*)

Goldback fern (*Pentagramma triangularis*)

Hart's tongue fern (*Asplenium scolopendrium*)

Hay-scented fern (*Dennstaedtia punctilobula*)

Holly fern (*Cyrtomium falcatum*)

Interrupted fern (*Osmunda claytonia*)

Japanese painted fern (*Athyrium nipponicum* 'Pictum')

Lacy tree fern (*Sphaeropteris cooperi*)

Lady fern (*Athyrium filix-femina*)

Maidenhair spleenwort (*Asplenium trichomanes*)

Male fern (*Dryopteris filix-mas*)

Marginal wood fern (*Dryopteris marginalis*)

Netted chain fern (*Woodwardia areolata*)

New York fern (*Thelypteris noveboracensis*)

Northern maidenhair fern (*Adiantum pedatum*)

Oak fern (*Gymnocarpium dryopteris*)

Ostrich fern (*Matteucia struthiopteris*)

River fern (*Thelypteris kunthii*)

Rock fern (*Polypodium virginianum*)

Royal fern (*Osmunda regalis*)

Sensitive fern (*Onoclea sensibilis*)

Shield fern (*Dryopteris carthusiana*)

Soft tree fern (*Dicksonia antarctica*)

Southern maidenhair fern (*Adiantum capillus-veneris*)

By the Water's Edge

If you have a small stream, pool, or pond on your property, you have the perfect opportunity to create a shady garden of moisture-loving plants. Be sure to place a bench somewhere in your oasis so you can enjoy this delightful garden environment.

Chances are, there already are trees near the stream or pond. Weeping willows are classic streamside trees with a beguiling grace, but they're not necessarily the most practical choice. Weeping willows grow huge with age, and their roots are greedy for water, making it difficult for less voracious plants to thrive nearby.

Plant Choices

Better choices to plant near a stream, pool, or pond include balsam fir (*Abies balsamea*), alders (*Alnus* species), serviceberry (*Amelanchier canadensis*), and the majestic American beech (*Fagus grandiflora*). Also consider planting one of the birches, especially the Heritage river birch (*Betula nigra* 'Heritage'), which has beautiful bark and is less susceptible to borers than white birches.

To create more privacy and enclosure along the water, add shrubs beneath the trees. Elderberry (*Sambucus canadensis*) and huckleberry (*Gaylussacia* species) offer small blue-black berries that make delicious jelly, if you have the patience to collect enough of them. They also nourish birds. You might prefer, instead, the decorative flowers of swamp azalea (*Rhododendron viscosum*) or viburnum.

Deep pink Japanese primroses (*Primula japonica*) thrive in the moist soil by the water's edge. Lavender-blue wild sweet William also has adapted to the moist environment.

The damp ground by the water's edge can become a symphony of color and lush foliage with herbaceous plants that love it wet. Possibilities include Japanese primrose (*Primula japonica*), astilbe, turtle-head (*Chelone* species), cardinal flower (*Lobelia cardinalis*), Joe-Pye weed (*Eupatorium purpureum*), and a host of ferns. In a warm environment, you could create a tropical look with the bold foliage of *Gunneramanicata*.

Some plants thrive with their feet in the water. Two irises, yellow flag (*Iris pseudacorus*) and blue flag (*Iris veriscolor*), are perfect for planting in shallow water in partial to light shade. For foliage interest, add the spiky green-and-cream-striped leaves of variegated sweet flag (*Acorus americanus* 'Variegatus') and the strangely beautiful horsetails (*Equisetum hyemale*). Horsetails can be invasive, so plant them in a container sunk in the ground to keep them from spreading.

If a simpler, low-maintenance approach is more to your liking, plant a shrub or two under the trees, and some moisture-loving ground covers, ferns, or ornamental grasses.

Yellow flag (*Iris pseudacorus*) is ideal for wet soil. It also will grow in shallow standing water.

Create a shady garden of moisture-loving plants if you have a small stream or pool on your property.

Types of Shade Gardens

Plants for Wet Places

These plants thrive in moist soil.

Trees and Shrubs
Alder (*Alnus* species)

American beech (*Fagus grandiflora*)

Balsam fir (*Abies balsamea*)

Bayberry (*Myrica pensylvanica*)

Birch (*Betula* species)

Blueberry (*Vaccinium* species)

Canadian rhodora (*Rhododendron canadense*)

Catawba rhododendron (*Rhododendron catawbiense*)

Chokeberry (*Aronia arbutifolia*)

Eastern hemlock (*Tsuga canadensis*)

Elderberry (*Sambucus canadensis*)

Huckleberry (*Gaylussacia* species)

Maple (*Acer* species)

Mountain ash (*Sorbus aucuparia*)

Mountain laurel (*Kalmia latifolia*)

Pin cherry (*Prunus pensylvanica*)

Pinxter azalea (*Rhododendron canescens*)

Raspberry (*Rubus* species)

Red oak (*Quercus rubrum*)

Red-osier dogwood (*Cornus sericea*)

Sassafras (*Sassafrass albidum*)

Serviceberry (*Amelanchier canadensis*)

Snowberry (*Symphoricarpos albus*)

Spicebush (*Lindera benzoin*)

Sumac (*Rhus* species)

Swamp azalea (*Rhododendron viscosum*)

Sweet pepperbush (*Clethra alnifolia*)

Viburnum species

White cedar (*Thuja occidentalis*)

White pine (*Pinus strobus*)

Winterberry (*Ilex verticillata*)

Ground Covers and Grasses
Bearberry (*Arctostaphylos uva-ursi*)

Bunchberry (*Cornus canadensis*)

Chameleon plant (*Houttuynia cordata* 'Variegata')

Mosses

Partridgeberry (*Mitchella repens*)

Ribbon grass (*Phalaris arundinacea* var. *picta*)

Striped St. Augustine grass (*Stenotaphrum secundatum* 'Variegatum')

Tufted hair grass (*Deschampsia caespitosa*)

Wintergreen (*Gaultheria procumbens*)

Flowers and Foliage
Arrow arum (*Peltandra virginica*)

Astilbe species

Blue beadlily (*Clintonia borealis*)

Cardinal flower (*Lobelia cardinalis*)

Christmas fern (*Polystichum acrostichoides*)

Cinnamon fern (*Osmunda cinnamomea*)

Cow parsnip (*Heracleum maximum*)

Elephant's-ear (*Colocasia esculentus*)

Forget-me-not (*Myosotis scorpioides*)

Goat's beard (*Aruncus dioicus*)

Goldthread (*Coptis* species)

Gunnera (*Gunnera manicata*)

Jack-in-the-pulpit (*Arisaema triphylla*)

Japanese iris (*Iris ensata*)

Japanese primrose (*Primula japonica*)

Japanese primrose (*Primula japonica*)

Marsh marigold (*Caltha palustris*)

Mayapple (*Podophyllum peltatum*)

Meadow beauty (*Rhexia virginica*)

Mistflower (*Eupatorium coelestinum*)

Netted chain fern (*Woodwardia areolata*)

Ostrich fern (*Matteucia pensylvanica*)

Rodgersia species

Royal fern (*Osmunda regalis*)

Rushes (*Juncus* species)

Sedges (*Carex* species)

Sensitive fern (*Onoclea sensibilis*)

Solomon's-seal (*Polygonatum* species)

Turtle-head (*Chelone* species)

Twinflower (*Jeffersonia diphylla*)

Umbrella plant (*Peltiphyllum peltatum*)

Wandflower (*Galax urceolata*)

Water figwort (*Scrophularia aquatica* 'Variegata')

Wood sorrel (*Oxalis* species)

Shallow Water
These plants can grow with their feet in shallow water.

Arrowhead (*Sagittaria latifolia*)

Blue flag (*Iris versicolor*)

Bulrush (*Scirpus* species)

Cattail (*Typha* species)

Golden club (*Orontium aquaticum*)

Horsetail (*Equisetum hyemale*)

Lizard's tail (*Sarurus cernuus*)

Papyrus (*Cyperus* species)

Spider lily (*Hymenocallis* species)

Sweet flag (*Acorus americanum*)

Water arum (*Peltandra virginica*)

Yellow flag (*Iris pseudacorus*)

Traditional Garden Styles

Free-flowing natural gardens are not to every gardener's taste, nor are they the most appropriate style for every shady setting. In an urban location, or a tightly developed suburb where lots are small and regular in shape, a more formal traditional garden probably is a better option. A traditional garden also would be more in keeping with a formal home on a larger property, at least one that's close to the house.

A traditional garden can express creativity. Traditional shade-garden styles include beds and borders of herbaceous perennials, annuals, and bulbs, mixed borders of shrubs and herbaceous plants, small gardens in city courtyards or next to decks and patios, and tiny pocket gardens tucked into corners and unusual spots.

Shapes for Beds and Borders

The kind of garden most familiar to many Americans is a simple rectangular plot that is placed in the backyard to grow vegetables or set along the foundation in front of the house to hold shrubs and annual flowers. Gardens can be much more. Vegetable gardens can be lush, colorful, edible landscapes pretty enough to be in the front yard. Beds of flowers, shrubs, and vines can be created in all sorts of places for all sorts of reasons.

For purposes of this book, traditional beds and borders differ from naturalistic gardens in that they're laid out in well-defined areas and planted with a variety of shade-tolerant plants chosen for form and color. They may not be native to or naturalized in the United States. Tra-

ditional gardens also are neatly maintained and not as wild-looking as naturalistic gardens.

A border can be defined as a garden area that delineates an edge of some sort and that usually is longer than it is wide. A border may be located along a property line, or used to separate one part of a property or one room of a garden from another. It may be placed next to a building, wall, fence, or hedge, or adjacent to a sidewalk, path, or driveway. Many borders are designed to be viewed primarily from one side. They may have straight or curved edges.

A bed is basically any other discrete area set aside for plants that is not a border. A bed can be a freestanding island surrounded by lawn or ground cover, or it may adjoin a structure or landscape feature. A bed may be dug at ground level or raised and given structured sides of wood, brick, or stone. A bed can be any shape you want—square, round, triangular, kidney-shaped, or free-form. It may stand on its own or combine with other beds laid out in an interesting overall pattern to create a garden.

Formal Gardens

Beds and borders may be formal or informal, without attempting to mimic the way plants grow in their natural habitats. Formal gardens are built on straight lines, precise patterns, and geometric shapes. Mathematic principles are used to lay them out. A formal garden is designed to appear stable and at rest, like a classically composed painting. It's usually built along two axes at right angles to one another, one of them the main axis along which the dominant features of the garden are arrayed, the

Garden beds don't have to be rectangular. This symmetrical bed of azaleas is outlined with mondo grass (*Ophiopogon japonica*).

ABOVE: This elegant formal garden is edged with carefully clipped boxwood topiaries. Scrupulous care is needed to maintain the neat look.

other serving as a secondary axis. The axes should lead the viewer's eye toward the house or other important features of the landscape.

The gardens of the great European palaces, such as Versailles, are formal. Many historic estates in the United States also have grand formal gardens. You can see them at places like Longwood Gardens in Pennsylvania; the Governor's Palace at Williamsburg, Virginia; Biltmore, in Nashville; and Filoli in Woodside, California.

Relaxing Formality

Formal gardens today are less lavish and fussy than those of centuries past, in part because lifestyles have changed and in part because grand formal gardens require armies of gardeners to maintain. Formal gardens still have a place, however, especially in sophisticated city settings and on the grounds of elegant formal homes.

If you want to design a formal garden, create beds of precise geometric shapes, edged with carefully groomed annuals or enclosed by a fence, wall, or hedge. To preserve the controlled appearance, the plants should be scrupulously maintained—dead leaves and flowers picked off, unruly branches removed, and soil kept clean of debris. Ornamental pruning techniques such as topiary and espalier are well-suited to appropriate trees and shrubs in formal gardens.

If you want a formal look, think straight lines and control. Remember, neatness counts!

LEFT: Stately spires of bear's breeches (*Acanthus mollis*) rise above the plant's bold leaves in this formal border.

Informal Gardens

Where a formal garden is all straight lines and symmetry, an informal garden is full of curves and movement. In the art world, curved lines are considered more dynamic than straight lines, and informal gardens are filled with them. The edges of informal beds and borders, although still neatly defined, are flowing, gracefully curved lines. They swirl and eddy and arc across the lawn in fluid shapes.

Another way to make a bed or border informal is to use plants to break a formal line. Along a straight-edged path, for example, allow some plants to spill out into the path at irregular intervals. This softens an otherwise stiffly formal line.

Informal gardens are at home in many settings, and perfectly in keeping with the busy, casual lifestyles so many gardeners embrace today.

Within a garden bed or border, plants can be arranged in informal, flowing drifts or irregular clumps—the predominant style now—or in well-ordered rows or precise patterns as in a Victorian carpet bed or an Elizabethan knot garden of herbs. The style you choose for your garden depends on who you are.

RIGHT: Flowing curves and irregular shapes typify informal garden beds and borders.
INSET: Soft drifts of perennials flow under trees. Wild sweet William (*Phlox divaricata*) and comfrey (*Symphytum grandiflorum*) bloom in the foreground.

Types of Shade Gardens

ABOVE: Poppies and thistles lean over a bench
to make a seated visitor feel part of the garden.

ABOVE: A path that curves adds an air of
mystery to the garden as strollers anticipate surprises
around every bend.

Mixed Beds and Borders

One way to create a uniquely engaging garden for a shady location is to combine woody and herbaceous plants in a single bed or border. These mixed gardens provide interest in several seasons and on a variety of visual levels. Ideal for locations where space is limited, they contain small trees or shrubs and perennials. Mixed gardens also can include annuals, bulbs, vines, and ground covers.

A mixed garden is more complicated to plan and plant than a bed or border of one type of plant, such as annuals, but you can develop it gradually. The easiest technique is to plant from the top down. Put trees or shrubs in place first, leaving enough room for them to grow to their mature size. The woody plants create the framework around which you'll build the rest of the garden.

You can use existing trees and shrubs, instead of planting new ones, and create the garden around them. The woody plants can serve as a backdrop for flowers and foliage plants. You also could plant a hedge of mixed shrubs to mature over time and surround the garden. If you're working with a backdrop of this sort, plant in increments toward the front of the garden. A single specimen—perhaps a favorite old apple tree or lilac bush—could serve as an anchor for the garden, around which you create your bed or border. In this case, build the garden to move gradually outward from the focal point.

As with any garden, consider the special qualities of the plants you'll put in the mixed border. Plants have forms, textures, colors, and seasons of bloom, and combining them in interesting ways makes a memorable garden. These design qualities of plants are discussed in Chapter 3. First, you'll need to consider the various kinds of beds and borders.

LEFT: Annual impatiens, assorted perennials, and evergreen shrubs combine to good effect in this rock garden.

ABOVE: Elegant mixed borders edge a lawn. On the right, gold-leaved *Hosta* 'Gold Standard' and a honeysuckle, *Lonicera* 'Baggesen's Gold,' light up the garden.
INSET: A stunning blue and gold theme is struck by hardy geranium and lady's mantle.

Plants for Beds and Borders

Trees

Cornelian cherry (*Cornus mas*)

Crab apple (*Malus* species)

Flowering dogwood (*Cornus florida*)

Fringe tree (*Chionanthus* species)

Hybrid dogwood (*Cornus* x *rutgersensis*)

Japanese maple (*Acer japonicum, Acer palmatum*)

Magnolia grandiflora 'Little Gem'

Mountain ash (*Sorbus* x *hybrida*)

Pacific dogwood (*Cornus nuttallii*)

Paperbark maple (*Acer griseum*)

Redbud (*Cercis canadensis*)

Sourwood (*Oxydendrum arboreum*)

Snowball (*Styrax* species)

Vine maple (*Acer circinnatum*)

Weeping cherry (*Prunus* species)

Weeping pear (*Pyrus salicifolia* 'Pendula')

Shrubs

Arborvitae (*Thuja* species)

Azalea (*Rhododendron* species)

Barberry (*Berberis* species)

Beautyberry (*Callicarpa* species)

Boxwood (*Buxus* species)

Bottlebrush buckeye (*Aesculus parviflora*)

Bush honeysuckle (*Diervilla sessilifolia*)

Camellia species

Carolina allspice (*Calycanthus floridus*)

Cotoneaster species

Dogwood (*Cornus alba* 'Elegantissima')

Dwarf conifers

Dwarf fothergilla (*Fothergilla gardenii*)

Enkianthus species

Fatsia japonica

Fuchsia species

Glossy abelia (*Abelia* x *grandiflora*)

Gold-dust plant (*Aucuba japonica*)

Heavenly bamboo (*Nandina domestica*)

Holly (*Ilex* species)

Hydrangea species

Japanese kerria (*Kerria japonica*)

Junipers (*Juniperus* species)

Korean forsythia (*Abeliophyllum distichum*)

Leucothoe species

Leatherleaf (*Chamaedaphne calyculata*)

Mock orange (*Philadelphus* species)

Oregon holly grape (*Mahonia* species)

Pieris species

Red-osier dogwood (*Cornus sericea*)

Rhododendron species and hybrids

Skimmia japonica

Snowball (*Syrax* species)

Spiraea species

St.-John's-wort (*Hypericum calycinum*)

Sweet box (*Sarcococca* species)

Sweet olive (*Osmanthus fragrans*)

Sweet pepperbush (*Clethra alnifolia*)

Viburnum species

Weigela species

Winter hazel (*Corylopsis* species)

Witch hazel (*Hamamelis* species)

Yew (*Taxus* species)

Vines

Boston ivy (*Parthenocissus tricuspidata*)

Clematis species and hybrids

Crimson glory vine (*Vitis coignetiae*)

Trumpet honeysuckle (*Lonicera sempervirens*)

Virginia creeper (*Parthenocissus quinquefolia*)

Winter creeper (*Euonymus fortunei*)

Perennials and Bulbs

Anemone species

Astilbe species

Balloon flower (*Platycodon grandiflorus*)

Barrenwort (*Vancouveria* species)

Bear's breeches (*Acanthus mollis*)

Bee-balm (*Monarda didyma*)

Bellflower (*Campanula carpatica, Campanula persicifolia*)

Bethlehem sage (*Pulmonaria saccharata*)

Black snakeroot (*Cimicifuga racemosa*)

Bleeding heart (*Dicentra* species)

Caladium (*Caladium* x *hortulanum*)

Calla lily (*Zantedeschia* species)

Christmas rose (*Helleborus niger*)

Columbine (*Aquilegia* species)

Coralbells (*Heuchera sanguinea*)

Corydalis species

Crested iris (*Iris cristata*)

Daffodil (*Narcissus* species and hybrids)

Daylily (*Hemerocallis* species and hybrids)

False dragonhead (*Physostegia virginiana*)

False Solomon's-seal (*Smilacina racemosa*)

Ferns

Foamflower (*Tiarella cordifolia*)

Forget-me-not (*Myosotis scorpioides*)

Foxglove (*Digitalis* species)

Gentian (*Gentiana* species)

Globeflower (*Trollius* species)

Goat's beard (*Aruncus dioicus*)

Goldenstar (*Chrysogonum virginianum*)

Grape hyacinth (*Muscari* species)

Hardy begonia (*Begonia grandis*)

Hardy cyclamen (*Cyclamen* species)

Types of Shade Gardens

Hardy geranium (*Geranium* species)

x *Heucherella tiarelloides*

Hosta species

Jacob's ladder (*Polemonium* species)

Japanese anemone (*Anemone* x *hybrida*)

Japanese iris (*Iris kaempferi*)

Lady's mantle (*Alchemilla* species)

Lenten rose (*Helleborus orientalis*)

Leopard's bane (*Doronicum cordatum*)

Ligularia species

Lily (*Lilium* species)

Lilyturf (*Liriope* species)

Lobelia species

Meadow-rue (*Thalictrum* species)

Meadowsweet (*Filipendula* species)

Monkshood (*Aconitum* species)

Narcissus species and hybrids

Oconee bells (*Shortia galacifolia*)

Phlox species

Polygonum bistorta 'Superba'

Primrose (*Primula* species)

Saxifrage (*Saxifraga* species)

Shooting star (*Dodecatheon meadia*)

Siberian bugloss (*Brunnera macrophylla*)

Siberian iris (*Iris sibirica*)

Snowdrop (*Galanthus nivalis*)

Spiderwort (*Tradescantia* x *andersoniana*)

Squill (*Scilla* species)

Stonecrop (*Sedum* species)

Sweet alyssum (*Lobularia maritima*)

Trout lily, fawn lily (*Erythronium* species)

Turtle-head (*Chelone* species)

Violet (*Viola* species)

Virginia bluebells (*Mertensia virginica*)

Annuals and Biennials

Baby blue-eyes (*Nemophila menziesii*)

Balsam (*Impatiens balsamina*)

Begonia, wax (*Begonia semperflorens-cultorum*)

Begonia, tuberous (*Begonia* x *tuberhybrida*)

Black-eyed Susan vine (*Thunbergia alata*)

Browallia speciosa

Caladium (*Caladium* x *hortulanum*)

Calendula officinalis

Canterbury bells (*Campanula medium*)

Chinese forget-me-not (*Cynoglossum amabile*)

Coleus species and hybrids

Cupflower (*Nierembergia hippomanica*)

English daisy (*Bellis perennis*)

Euphorbia species

Exacum affine

Flowering tobacco (*Nicotiana alata*)

Forget-me-not (*Myosotis sylvatica*)

Foxglove (*Digitalis* species)

Fuchsia hybrids

Impatiens hybrids

Lobelia (*Lobelia erinus*)

Pansy (*Viola* x *wittrockiana*)

Polka-dot plant (*Hypoestes phyllostachya*)

Scarlet sage (*Salvia splendens*)

Victoria salvia (*Salvia farinacea* 'Victoria')

Wishbone flower (*Torenia fournieri*)

Ornamental Grasses

Amur silver grass (*Miscanthus sacchariflorus* 'Aureum')

Blue oat grass (*Helictotrichon sempervirens*)

Bottlebrush grass (*Hystrix patula*)

Bulbous oat grass (*Arrhenatherum elatus* var. *bulbosum* 'Variegatum'

Cloud grass (*Agrostis nebulosa*)

Fescue (*Festuca* species)

Gardener's garters (*Phalaris arundinacea* var. *picta*)

Hair grass (*Koeleria cristata*)

Hakonechloa macra 'Aureola'

Hare's tail grass (*Lagurus ovatus*)

Melic grass (*Melica* species)

Ribbon grass (*Oplismenus hirtellus*)

Spangle grass (*Chasmanthium latifolium*)

Striped St. Augustine grass (*Stenotaphrum secundatum* 'Variegatum')

Tufted hair grass (*Deschampsia caespitosa*)

Variegated velvet grass (*Holcus lanatus* 'Variegatus')

Wood millet (*Milium effusum* 'Aureum')

Ground Covers

Baby's tears (*Soleriolia soleirolii*)

Bearberry (*Asarum* species)

Bugleweed (*Ajuga reptans*)

Bunchberry (*Cornus canadensis*)

Creeping forget-me-not (*Omphalodes verna*)

Creeping Jenny (*Lysimachia nummularia*)

Creeping mahonia (*Mahonia repens*)

Creeping phlox (*Phlox stolonifera*)

Creeping speedwell (*Veronica repens*)

Epimedium species

Leadwort (*Ceratostigma plumbaginoides*)

Lilyturf (*Liriope* species)

Lungwort (*Pulmonaria* species)

Mondo grass (*Ophiopogon japonicus*)

Partridgeberry (*Mitchella repens*)

Periwinkle (*Vinca minor*)

Spotted dead nettle (*Lamium maculatum*)

Sweet woodruff (*Galium odoratum*)

Wild ginger (*Asarum* species)

Wintergreen (*Gaultheria procumbens*)

Herbaceous Beds and Borders

Herbaceous plants are those whose top growth dies back to the ground each year in autumn or winter. In perennials and bulbs, the root systems live underground in climates where the plants are hardy, and new leaves, stems, and flowers are produced each year. Annuals, as the name implies, live for just one year. After flowering and ripening their seeds, the plants die. Biennials live for two years, flowering and going to seed in their second year.

Herbaceous beds and borders are what once were called flower beds. You can create a lovely bed or border entirely from annuals, bulbs, or perennials. Mixing all three types together gives you more variety, however, and makes it easier to create a garden that's filled with color and interest from spring to fall.

Perennials have their particular time of bloom, and most flower for about three or four weeks. The seasonal flowering habit makes perennials dependable. Unless the weather is especially severe or an unusually large pest population invades your garden, you can expect your forget-me-nots to bloom in May, the astilbes in June, and the hostas in July and August.

Bloom Times

Flowering time varies according to species, variety, and location, but after a few years you'll know when your perennials bloom. Some bloom for a month or more, and these are exceptionally valuable in the garden. Fringed bleeding heart, for example, flowers through much of the summer. Except for those few glorious, all-too-brief weeks, most perennials are masses of greenery. One of the secrets of good perennial garden design is effectively combining the masses of foliage as well as the flowers.

Adding bulbs and annuals to the garden can simplify the task of designing a bed or border that's beautiful all season. Many hardy bulbs bloom early, bringing color to the garden while perennials are just beginning to grow. After they flower, however, bulbs only produce leaves, and bulb foliage usually is unattractive. As a bulb grows, its leaves become long and soft, flopping all over the garden. What's worse, the foliage must be left in place until it dies a month or so later, to nourish the bulb so it can produce the next year's flowers. On English estates, gardeners in the old days braided the leaves of daffodils and narcissus to keep them neat. It's a nice idea, but not one that many gardeners have time for today.

Mixing Bulbs and Annuals

A better solution to the problem of messy bulb foliage—and a bonus for beds and borders—is to plant annuals among the bulbs. Most annuals can be planted without harming the bulbs deeper in the ground. As they grow, annuals will hide the ruins of the bulb leaves. True workhorses in the garden, annuals frequently bloom from summer until frost. Their colorful foliage lasts all season, too.

In the past, so-called serious gardeners often rejected annuals, believing they were too coarse and garish to deserve a place in sophisticated gar-

This garden combines bulbs (tulips), perennials (wild sweet William), and ferns. The feathery ferns hide maturing tulip foliage after the flowers finish blooming.

OPPOSITE: An assortment of hostas keeps this garden interesting throughout the growing season. The red flowers of fringed bleeding heart bloom through much of the summer.

dens. As a result, annuals weren't planted or were relegated to beds of their own or stuck out back in the vegetable garden. Opinions are changing, however, and annuals are beginning to gain more recognition and approval.

Annuals bloom their hearts out week after week, and breeders are producing more interesting colors and more delicate forms. A good example is scarlet sage (*Salvia splendens*), originally an intensely brilliant red that's difficult to combine with other flowers in the garden. Today, scarlet sage also is available in softer shades of pink, white, and purple.

New Annuals Abound

Many other annuals also are finding their way into the market, so you have more options for a shady garden than impatiens and wax begonias. You can find wishbone flower (*Torenia fournieri*), cupflower (*Nierembergia hippomanica*), sweet potato vine (*Ipomoea batatas* 'Blackie'), and many other interesting annuals to grow in shade gardens.

Expand your horizons by using annuals creatively. Sweet alyssum, for example, makes a charming edging plant and often is used that way. A more unusual and interesting approach, however, would be to plant it in drifts among taller plants, to give the effect of a snowy ground cover. If you're looking for a dash of pink in the front of your garden but are bored with wax begonias, substitute polka-dot plant (*Hypoestes phyllostachya*).

Using Plants Imaginatively

Even an old standby like impatiens still can look fresh if you use it in an interesting way. Two popular impatiens colors of recent origins are

TOP: A prolific bloomer, scarlet sage (*Salvia splendens*) is available in a variety of attractive hues, including salmon.
BOTTOM: Traditionally preferred as an edging, sweet alyssum offers a striking contrast when planted among taller shade-lovers, such as impatiens.

maroon and red-violet. Either color can set your teeth on edge when planted with a mass of other mixed impatiens. Planting maroon or red-violet impatiens next to coleus, with its yellow-green foliage, or next to the spring green leaves of *Sedum* 'Autumn Joy' provides a new and exciting look. When you're working with a limited palette, as you'll need to in a shady bed or border, combining perennials, bulbs, and annuals gives you more options.

Be creative when choosing locations for beds and borders, too. Don't limit yourself to a rectangle in front of the house. Put beds and borders in a front, back, or side yard, or in front of a hedge, fence, or wall. Carve out an island bed in an expanse of lawn—and have less lawn to mow. Place a garden along a property line or next to a driveway. Plant in the strip of grass between the sidewalk and the street or at the end of a driveway. Tuck plants into a corner next to the front steps, or by the back door, or in the narrow strip between your house and the house next door.

Use your imagination. Putting plants in unexpected places adds to the fun of gardening.

Gardens for Small Spaces

Some of the smallest, most intimate spaces on your property are likely to be shady, and they can be ideal places for tiny gardens. One of the best is where you enter and leave the house. Plants add a gracious note of welcome near the front door or another entrance to your home.

Plant a small dooryard garden with dwarf conifers and flowers, or a compact border along a walk or path leading to the door. Put a small raised bed or a planter box next to the stoop, if you don't have a porch.

For a less permanent planting, create a miniature flower garden in a wooden tub, or place a neatly trimmed small evergreen or topiary on each side of the door. Yew, boxwood, arborvitae, Japanese holly, and privet will grow nicely in light to half or even full shade.

Mass small pots together to create a gardenlike effect. If the steps leading to a porch or deck are wide enough, set a potted plant on each one.

Plants for Entries

Shade-loving annuals are a good choice for an entry garden. You can use different plants each year to change the look. Impatiens, browallia, Persian violet, ferns, lobelia, tuberous begonias, torenia, caladiums, coleus, fuchsias, and ivy all thrive when grown in containers. So do ferns. See the list of annuals under Plants for Beds and Borders on page 53 for more suggestions.

Don't limit entrance gardens to the front door. Put plants near the entries you use the most. You could have a pocket garden next to the front door or a side door, or along the

ABOVE: Tuberous begonias, impatiens, and a fern make a cheerful tiny garden in containers.
BELOW: In this inviting entry, polyanthus primroses line the walk, and pots of cyclamen and other plants dress up the porch.

path leading from the garage to the house. All can be dressed up with the addition of some plants.

You can even bring the garden onto the porch, by mounting window boxes atop the wall or railing enclosing the porch. Lushly planted boxes will let you look out over refreshing greenery and colorful blossoms as you sit on the porch on a summer day.

To create a living screen and give porch sitters some shade and privacy, suspend hanging baskets at different levels directly above the window boxes. Attach hangers to the under-

A lovely compact ground cover for West Coast gardens is blue star creeper (*Laurentia fluviatillis*).

A planter filled with colorful coleus, fuchsias, and trailing variegated vinca brings a romantic touch to a wooden screen.

side of the porch roof, close to the edge. Fill the baskets with cascading plants such as fuchsias and trailers such as ivy or vinca that will dangle toward the plants in the window boxes.

Another place to tuck small plants is in little pockets left between flagstones or bricks in a patio or path, or between stones in a dry stone wall. In a path or patio, space stones far

enough apart to allow for insertion of plants here and there, or leave out an occasional brick or stone. Scoop out the soil and replace it with a good all-purpose potting mix or a well-drained blend of good garden loam, peat moss, and sharp builder's sand. Place a small plant in each pocket of soil.

Only plants that remain small—preferably those that grow in a low rosette or mound and stay close to the ground—will do for this type of garden. Possibilities include violets, Corsican mint (*Mentha requienii*), lobelia, sweet alyssum, small hostas, ground ivy (*Glechoma hederacea*), bluets (*Houstonia caerulea*), bugleweed (*Ajuga* species), and mosses. In warm climates, plant baby's tears (*Soleirolia soleirolii*).

To create a feeling of intimacy and enclosure for an open patio, plant a

low hedge around the perimeter. For a lush feeling, add trellises or lattice panels next to the wall of the house from which the patio projects and train vines on them.

If your house is made of stone, brick, or stucco, you can grow clinging vines directly on the wall. English ivy (*Hedera helix*), Boston ivy (*Parthenocissus tricuspidata*), Virginia creeper (*Parthenocissus quinquefolia*), and winter creeper (*Euonymus fortunei*) will climb a rough-surfaced wall unaided. Gardeners in warm climates can cover walls with creeping fig (*Ficus pumila*) or Algerian ivy (*Hedera canariensis*).

If you grow vines directly on a wall, prune when necessary to keep vines away from wood trim, window frames, rain gutters, and shingles. The aerial roots of vines can damage wood, and the plants can clog rain gutters.

Vegetable and Herb Gardens

As a rule, vegetables and herbs love the sun. If you use some clever tactics and choose plants carefully, however, you can grow a surprising number of vegetables, herbs, and edible flowers in partial to light shade. Leafy greens, especially, perform well in a bright, shaded environment.

Chives

Shade can be beneficial for some edibles, especially where the summer sun is hot and intense and the air is clear and dry. Even in more moderate climates, some shade, particularly in the afternoon, allows leafy crops to develop a mild taste and succulent texture, without the bitterness or coarseness they sometimes take on when grown in hot conditions. Shade can extend the harvest, too, delaying the bolting of crops like lettuce. Plenty of moisture also helps.

Leaf vegetables and root crops can take more shade than fruit-bearing crops. You can grow carrots, beets, turnips, and potatoes without full sun.

Fruit-bearing crops generally need full sun, so don't plan on bumper crops of tomatoes, squash, peppers, corn, or beans from a shady plot. The plants will be taller and less bushy than those that receive full sun, and

Frilly leaf lettuce is ornamental as well as edible when combined with flowers in a small bed.

Edibles for Shade

Plants marked with an asterisk (*) will tolerate partial to light shade. The rest are recommended for partial shade.

Angelica*	Celery	Leaf lettuce*	Saffron crocus
Arugula	Chamomile	Lemon balm	Salad burnet
Beans	Chervil*	Lovage	Salsify
Bee-balm*	Chives	Mints	Sorrel
Beets	Coriander	Nasturtium	Spinach*
Borage	Costmary	Parsley	Summer squash
Broccoli	Cress*	Parsnips	Sweet cicely*
Brussels sprouts	Endive*	Peas	Sweet woodruff*
Cabbage	Garlic	Potatoes	Tarragon*
Calendula	Garlic chives	Pumpkins	Thyme
Caraway*	Ginseng*	Purslane*	Turnips
Catnip	Goldenseal*	Radishes*	Valerian
Cauliflower	Kohlrabi	Rhubarb	Wintergreen*

they'll produce a smaller, later harvest. If you want to try these sun-lovers, choose early maturing varieties, and plant them where they will get sun from 10 a.m. to 2 p.m., when the light is strongest.

Brighter Is Better

When you design a garden of edibles for a shady location, pick the brightest spot available. Space plants farther apart than the distance recommended, because they'll sprawl and spread more in the lower light. If your location is shady during the peak sun hours, try some of the techniques recommended in Chapter 1 for bouncing additional light into the garden.

Your harvest will be smaller and later from your shady garden, but you'll get a harvest nonetheless. For a gardener, that's gratifying.

CHAPTER THREE

Elements of Design

Whatever kind of shade garden you decide to create, basic design principles can help you put the plants together attractively. Thoughtful design is what turns a collection of plants into a garden. Whether you're designing a naturalistic or a more traditional garden, you'll enjoy better results if you think about color schemes, seasonal interest, plant forms and textures, and planting patterns when creating the garden.

Color Schemes

Working with color can be the most enjoyable part of designing a garden. Color theory is complicated, and it takes artists years of study to understand it fully. Gardeners can apply the basic principles in their choice of plants to create wonderful effects. We all have ideas about the kinds of colors that appeal to us and the colors we like to see together. The most important rule in choosing colors for your garden is to choose ones that you like. Don't be afraid to bend the rules. If you don't like the guidelines you find below, ignore them and plant whatever combination of colors you like. It's your garden, and you should please yourself first.

That said, you need to ask yourself some questions before deciding on color schemes. First, do you prefer subtle combinations of colors that harmonize with one another, or do you like contrasting colors? Do you have a favorite color that you'd like to predominate in the garden from spring to fall, or would you rather see several different colors working together? What color scheme have you used to decorate the inside of your home? You might want to repeat one or more of those colors in the garden.

Color Palette

If you're planning a wildflower garden or one composed primarily of perennials, your color palette will be somewhat limited. Shade-loving plants tend to bloom in soft colors. There are many shades of pink; a number of blues, lavenders, and violets; lots of white, and even a few yellows for shade gardens. Except for cardinal flower, you won't find much bright red or orange. By including annuals in

Soft pastel colors—blue phlox, white foamflower, and pink azaleas—light up a woodland garden in spring.

the garden, however, you can bring hot reds, oranges, and golds, and softer shades of yellow, peach, and salmon to a shady garden with tuberous begonias, impatiens, and coleus.

One way to create a harmonious blend of colors is to grow several varieties of one type of flower—columbines, for example, or phlox or begonias. The colors among varieties may differ in hue and intensity, but they'll almost always harmonize with one another. One notable exception is impatiens.

The impatiens spectrum ranges from hot reds and oranges to cool lavenders. There are both warm pinks and cool, bluish pinks among the group. Although the impatiens clan includes many lovely pastels, some of the stronger colors would clash if planted together. You probably wouldn't want to see a red-violet next to a bright, clear orange or red, for example. If you love strong con-

Impatiens come in many colors, most of which harmonize or contrast beautifully with one another.

trasts, however, you might enjoy the combination. It's simply a matter of personal taste.

Contrasting color schemes can be jarring, but it's possible to achieve the liveliness of contrasting colors in ways that are easy on the eye. These are discussed later in this chapter, under Contrasting Color Schemes.

Whether you opt for harmonious or contrasting colors, take into account the colors of other landscape features outside the garden. The colors of foliage plants and flowers should work with the colors of near-

by outbuildings, fences, walls, pavement, and trees and shrubs, as well as those of other garden plants. When all the landscape colors work together, the design becomes a coherent, integrated whole.

Single-Color Gardens

The simplest kind of color scheme—and generally the easiest kind for new gardeners to develop—is monochromatic, built on shades of a single color. Sometimes a second color is added in small amounts as an accent. Many gardeners love the freshness of an

all-white garden, especially in a shady environment. A garden in shades of pink also is relatively easy to design for a shady location.

A single-color garden gives a sense of openness and space to a small shady site, and it need not be boring. You can vary the types of flowers, plant heights, shapes, foliage textures, and tones of color (pale, bright, or dark). In fact, in a monochromatic garden, you're better able to appreciate the subtleties of plant form and texture, because you're less distracted by a rainbow of colors.

This monochromatic summer garden in shades of pink and red includes impatiens, purple coneflower, lilies, and fuchsia.

An all-white garden brings sparkle to a shady spot. Here, hydrangeas and a white-edged hosta cultivar keep company.

Harmonious Colors

Gardens of related or harmonious (also called analagous) colors appeal to many people. Harmonious colors are located close together on an artist's color wheel and contain pigments in common. For example, a garden containing flowers of lavender, blue, and cool pink harmonize

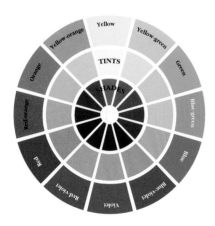

well because all the flowers contain some blue, even the pink ones. Another harmonious combination is purple, rose, and warm pink, all of which contain some red.

Contrasting Colors

Contrasting colors are farther apart on a color wheel. Complementary colors lie opposite one another on the color wheel and contrast more strongly than any other combination of colors. Orange and blue are complementary colors, as are yellow and violet, and red and green.

Contrasting colors have interesting effects on one another. Some contrasting colors have a modifying effect on each other when planted together. For example, blue flowers tend to cast a yellowish shadow on neighboring blossoms and can make white flowers appear closer to an ivory color. When the contrasting colors are pure hues of the complements, however, the contrast is exaggerated. The right shade of green foliage makes red flowers look redder.

It's generally best to avoid mixing pure contrasting colors in the garden. They'll work better visually if you use a deep shade of one color and a pale tint of the other. For example, if you want to mix purple and yellow flowers, you may find the combination more appealing if you combine deep purple with soft yellow, or lavender with rich gold. To mix blue and orange, try softening the orange to peach or deeping the blue to violet.

When combining contrasting colors, use one strong color as an accent, in small doses, and spread the softer color or colors over a larger area.

If you want to mix several strong colors in an intense blend of impatiens, perhaps, or coleus, put them

ABOVE: A pink and lavender scheme pairs wood hyacinth, or Spanish bluebell, with azaleas of clear pink.
BELOW: Red and green intensify when they're placed next to one another.

where they'll be viewed across an expanse of lawn or ground cover. All that green will make the colors appear less strident. If they're planted where you'll see them up close, the colors could be jarring.

Seasonal and Multiseason Color

Part of choosing colors for your garden is deciding when those colors will appear. If you're planning a woodland garden or mixed border with shrubs and wildflowers, the peak season of bloom probably will be in spring.

Tips for Handling Color

◆ Plant in drifts of color for visual impact. Single plants get lost.

◆ Use a simple color scheme that relates to other landscape elements and the site.

◆ Employ solid-color flowers of several hues in gardens. Bicolored flowers are more difficult to work with.

◆ Allow adjacent areas of color to intermingle along the edges for a softer look.

◆ Plant light colors in shade gardens. Dark colors are harder to see.

◆ Select flowers in a harmonious mixture of cool colors for a soothing, restful feeling.

◆ Create the illusion of more space in a small garden by planting warm colors in front and cool colors in back.

◆ Lighten up dim areas with white and pastels. Use white in deeply shaded gardens.

◆ Use whites and pastels to make your garden glow at dusk. Stronger colors disappear in the fading light.

◆ Soften strong colors or harsh contrasts by surrounding them with lots of white flowers or deep green foliage.

Splashes of contrasting yellow wake up this otherwise subtle pink and purple garden.

Spring-Blooming Flowers

In addition to many wildflowers, some of the most beautiful shade-tolerant perennials also bloom in spring. Hybrid columbines (*Aquilegia*), bergenia (*Bergenia cordifolia*), Siberian bugloss (*Brunnera macrophylla*), bleeding heart (*Dicentra* species), globeflower (*Trollius* species), leopard's bane (*Doronicum cordatum*), primroses (*Primula* species), and clivia (*Clivia miniata*) flower in spring. Spring color also can be obtained from ground covers like bugleweed (*Ajuga* species), *Epimedium* species, and lily-of-the-valley (*Convallaria majalis*).

If you garden under deciduous trees, where it is sunny in spring, you can have masses of color from hardy bulbs like daffodils, narcissus, tulips, and grape hyacinths (*Muscari*

Bugleweed becomes a carpet of rich violet when the plants bloom in spring.

Blue phlox makes a lovely companion for spring tulips and violas.

species). Azaleas, rhododendrons, and camellias burst into glorious shades of pink, rose, red, and white. Azaleas offer sunny yellow and flaming orange as well. Other spring-blooming shrubs include kerria, Carolina allspice (*Calycanthus floridus,* which has aromatic brownish-red flowers), mountain laurel (*Kalmia latifolia*), leucothoe, pieris, evergreen clematis (*Clematis armandii*), Carolina jessamine (*Gelsemium sempervirens*), and sweetly fragrant *Jasminum polyanthum.*

Summer Color

Although spring is a season of riches in shade gardens, color abounds in summer as well. Annuals will flower throughout the summer, and their colors are rich and varied. A host of perennials are available for summer color, and some bulbs, too. The airy spires of astilbe and goat's beard (*Aruncus dioicus*) bring soft masses of color. The upright spikes of foxglove (*Digitalis grandiflora*), bear's breeches (*Acanthus mollis*), black snakeroot

Sweet-scented lily-of-the-valley sends out its delicate white bells for an all-too-brief period in May.

Plants for Spring Color

Perennials and Bulbs

Bergenia (*Bergenia cordifolia*): pink, white

Bethlehem sage (*Pulmonaria saccharata*): reddish violet, blue, white

Bleeding heart (*Dicentra spectabilis*): pink, white

Bluebells (*Endymion* species, *Hyacinthoides* species): blue, pink, white

Bugleweed (*Ajuga* species): blue, purple, white

Christmas rose (*Helleborus niger*), cool climates: white to pinkish

Clivia species, warm climates: orange-scarlet

Columbine (*Aquilegia* species and hybrids): red, rose, pink, yellow, violet, purple, blue, white

Creeping phlox (*Phlox stolonifera*): purple, blue, pink, white

Crested iris (*Iris cristata*): purple

Cyclamen, some species: red, rose, pink

Epimedium species: red, pink, yellow, white

Forget-me-not (*Myosotis* species): sky blue

Fritillary (*Fritillaria* species): pink, purple, brownish

Globeflower (*Trollius* species): yellow, orange

Glory-of-the-snow (*Chionodoxa* species): blue

Grape hyacinth (*Muscari* species): blue, violet

Jacob's ladder (*Polemonium* species): violet-blue

Lady's mantle (*Alchemilla* species): yellow-green

Lenten rose (*Helleborus orientalis*): greenish white to rose-purple

Leopard's bane (*Doronicum cordatum*): yellow

Lily-of-the-valley (*Convallaria majalis*), fragrant: white

Marsh marigold (*Caltha palustris*): yellow

Narcissus and daffodil (*Narcissus* species and hybrids), some fragrant: yellow, cream, white

Oconee bells (*Shortia galacifolia*): white

Periwinkle (*Vinca minor*): blue to violet

Primrose (*Primula* species): red, rose, pink, yellow, orange, blue, violet, white

Siberian bugloss (*Brunnera macrophylla*): sky blue

Solomon's-seal (*Polygonatum* species), some fragrant: white

Spring snowflake (*Leucojum vernum*): white

Squill (*Scilla* species): blue, pink

Striped squill (*Puschkinia* species): blue, white

Trillium species: white, yellow, pink

Trout lily (*Erythronium* species): white, yellow, purple

Tulip (*Tulipa* species and hybrids): red, rose, pink, purple, orange, yellow, white

Violet (*Viola* species): white, blue, purple, yellow

Virginia bluebell (*Mertensia virginica*): lavender to blue

Wild geranium (*Geranium maculatum*): lilac-pink

Wild geranium

Daffodil

Wild strawberry (*Fragaria* species): white

Wild sweet William (*Phlox divaricata*): lavender-blue, white

Wood anemone (*Anemone nemorosa*): purple, blue, pink, white

Shrubs and Vines

Azalea (*Rhododendron* species and hybrids), some fragrant: red, rose, pink, yellow, orange, white

Camellia (*Camellia japonica*): red, rose, pink, white

Carolina allspice (*Calycanthus floridus*), fragrant: brownish red

Carolina jessamine (*Gelsemium sempervirens*): yellow

Drooping leucothoe (*Leucothoe fontanesiana*): white

Evergreen clematis (*Clematis armandii*), fragrant: white

Fothergilla species: white

Japanese kerria (*Kerria japonica*): yellow

Jasminum polyanthum: white, fragrant

Korean forsythia (*Abeliophyllum distichum*): white

Mountain laurel (*Kalmia latifolia*): pink, rose-red, white

Pieris species: white

Rhododendron (*Rhododendron* species and hybrids): red, rose, pink, lavender, white

Viburnum species: white

(*Cimicifuga racemosa*), *Rehmannia*, and monkshood (*Aconitum* species) add vertical line and height. Most daisies need sun, but if you love daisy-like flowers, you can enjoy some in summer with purple coneflower (*Echinacea purpurea*), golden groundsel (*Ligularia dentata*), or annual cinerarias. The lavish blooms of hydrangeas and Siberian and Japanese irises lend a more classic elegance to a shady garden, giving it more of the feeling of a traditional bed or border. Lilies, too, contribute to a more clas-

Summer bloomers include purple coneflower, bee-balm, and astilbe.

Shade-loving annuals such as fancy-leaved caladiums and ever-popular impatiens bring color to the garden all summer long.

sic look, as do the lilylike blooms of lily of the Nile (*Agapanthus* species). To bring some color up off the ground, plant summer-blooming vines in a lightly shaded garden. Hybrid clematis is available in many colors, and species clematis such as Italian clematis (*Clematis viticella*) offer more delicate flower forms. Later in the season, silver-lace vine (*Polygonum*

aubertii) or sweet autumn clematis (*Clematis paniculata*) will blanket a fence with masses of small white flowers that cover the plants like billows of foam. Those of sweet autumn clematis are lightly fragrant, too. You also could plant climbing hydrangea (*Hydrangea anomala* subspecies *petiolaris*) up a tree trunk. Once established, it climbs by itself.

Autumn Color

Autumn is almost synonymous with chrysanthemums in the United States, but mums need to grow in full sun. You could purchase plants already in bud to pop into the shade garden, but there are other, more natural ways to have autumn color in your shady plot. Ultimately, growing plants adapted to the shade that are

Elements of Design

Plants for Summer Color

Wood lily

Perennials and Bulbs

Astilbe species: red, rose, pink, white

Bear's breeches (*Acanthus mollis*): lavender, pink, white

Bee-balm (*Monarda didyma*): red, rose, pink, purple, white

Bellflower (*Campanula* species): blue, violet

Black snakeroot (*Cimicifuga racemosa*): white

Cardinal flower (*Lobelia cardinalis*): red

Daylily (*Hemerocallis* species and hybrids), some fragrant: red, pink, orange, salmon, yellow, cream

Foxglove (*Digitalis grandiflora*): yellow

Goat's beard (*Aruncus dioicus*): white

Golden groundsel (*Ligularia dentata*): yellow

Goldenstar (*Chrysogonum virginianum*): yellow

Hosta species and hybrids (some fragrant): lavender, white flowers

Japanese iris (*Iris kaempferi*): red-violet, purple, blue-violet

Lily of the Nile (*Agapanthus* species): blue, violet, white

Lilyturf (*Liriope* species): blue-violet

Meadow lily (*Lilium canadense*): red, yellow-orange, yellow

Meadow-rue (*Thalictrum* species): lavender, pink, white

Monkshood (*Aconitum* species): blue, violet

Purple coneflower (*Echinacea purpurea*): pinkish purple

Rehmannia elata: rose-pink

Spiderwort (*Tradescantia* species): blue-violet, rose-pink

Summer hyacinth (*Galtonia candicans*), fragrant: white

Turk's-cap lily (*Lilium superbum*): orange

Turtle-head (*Chelone* species): pink, white

Wood lily (*Lilium philadelphicum*): orange-red

Annuals and Biennials

Balsam (*Impatiens balsamina*): red, pink, orange, purple, white

Browallia (*Browallia speciosa*): blue-violet, white

Caladium (*Caladium* x *hortulanum*): red, rose, pink, white, green leaves

Clarkia species: red, pink, white

Cineraria (*Senecio* x *hybridus*): red, pink, purple, blue, white

Coleus hybrids: maroon, red, pink, bronze, yellow, chartreuse, green foliage

Cupflower (*Nierembergia hippomanica*): purple, blue, white

Foxglove (*Digitalis purpurea*): lavender, pink, white

Fuchsia hybrids: red, rose, pink, purple, white

Impatiens hybrids: red, rose, pink, lavender, orange, salmon, red-violet, white

Johnny-jump-up (*Viola tricolor*): purple, blue, yellow

Lobelia (*Lobelia erinus*): blue, white

Monkey flower (*Mimulus* species): red, yellow

Nicotiana species, some fragrant: red, rose, pink, white, green

Pansy (*Viola* x *wittrockiana*), blooms in cool weather: red, rose, pink, purple, blue, orange, yellow, white

Persian violet (*Exacum affine*): lavender-blue

Polka-dot plant (*Hypoestes phyllostachya*): pink and green leaves

Tuberous begonia

Scarlet sage (*Salvia splendens*): red, pink, purple, white

Sweet alyssum (*Lobularia maritima*), fragrant: white, purple

Tuberous begonia (*Begonia* x *tuberhybrida*): red, rose, pink, yellow, orange, salmon, white

Wax begonia (*Begonia* x *semperflorens-cultorum*): red, pink, orange, salmon, white

Wishbone flower (*Torenia fournieri*): purple, rose-pink, white

Shrubs and Vines

Azalea (*Rhododendron* species and hybrids), some fragrant: red-orange, orange, yellow, pink, white

Clematis species and hybrids: red, rose, pink, yellow, blue, purple, violet, white

Glossy abelia (*Abelia grandiflora*): white, pink

Hydrangea (*Hydrangea* species): pink, blue, white

Silver-lace vine (*Polygonum aubertii*): white

Sweet pepperbush (*Clethra alnifolia*), fragrant: white

Azalea

interesting in fall will be more satisfying than planting mums, which don't really belong there and won't look quite right. Many annuals will keep blooming in fall right up until the first frost. Some perennials and bulbs also flower as the days grow shorter. Three of the best are hardy cyclamen (*Cyclamen hederifolium, Cyclamen cilicium,* and *Cyclamen europeaum* are autumn bloomers), Japanese anemone (*Anemone* x *hybrida* blooms in late summer in sunnier gardens), and autumn snowflake (*Leucojum autumnale*). Gardeners in mild climates can

Deciduous trees and shrubs such as this witch hazel are one way to bring autumn color to the landscape.

The elegant white flowerheads of peegee hydrangea fade to a lovely salmon-pink in fall, for two seasons of garden color.

enjoy the lovely blossoms of sasanqua camellia. Ornamental grasses come into their own in autumn, when their plumy seedheads wave gracefully in the breeze.

Fall also is the season when the leaves of deciduous trees and shrubs turn to warm shades of red, orange, russet, and gold, before dropping as the plants prepare for their winter dormancy. In the shade garden, Virginia creeper and Boston ivy turn brilliant red and scarlet in fall, as do many Japanese maples. The leaves of bishop's hat turn reddish, too. Even evergreens may take on a different color when the weather turns cold.

Plants for Autumn Color

Perennials and Bulbs

Autumn snowflake (*Leucojum autumnale*): white

Cyclamen species: rose, pink, white

Epimedium species: reddish leaves

Goldenrod (*Solidago* species): yellow

Italian arum (*Arum italicum* 'Pictum'): red berries

Japanese anemone (*Anemone* x *hybrida*): rose, pink, white

Ornamental grasses: seedheads in shades of gold, tan, cream

Plumbago (*Ceratostigma plumbaginoides*): blue

Toad lily (*Tricyrtis hirta*): white

Wood aster (*Aster cordifolius*): blue

Annuals

Many annuals still blooming, many colors

Shrubs and Vines

Bearberry (*Arctostaphylos uva-ursi*): red berries

Boston ivy (*Parthenocissus tricuspidata*): red to orange leaves

Bunchberry (*Cornus canadensis*): red berries

Sasanqua camellia (*Camellia sasanqua*): red, rose, pink, white

Sweet autumn clematis (*Clematis paniculata*): white, fragrant

Virginia creeper (*Parthenocissus quinquefolia*): red leaves

Winter creeper (*Euonymus fortunei* 'Colorata'): reddish-purple leaves

Wintergreen (*Gaultheria procumbens*): red berries

Virginia creeper

Those of *Euonymus fortunei* 'Colorata' turn reddish purple in fall and winter.

Finally, colorful berries are another feature found in the garden in autumn. Wintergreen (*Gaultheria procumbens*), bearberry (*Arctostaphylos uva-ursi*), partridgeberry (*Mitchella repens*), and bunchberry (*Cornus canadensis*) produce red berrylike fruit close to the ground.

Winter Interest

In winter, the garden is quiet in cold climates, but even snowy landscapes offer plenty to see. Hollies and, especially, winterberry (*Ilex verticillata*) hold their bright red berries through much of the winter if the birds don't eat them. Some trees and shrubs have decorative bark that's easiest to appreciate when the leaves are gone. Climbing hydrangea, red-osier dogwood (*Cornus sericea*), and 'Heritage' river birch (*Betula nigra* 'Heritage') are three outstanding examples. Later, the fragrant flowers of witch hazels (*Hamamelis* species) offer clusters of little yellow or orange ribbons.

Gardeners in the South have a large array of plants in winter. Christmas rose (*Helleborus niger*), primroses, pansies, camellias, and Carolina jessamine (*Gelsemium sempervirens*) bloom in mild winter climates.

Multiseason Interest

How do you put all these seasonal specialties together? You can plan your garden to put on its biggest show in one season by primarily growing plants that bloom at that time of year. For multiseason interest, however, you need to include plants for different seasons. This is easier to accomplish if you work with different types of plants. For example, you might combine hardy bulbs and summer perennials, or spring and summer perennials and autumn foliage. You could focus on shrubs, including some that bloom in spring and summer and some with colorful leaves or berries in fall. If you love perennials, you could include some for each season in an herbaceous bed or border.

For many gardeners, a dazzling display in one season isn't enough. If you want a garden filled with color all season long, you'll need to select plants that are colorful throughout the growing season. They are basically of three types: annuals, foliage plants, and ornamental grasses. Ferns, too, are foliage plants, and they're beautiful and interesting. Their beauty, however, like the appeal of perennials when out of bloom, is quieter. The subtler qualities of foliage are discussed later in this chapter, under Plant Forms and Foliage Textures. For a garden of nonstop color, combine the colorful foliage plants discussed below with shade-tolerant annual flowers.

Foliage Color

Foliage is an important part of any garden, and it functions as an element of garden design in many ways. Leaves provide a backdrop for flowers, a field of green against which the brighter colors of blossoms are displayed. Because plants are mostly foliage when they're not in bloom—which for many plants is most of the growing season—leaves often are what we see when we look at plants.

New gardeners tend to ignore leaves. As gardeners spend more time in the garden, however, they begin to

---

Plants for Winter Interest

Camellia (*Camellia japonica*), warm climates: red, rose, white

Carolina jessamine (*Gelsemium sempervirens*), warm climates: yellow

Christmas rose (*Helleborus niger*), warm climates: greenish white or pinkish

Climbing hydrangea (*Hydrangea anomala* subspecies *petiolaris*): attractive bark

Heritage river birch (*Betula nigra* 'Heritage'): attractive bark

Hollies (*Ilex* species): red berries

Pansy (*Viola* x *wittrockiana*), warm climates: red, rose, pink, orange, yellow, purple, blue, white

Red-osier dogwood (*Cornus sericea*): red stems

Winterberry (*Ilex verticillata*): red berries

Winter hazel (*Corylopsis* species): yellow

Witch hazel (*Hamamelis* species). fragrant: yellow, orange

Winterberry

pay more attention to the many shapes and textures of foliage. These qualities are important design elements and are discussed in the next section of this chapter.

In addition to their forms and textures, some leaves contribute color to the garden equation. You can use colored foliage to work with the colors of flowers in the garden, or you can create a garden devoted entirely to foliage plants. Even in a shady garden there is a surprising range of plants from which to choose.

Types of Color

Foliage color is of two basic types. Leaves may be primarily green and variegated with a second color, or they may be a color or combination of colors other than green.

Variegated leaves are striped, edged, mottled, or splashed with creamy white or yellow. The variegation is caused by a lack of chlorophyll in those parts of the leaves.

Sometimes, variegation is caused by disease or lack of certain nutrients. This sort of pale or yellowish color usually is known as chlorosis, and it's not a desirable condition. Plants with variegated leaves often occur as a genetic mutation, and may not be reproducible if the next generation of plants is grown from seed. Thus, many variegated cultivars must be propagated vegetatively—by cuttings, layering, or some other means—to preserve the variegation.

Plants with colored leaves, on the other hand, get their color from pigmentation. Unusually colored leaves also often result from mutations, and these plants may or may not revert to their natural green color when grown from seed.

Plants with colored or variegated leaves can add considerable interest to the garden. Because the leaves are colorful throughout the growing season, these foliage plants can provide continuity between bursts of floral color, they can serve as accents or highlights in the garden, or they can

TOP: Marrying chartreuse and deep green varieties of hostas forms a subtle all-green garden union.
BOTTOM: The green leaves of lungwort are splotched with silvery white, as if dusted with sugar. The colored leaves of caladiums often are veined with contrasting colors.

Elements of Design

Colorful Foliage

The plants listed here have variegated or colored leaves, and tolerate or prefer some degree of shade.

Algerian ivy (*Hedera canariensis* 'Variegata'): edged in ivory

Amur silver grass (*Miscanthus sacchariflorus* 'Aureum'): silver

Arborvitae (*Thuja occidentalis* 'Rheingold'): golden

Bethlehem sage (*Pulmonaria saccharata*): spotted with white

Bishop's weed (*Aegopodium podagraria* 'Variegatum'): variegated with white

Blue oat grass (*Helictotrichon sempervirens*): blue-green

Bulbous oat grass (*Arrhenatherum elatius* var. *bulbosum* 'Variegatum'): striped in cream and blue-green

Bugleweed (*Ajuga reptans*) 'Bronze Beauty': bronze-purple

Bugleweed (*Ajuga reptans*) 'Burgundy Glow': combination of ivory, pink, and green

Bugleweed (*Ajuga reptans*) 'Royalty': dark purple

Bugleweed (*Ajuga reptans*) 'Variegata' ('Silver Beauty'): variegated with white

Caladium (*Caladium* x *hortulanum*): green with red, pink, or white

Chameleon plant (*Houttuynia cordata* 'Variegata'): green mottled with reddish purple and cream

Coleus (*Coleus* hybrids): combinations of maroon, red, pink, salmon, yellow, chartreuse, cream, and green

Creeping Jenny (*Lysimachia nummularia* 'Aurea'): golden

Cyclamen species: some are variegated with silver

English ivy (*Hedera helix*) 'Glacier': splotched with white and silver

English ivy (*Hedera helix*) 'Goldheart': dark green with gold center

English ivy (*Hedera helix*) 'Pixie': variegated with white

English ivy (*Hedera helix*) 'Silverdust': variegated with white

English yew (*Taxus baccata* 'Standishii'): yellow-green

Fescue (*Festuca ovina* var. *glauca*): blue-green

Gardener's garters (*Phalaris arundiacea* 'Picta'): striped with creamy white

Gold-dust plant (*Aucuba japonica* 'Variegata' and *Aucuba japonica* 'Maculata'): spotted and splashed with gold

Golden wood millet (*Milium effusum* 'Aureum'): yellow-green

Hakonechloa macra 'Aureola': gold striped with green

Hosta (*Hosta* species and hybrids): combinations of green, blue-green, chartreuse, gold, and white

Italian arum (*Arum italicum* 'Pictum'): green with light green veins and mottling

Japanese painted fern (*Athyrium nipponicum* 'Pictum'): tinged with purple and overlaid with silver

Japanese pieris (*Pieris japonica* 'Variegata'): edged with white

Japanese sedge (*Carex morrowii* 'Variegata': striped with cream

Japanese sedge (*Carex morrowii* 'Aureo-variegata': green and yellow striped

Lilyturf (*Liriope muscari* 'Variegata'): striped with cream

Mock orange (*Philadelphus coronarius* 'Aureus'): new leaves are golden in spring

Pachysandra (*Pachysandra terminalis* 'Variegata'): edged in white

Palace Purple alumroot (*Heuchera micrantha* 'Palace Purple'): deep purple-bronze

Pittosporum (*Pittosporum tenuifolium* 'Silver Queen'): silvery edges

Polka-dot plant (*Hypoestes phyllostachya*): splashed with pink

Spotted dead nettle (*Lamium maculatum*): spotted and splashed with silvery white

Spotted dead nettle (*Lamium maculatum*): 'Beacon Silver': variegated with silver and edged in green

Striped St. Augustine grass (*Stenotaphrum secundatum* 'Variegatum'): variegated white and light green

Sweet flag (*Acorus americanus* 'Variegatus'): striped with yellow

Velvet grass (*Holcus lanatus* var. *variegatus*): green and white striped

Vinca (*Vinca major* 'Variegata'): irregularly edged in pale yellow to cream

Winter creeper (*Euonymus fortunei*) 'Emerald Gaiety': variegated with white

Winter creeper (*Euonymus fortunei*) 'Emerald 'n' Gold': variegated with yellow

Winter creeper (*Euonymus fortunei*) 'Golden Prince': variegated with yellow

Winter creeper (*Euonymus fortunei*) 'Ivory Jade': variegated with white

Yellow flag (*Iris pseudacorus* 'Variegata'): striped with yellow

Yew (*Taxus baccata* 'Aurea'): young leaves are golden

Polka-dot plant

form the basis of the garden and provide most of the color.

If you decide to include plants with colored or variegated leaves in your garden, don't overuse them. In a bed or border of flowering plants, too much colorful foliage will detract from the impact of the blossoms and make the whole scene look too busy. Even an all-foliage garden will work best if you include lots of green plants with the colored or variegated ones. Using colored foliage in dashes is more visually striking.

By combining plants with a variety of foliage textures, this gardener has created a garden that's interesting even when plants aren't in bloom.

Some varieties of hostas are striped with creamy white, like these, or edged or streaked with lime green, deep blue-green, or gold.

When combining plants with colorful foliage, consider the shapes and textures of the leaves as well as the colors. Mix the plants in interesting ways, as described in the next section.

Plant Forms and Foliage Textures

Plants have form and texture on different levels. First, there's the overall form of the plant. You discern the forms of plants when you see their outline against the empty space immediately surrounding them, or in contrast to a lighter or darker plant against which they are silhouetted. In a mature garden, the forms of the individual plants intermingle and come together in a total composition.

Shade Plant Forms

Some plants have a mounded form created by a low, dense, rounded clump of foliage. Others, especially plants used for ground cover, are low and spreading, staying close to the ground and often growing wider than they are high. Some plants, particularly grasses, plants with narrow, grasslike leaves, and plants that produce their flowers in spikes, have a vertical, upright form. These valuable plants add vertical lines to break up the lower, rounded forms of other plants. Still other plants are branched and bushy, growing upward but in a spreading rather than in a narrowly vertical way.

A plant's form may change when it comes into bloom. For example, a foxglove in bloom, with its tall spike of flowers, has a strong vertical line to it. Before the plant flowers, however, it is a rosette (cluster) of leaves close to the ground. The Plant Forms list opposite includes some notable examples of plants whose form changes dramatically when they are in bloom.

When you design your garden, include plants with different forms to add interest to the overall picture. Interspersing spiky plants among mounded and bushy ones will bring a sense of movement and life. You also can use a group of spiky plants to draw the viewer's eye upward toward a particularly handsome tree, or a vine growing overhead. Similarly, low, spreading plants that trail outward from the main garden can lead the eye

Elements of Design

Foxglove

Upright, Spiky, Vertical

Astilbe, in bloom

Bear's breeches (*Acanthus mollis*), in bloom

Black snakeroot (*Cimicifua racemosa*), in bloom

Cardinal flower (*Lobelia cardinalis*)

Clivia

Daylily (*Hemerocallis* species and hybrids)

False dragonhead (*Physostegia virginiana*)

Foxglove (*Digitalis* species), in bloom

Goat's beard (*Aruncus dioicus*), in bloom

Irises

Lilies

Lilyturf (*Liriope* species)

Monkshood (*Aconitum* species)

Ornamental grasses

Scarlet sage (*Salvia splendens*)

Spiderwort (*Tradescantia* species)

Summer hyacinth (*Galtonia candicans*)

Turtlehead (*Chelone* species)

Bushy, Branched

Balloon flower (*Platycodon grandiflorus*)

Balsam (*Impatiens balsamina*)

Baneberry (*Actaea* species)

Bee-balm (*Monarda didyma*)

Plant Forms

Browallia (*Browallia speciosa*)

Bugloss (*Anchusa capensis*)

Calendula (*Calendula officinalis*)

Chinese forget-me-not (*Cynoglossum amabile*)

Clarkia (*Clarkia amoena*)

Coleus (*Coleus* hybrids)

Dame's rocket (*Hesperis matronalis*)

False Solomon's-seal (*Smilacina racemosa*)

Goldenrod (*Solidago* species)

Hardy begonia (*Begonia grandis*)

Hellebores (*Helleborus* species)

Jacob's ladder (*Polemonium caeruleum*)

Meadow-rue (*Thalictrum* species)

Meadowsweet (*Filipendula* species)

Monkshood (*Aconitum*)

Nicotiana (*Nicotiana* species and hybrids)

Persian violet (*Exacum affine*)

Wishbone flower (*Torenia fournieri*)

Mounded

Alumroot (*Heuchera* species)

Astilbe (*Astilbe* species and hybrids)

Anemone (*Anemone* species)

Bear's breeches (*Acanthus mollis*)

Black snakeroot (*Cimicifuga racemosa*)

Bleeding heart (*Dicentra* species)

Columbine (*Aquilegia* species and hybrids)

Cranesbill (*Geranium* species)

Forget-me-not (*Myosotis* species)

Forget-me-not

Globeflower (*Trollius* species)

Hardy cyclamen (*Cyclamen* species)

Hosta (*Hosta* species and hybrids)

Impatiens (*Impatiens* hybrids)

Lady's mantle (*Alchemilla* species)

Marsh marigold (*Caltha palustris*)

Oconee bells (*Shortia galacifolia*)

Pansy (*Viola* x *wittrockiana*)

Primrose (*Primula* species)

Saxifrage (*Saxifraga* species)

Shooting star (*Dodecatheon meadia*)

Siberian bugloss (*Brunnera macrophylla*)

Wandflower (*Galax urceolata*)

Low and Spreading

Bearberry (*Arctostaphylos uva-ursi*)

Bethlehem sage (*Pulmonaria saccharata*)

Bugleweed (*Ajuga* species)

Bunchberry (*Cornus canadensis*)

Chameleon plant (*Houttuynia cordata* 'Variegata')

Creeping phlox (*Phlox stolonifera*)

Dead nettle (*Lamium maculatum*)

Epimedium (*Epimedium* species)

Fairy bells (*Disporum* species)

Foamflower (*Tiarella cordifolia*)

Goldenstar (*Chrysogonum virginianum*)

Ivy (*Hedera* species)

Lily-of-the-valley (*Convallaria majalis*)

Pachysandra (*Pachysandra* species)

Periwinkle (*Vinca* species)

Polka-dot plant (*Hypoestes phyllostachya*)

Sweet alyssum (*Lobularia maritima*)

Sweet woodruff (*Galium odoratum*)

Violet (*Viola* species)

Wild ginger (*Asarum* species)

Wild sweet William (*Phlox divaricata*)

Bold hostas mingle with small-leaved azaleas, delicate ferns, and other plants in a graceful composition of textures and forms. The spiky foliage of narcissus adds vertical accents for a few weeks in late spring.

textures include smooth, fuzzy, hairy, bristly, thorny, pebbly, quilted, puckered, sticky, and slippery.

All leaves possess these textures. Becoming aware of the textures of plants brings new richness to the experience of a garden. Garden designers are able to manipulate plant textures to create subtle qualities that may go unnoticed by less-practiced eyes, but which combine to create a garden that works in ways the rest of us recognize and appreciate without fully understanding.

There is an art to combining foliage textures in the garden, and it can take a lifetime to truly master it. Even moderately experienced gardeners, however, can have fun playing with texture. Work a few different kinds of plant textures into your garden, and your composition of plants will be more interesting.

As you gain experience, you may even learn to create special effects. For example, plants of tropical origin often have big, bold, sculptural leaves. To create a garden with a tropical feeling, you could build it around bold-leaved plants like elephant ears (*Colocasia*), caladiums, *Gunnera manicata*, and Italian arum (*Arum italicum* 'Pictum').

Sculptural plants also have a contemporary feeling that can work well in a garden for a house of modernistic or avant-garde design. In addition to plants with large leaves, look for those with sleek, smooth textures and spiky forms for a contemporary-looking garden. Ornamental grasses are good choices, too.

Flowering perennials with handsome, interesting leaves are doubly valuable in the garden. Bergenia, Siberian bugloss (*Brunnera macrophylla*), and golden groundsel (*Ligularia*

horizontally across the ground toward another garden, a specimen shrub, or another feature of the landscape.

You can combine plant forms in a couple of ways. For the most naturalistic look, mimic the way plants grow together in nature. This is especially appropriate in a woodland or other environment-based garden, where you're attempting to create a look reminiscent of a natural setting. The other way to combine plant forms is aesthetically, mixing and matching mounds, bushes, verticals, and carpets to get a combination that pleases you.

Plant Textures

A plant's texture is largely determined by the size, shape, and surface quality of its leaves. Leaves possess two kinds of texture: visual and tactile.

Visual texture comes from the way leaves look, their outline in space, and the way they're affected by light. The visual texture of a plant's leaves might be described as bold, sculptural, sleek, delicate, lacy, fluffy, feathery, dense, sparse, glossy, or dull.

Tactile textures describe the way leaves would feel if you were to touch them. Words used to describe tactile

ABOVE: This perennial garden
is a marvelous symphony of foliage
shapes and textures.

INSET: The stunning green-and-gold-striped
foliage of an ornamental grass is like a shaft of
sunlight in this shady garden.

dentata) have large, sculptural leaves. Columbines (*Aquilegia* species and hybrids) are graced with mounds of delicate, attractively scalloped foliage. The leaves of fringed bleeding heart (*Dicentra eximia*) and astilbes are fine-ly cut and lacy, like fern fronds. Siberian iris and lilyturf (*Liriope* species) have sleek, narrow, grassy leaves that introduce vertical line to a flower bed or border. As you spend time working among your plants and come to know them better, you'll begin to appreciate the differences between their leaves. You'll be able to include foliage in your plans when you start a new garden or expand an existing one.

Planting Patterns

Within the confines of the garden, whatever its style, there are different ways of arranging plants. When laying out planting patterns, you need to consider three factors:

• the visibility of the plants in the garden in relation to positions from which they will likely be viewed;

• accessibility, so you can get into the garden to weed, deadhead, and perform other maintenance; and

• the visual impact of the plants themselves in relation to one another.

To allow all of the plants to be visible outside the garden, assuming the garden area is level, put the tallest plants in the back of the garden and work out toward the front of the garden in gradually decreasing heights, with the lowest plants along the front edge. In an island bed that will be viewed from all sides, place the tallest plants in the center of the garden and work out toward the edges on all sides.

Breaking Ranks

For the most natural, appealing look, allow plants to break out of their ranks a bit, and stagger the edges of plant groups to avoid creating rigid groups. You also can put taller plants in front of shorter ones, if the taller plants are open enough in their structure to allow you to see through them to the plants behind. Using tall, airy plants as scrims also creates an illusion of greater depth, a trick that can come in handy where space is limited.

To achieve visual impact from flowers and foliage plants, plant more than one of each, and plant them together in groups. A single astilbe placed by itself here or there will get lost in the overall design and won't be noticed. If you plant the entire garden that way, dotting the plants all about the plot, the result will look like confetti—no design pattern will be apparent. If you plant the astilbes or cinnamon ferns or columbines in concentrated groups, however, each will become a presence in the garden.

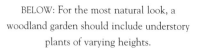

ABOVE: Placing small, delicate plants in the front of the garden and larger, bolder plants in back helps create depth.

BELOW: For the most natural look, a woodland garden should include understory plants of varying heights.

This border shows skillful use of color, form, texture, and plant
height. The plants unite in an artful composition.

ABOVE: Stepping-stones placed at a comfortable distance for walking make an attractive informal path.

Drifts of Color

If your garden is large, plant the flowers in flowing drifts. A drift is similar to an elongated clump or a wide band with softly curved sides and an undulating shape. A drift can be wide in the middle and narrow toward the ends, and adjoining drifts of flowers melt into one another, with a few plants intermingled along the edges.

LEFT: In a small garden, set plants in clumps of three or five to gain visual impact.

In a garden of any appreciable size, the colors will be most appealing when they're concentrated in these soft drifts.

In a large garden, it takes numerous plants to fill out a drift. If your funds are limited, plant a few good drifts of flowers in one part of the garden and expand the plantings year by year. That approach will give you a better display than just putting a few plants in each future drift throughout the garden. You may want to sketch the outlines of the drifts on the ground before you begin planting, by sprinkling lime through your fingers or by laying out lengths of rope or garden hose.

In a small garden where there's no room for sweeping drifts of color, group the plants into clumps. For the most natural look, try to make each clump irregular in shape. Don't put the plants in boxes or rings. Some gardeners toss a handful of stones into the air and position the plants where the stones land.

You'll find it easier to make an asymmetrical clump if you put an odd number of plants in each. Plant in groups of five, seven, nine, eleven, or more. Even in the tiniest garden, plant in groups of three or more. This rule applies even to accent colors used sparingly. It will work better to plant five groups of three plants in the accent color than to set out 15 single plants by themselves.

If you're striving for a precise, formal effect, perhaps to create a geometric pattern in a carpet bed, you can lay out the plants in straight lines. You'll need to mark the planting pattern on the ground before you plant, and measure carefully. Lay out the design with stakes and string, or by carefully sprinkling lime.

Elements of Design

A neatly mowed strip of lawn meanders through this well-tended
garden. The thick turf invites a barefoot stroll.

Paths and Walkways

If your garden is reasonably large, or if it's composed of several beds or borders, you'll need to put some sort of path or walkway through it. A path is an important part of a garden's overall design and shouldn't be treated as an afterthought. In fact, you should plan where paths will go before you ever put spade to soil.

Paths play many roles in the garden. First and foremost, they allow access. Whether a path winds through a woodland or simply divides a pair of small, neat beds, it allows visitors to stroll along and look at the plants. A path also gives the gardener access to plants to deadhead, weed, and perform other necessary maintenance.

A path can connect separate gardens located some distance from one another. In a formal garden designed in regular, geometric units, paths are prominent elements, helping to create the structure and framework of the garden. A path can lead the eye to a special feature or focal point of the garden, perhaps a sundial or birdbath, or it can direct the visitor to a comfortable bench in a shady corner.

Inconspicuous Paths

A path can be designed to be less noticeable, depending on the setting. In a naturalistic garden, for example, a path should allow access without being obtrusive. In a large, broad border, you may need to place a narrow path along the back of the border, hidden by plants, so you can care for plants you can't reach from the front of the garden.

OPPOSITE: Flagstones set in mulch make a naturalistic path through a woodland garden.

One of the keys to designing a successful path is to understand the function it will serve in the garden. When you know what the path is supposed to do, you can plan it to best serve its designated purpose.

Design Guidelines

Paths can take many forms, and you can choose from a diverse assortment of materials for surfacing them. Different materials tend to work best in different settings, so the type of garden you are planning will determine where the paths will be placed and how they will look.

In a naturalistic garden, paths are essential. If you're creating a garden in an existing woodland or wetland, one of the first things you'll have to do is blaze a trail through the garden site. The path may wind in and out among trees, and up and over a hillside. In this situation, you have to consider where the best footing can be had when deciding where the path will go. It's not just a matter of aesthetics. This kind of path cannot be designed on paper. You'll have to create it on-site, working your way through the garden-to-be.

A path through a naturalistic garden should be easy for visitors to follow without drawing undue attention to itself. In a woodland garden, the path will have to avoid large, shallow tree roots and small rocks that could trip unsuspecting feet. In a wetland or boggy area, the path will have to allow feet to stay dry.

Don't necessarily plot the path to traverse the shortest distance through the garden. A path that bends and winds is far more interesting. When

An unobtrusive path meandering among the trees is ideally suited for this woodland garden.

the stroller cannot see what's beyond the next curve, a sense of mystery and anticipation is created. The garden also seems larger because you can't see all of it at once. A winding path allows more of the plants to be viewed up close. If your garden is large enough, you may want to design a main path and one or more smaller side paths that branch off from it.

Path Styles

In a naturalistic garden, you want the path to blend into the landscape. The surface material has as much to do with the path's visual effect as the course it follows. A good way to tell if the finished path meets its visual objectives is to squint as you look at it. If the path is difficult to see through narrowed eyes, you've done a good job. If it stands out against the landscape as a dark or light line, it's too obvious. Use a different surface material.

In a more traditional or formal garden of beds and borders, you can plan paths when you design the garden on paper. A straight path works as part of the garden design, forming one of the axes along which the garden is structured, or leading the eye to a carefully planned focal point. A straight path often is especially nice when you allow some of the low plants in the front of the garden to spill out into the path to soften the edges. If this look appeals to you, make sure the path is wide enough to allow people to walk comfortably without stepping on the plants.

Whatever type of path your garden will have, take the time to plan it carefully so it works for you. Make the path wide enough so you can walk comfortably along it. A 2-foot-wide path will accommodate one person; a

A well-placed chair offers a comfortable spot
to rest after a stroll through the garden.

To soften the sharp lines of a straight, formal path,
allow clumps of plants to spill over its edges.

Elements of Design

path 3 to 4 feet wide will allow two people to stroll side by side. It's a good idea to make the path a bit wider where it curves. The path also should be well-drained, so you won't get muddy feet when walking on it. To prevent puddles from collecting on a flat path after rain, make the center of the path slightly higher, like a crowned road surface, so the water runs off to either side.

Keep the path a couple of feet away from large shrubs, trees with low branches, walls, and hedges, to avoid a feeling of confinement. You may need to remove some of the lower branches of large, mature trees so you can walk underneath without bumping into them.

Finally, choose a surface material that suits the type of garden, its location, and the amount of traffic the path will carry.

Surface Materials

You can use any number of materials to surface paths and walkways in the garden. Prices vary, some materials are more permanent than others, and different materials look best in different kinds of gardens. Choose from hard materials such as brick, flagstone, and concrete pavers; various kinds of loose stone; wood-based materials such as tree rounds and bark chips; and living surfaces such as ground covers, lawn grass, or moss.

In a naturalistic garden, natural materials look best. Surface the path with a material that might naturally be found in such an environment. In a woodland garden, tree rounds (horizontal slices cut from logs), shredded bark, wood chips, pine needles, and shredded leaves make good path materials. In a desert garden, gravel or stone would be more appropriate. For

a path through a shady seaside garden, consider light-colored pebbles. If the environment is closer to woodland or pine barrens, use pine needles. In a boggy garden, the path must be elevated to keep feet out of the muck. You could place large, flat-topped stepping-stones at a comfortable stepping distance apart, or construct sections of raised boardwalk to traverse the wettest areas. Use rot-resistant or treated wood.

Slate and Flagstone

Two of the most versatile paving materials, slate and flagstone can work in both formal and informal gardens. Set the stones a comfortable distance apart, in whatever pattern appeals to you. To soften the look of a slate or flagstone path and give it an old, weathered look, plant moss around and between the stones, if your soil is sufficiently moist and acidic. You also could plant another small-leaved ground cover, such as Corsican mint (*Mentha requienii*), or, in a warm climate, baby's-tears (*Soleirolia soleirolii*).

Brick and Concrete

Brick and concrete pavers will give your path the most formal look and will hold up well for years under heavy traffic. Brick can be laid in a variety of patterns, including herringbone, running bond, and straight bond. Concrete pavers also come in a variety of patterns and are designed with interlocking edges.

Ground Covers and Grass

If the soft, green look of ground covers or grass appeals to you, consider how much traffic the path will carry. For a heavily traveled path, lawn grass holds up best. To carry very heavy

Flagstone is a durable paving material that works in both formal and informal gardens.

A course of weathered local stones creates the look of a river made of stone and provides an interesting—if lumpy—path.

Brick can be laid in a variety of patterns and holds up well under foot traffic.

Making a Path

To build a path, begin by laying out its course. Use stakes and string to lay out a straight path, or lengths of rope or garden hose to lay out a curved path. Next, excavate the path area. If your path will be made of brick, stone, or concrete pavers, dig to a depth of 6 inches. For a mulched path, dig 3 to 4 inches. If the path will be of grass or ground covers, just prepare the soil for planting.

Tamp down the soil in an excavated path. To prevent weeds, cover with a weed barrier fabric or black plastic sheeting. Install an edging to keep path materials in place. Use plastic edging strips, treated lumber, or bricks set on edge for paths made of brick, concrete pavers, stone, or mulch. Hammer in wood or metal stakes to hold edging boards in place. Edge grass or ground-cover paths with metal or plastic edging strips.

Spread 2 inches of sand as a base for brick, concrete pavers, or stone. Tamp it down and level it with the edge of a board.

If you're using loose stone, spread a 2-inch layer of it, then roll it with a lawn roller to pack it in place. Spread the remaining 2 inches and roll again.

If you're using bricks or concrete pavers, set them in place one at a time, tapping each one into place with a rubber mallet. Cover the finished path with a thin layer of sand, then sweep with a broom so the sand fills the cracks between bricks or pavers. Water to settle the sand and clean the path.

To install flagstone, fieldstone, or slate, lay each stone on the ground and trace its outline with the tip of a trowel. Excavate the soil within the outline deep enough so the top of the stone will be level with the surrounding soil, plus 2 inches. Lay 2 inches of sand in the bottom of the hole, then set in the stone.

Steps

If your path travels a slope with a grade of more than 10 degrees, you probably will need to build steps. If the grade is steep, you'll need to add a railing, to make the climb easier. For comfort, make the steps the same width as the path, about 6 inches high and 12 inches deep. You can make the risers of logs set horizontally into the hillside. The stair treads can be surfaced with gravel, wood chips, or perhaps moss or a ground cover.

To build steps, begin by sinking two parallel upright stakes into the ground at each end of the first step. Fit a log or railroad tie cut to the proper length behind the stakes, and hammer it into place. Pack gravel or dense clay soil behind the wood riser to make a terrace that becomes the stair tread and forms the base of the next step. Repeat the procedure until you get to the top of the hill.

When the stairs are finished, plant ground covers along the sides and trailing off into the garden to tie the steps into the landscape.

If the steps will be used at night, install lighting and a railing.

If you want to enjoy evening walks through the garden, install lights along the path.

traffic—even vehicles—lay plastic reinforcing cells, and plant grass to grow up through them. The drawback is that a grass path will need maintenance, just like a lawn. You'll have to mow and fertilize, and the path will need sturdy edging strips to keep the grass from spreading beyond the path. The path will have to be wide enough to accommodate a lawn mower, too.

For a path that is traveled less often, consider planting a ground cover that tolerates light traffic. Roman chamomile (*Chamaemelum nobile*), *Mazus reptans*, and, in the warm cli-

mates of zones 9 and 10, brass buttons (*Cotula squalida*) are three possibilities. Moss is a lovely cover for a path, and positively delightful under bare feet, but it needs a specific set of conditions in order to thrive. In addition to shade, moss needs soil that is moist, humusy, and low in pH. If moss grows naturally on your property, you may be able to transplant enough of it into a path area that it will take hold and eventually carpet the path. Unless all of the necessary growing conditions are present, however, trying to create a moss-covered path will be an exercise in futility.

The stairs in this path are just wide enough to step on and unobtrusive in the garden.

Making a Plan

Now you're ready to draw a garden plan. Begin with the property or site map described in the beginning of Chapter 2. Make enlarged copies of the map so you can sketch out your garden in more detail.

Draw in the outlines of beds and borders or naturalistic gardens in the areas you have chosen as the best sites. Experiment with different shapes and sizes until you find what looks best to you.

When the outlines and measurements are in place, choose your color scheme. Draw in drifts or clumps of the colors you have chosen, to create a pleasing arrangement. Colored pencils come in handy for this phase of the process.

Choosing Plants

When you've got the colors plotted, choose plants for each area. It's important to work more or less to scale so you can determine the size of each drift or clump of plants and, in turn, how many plants you'll need.

This is the time to let your imagination run free, and to try out as many ideas as you like. It's easy to make changes when you're working on paper.

Remember, as you work, that your goal is to create a design that *you* like. Remember, too, that gardens evolve and change over time. If you're just not sure what you want, you can plant a little each year, and build your garden gradually. Every gardener has a different way to work, and you should find the method that's most enjoyable for you.

These well-weathered stone stairs are wide and comfortable, inviting an easy, relaxed pace.

Plants for Shade Gardens

This chapter contains descriptions and basic cultural information for more than 250 of the best plants to grow in shade gardens. Most are adaptable to a range of climates. Each entry discusses where the plant is hardy, the degree of shade it prefers or can tolerate, soil and moisture conditions, planting tips, and suggestions for using the plant effectively in your garden.

Trees and Shrubs

Trees and shrubs form the basic structure, the "bones" of a well-planned garden, especially a formal garden or a mixed bed or border. Because they are large and remain visible all year, their form and placement create a framework around which the rest of the garden can be planned.

Trees and shrubs add height and vertical lines to a garden, and bushy shrubs add mass. They contribute foliage that is green, variegated, or colored in autumn or throughout the growing season. Woody plants also provide flowers, interesting bark, and ornamental or edible fruit.

Abelia

Glossy abelia (*Abelia* x *grandiflora*) is a bushy shrub that grows to 8 feet tall and about 5 feet wide. Its graceful, arching branches bear pale pink or white flowers in summer and glossy green, oval leaves that turn bronze in autumn. Glossy abelia is hardy in zones 6 to 10.

Give glossy abelia partial shade to full sun, and well-drained soil with an acid pH. Prune in late winter or early spring to remove any dead or damaged wood.

Use glossy abelia in mixed beds and borders, as a specimen plant, or as a screen or divider.

Abeliophyllum

Korean forsythia or **white forsythia** (*Abeliophyllum distichum*) bears clusters of fragrant white or pink-tinged flowers similar to those of forsythia in spring before the oval leaves appear. It grows to 6 feet tall and equally wide. It is hardy in zones 5 to 8.

Plant Korean forsythia in very light shade to full sun, in moist but well-drained soil rich in organic matter. Prune in late winter to early spring to remove dead and damaged wood, and after blooming to promote bushier growth and improve the form.

Korean forsythia is a nice addition to a mixed border, or you can plant it along the edge of a woodland or as a background for spring bulbs.

Abies

Balsam fir (*Abies balsamea*) is more shade tolerant than other firs. It is pyramidal to cone shaped when young, becoming more irregular with age. Balsam fir grows to 75 feet tall and 20 to 25 feet across. The dark green needles are pleasantly aromatic. It is hardy in zones 3 to 5 and in mountainous regions farther south.

Glossy abelia (*Abelia* x *grandiflora*)

Korean forsythia/White forsythia (*Abeliophyllum distichum*)

Balsam fir (*Abies balsamea*)

Plant balsam fir in light shade to full sun. Like other firs, it needs soil that is moist but well drained and rich in organic matter with an acid pH. It grows best where summers are cool and the air is humid.

Balsam fir makes a good specimen tree to plant on a lawn, or you can include it in a woodland garden.

Acanthopanax

Five-leaf aralia (*Acanthopanax sieboldianus*, also known as *Eleutherococcus*), is a deciduous shrub that grows to 10 feet tall and equally wide. Its bright green leaves are palmately compound, with five oval leaflets splayed out from a central point. The arching stems eventually dip over to give the plant a rounded shape. Five-leaf aralia is hardy in zones 4 to 8.

Five-leaf aralia
(*Acanthopanax sieboldianus*)

Plant the shrub in full shade to full sun, in well-drained, preferably sandy, soil. It is tolerant of poor, dry soil and will grow in a range of conditions.

Five-leaf aralia withstands pollution and is a good choice for city gardens. You also can plant it as a screen.

Acer

Maples (*Acer* species) are outstanding trees for making shade, and some of them tolerate shade as well. Some maples, such as Norway maple, have shallow roots that greedily suck up moisture and nutrients from the soil and make it difficult for other plants to grow nearby. The species listed here are more congenial, and better choices for gardens and landscapes.

Amur maple (*Acer ginnala*) grows to 15 or even 20 feet tall with an equal spread, but pruning can keep it smaller. You can treat it either as a small tree or a large shrub. Its leaves are toothed and lobed like those of other maples, with the central lobe longer than the other two. The leaves turn yellow to red in fall. In spring there are fragrant pale yellow flowers—unusual in maples. Amur maple is hardy in zones 3 to 8, but performs best in the South.

Plant Amur maple in full sun to partial or light shade, in moist but well-drained soil. It grows well in a range of soils and pH values.

Amur maple is an excellent tree for small gardens and can even be grown in a container. Or plant several in a row as a hedge or screen. Dwarf cultivars make the best hedges.

Paperbark maple (*Acer griseum*) grows slowly to about 30 feet in height, with a spread of 15 to 30 feet. Its notable feature is its peeling, russet-colored bark. Paperbark maple has three-lobed leaves with toothed margins; in autumn they turn bronze to orangy red or red, and can be especially colorful in some cultivars. The tree has a round to oval shape and an open habit. It is hardy in zones 5 to 8.

Give paperbark maple partial shade to full sun, and moist but well-drained soil rich in organic matter. It tolerates a range of soils and pH, but does not do well in drought.

Plant paperbark maple as a specimen tree for a small yard or as an addition to mixed beds and borders. It also is attractive planted in small groups.

Japanese maple (*Acer palmatum*) has graceful leaves with five slender, toothed leaflets arranged like the fingers on a hand. Some cultivars have burgundy-colored leaves; in others the delicate foliage is deeply serrated and finely cut. Many Japanese maples have good fall color. Trees grow to 25 feet in height, depending on the cultivar, and may be as wide or wider than they are high. Most are hardy in zones 5 to 9.

Plant Japanese maple in partial shade (dappled shade is preferred), in moist but well-drained soil containing plenty of organic matter. It makes a lovely specimen tree and is perfect in a small yard, near a patio, or in a mixed bed or border.

Japanese maple (*Acer palmatum*)

Amur maple
(*Acer ginnala*)

Amelanchier

Serviceberries (*Amelanchier* species) are small trees valued for their spring blossoms and summer fruit. They are attractive to birds, and good additions to home landscapes.

The **downy serviceberry** (*Amelanchier arborea*) usually reaches a height of 15 to 25 feet. In spring it bears lovely drooping clusters of white flowers. The oval green leaves turn spectacular shades of yellow, orange, and deep red in fall. Sweet purple-black fruits ripen in summer. Downy serviceberry may grow as a small tree or a large shrub, with a bushy, rounded form. It is hardy in zones 4 to 9.

Give downy serviceberry a location in partial to light shade to full sun, in moist but well-drained soil with an acid pH.

Serviceberry (*Amelanchier canadensis*) is very similar to downy serviceberry but more often takes the form of a large shrub. It grows to 20 feet tall and spreads by producing suckers around the base. It, too, has clusters of white spring flowers, but they stand upright. The oval green leaves turn yellow in fall. Edible purple-black fruits are produced in late spring to early summer. Serviceberry is hardy in zones 3 to 7.

Plant serviceberry in partial shade to full sun, in moist, humusy soil.

Serviceberries are at home along the edge of a woodland garden, next to a stream or pond, or in a border of mixed shrubs and small trees. You also can grow them by themselves, as specimen trees.

Aronia

Red chokeberry (*Aronia arbutifolia*) is an upright shrub that grows 6 to 10 feet high and spreads by suckers to form a thicket. Its oblong leaves turn bright red in autumn, when the plant also bears masses of small red fruits. The plant is hardy in zones 4 to 9.

Plant red chokeberry in light shade to full sun, in any average garden soil. It tolerates a range of soils, including those of poor quality. Cut older stems back to the ground from time to time so the plants remain vigorous.

Red chokeberry is most valuable for its colorful berries. It looks best planted in masses or in a mixed border or hedgerow along with other shrubs.

Berberis

Barberries are compact, spiny shrubs that are often used as barriers and low hedges. Two good barberries for shady locations are Korean barberry and mentor barberry.

Korean barberry (*Berberis koreana*) grows 4 to 6 feet high and about 4 feet across, with deciduous oval leaves that turn red in fall, and spiny stems.

Its small, bright red fruits are colorful in fall and winter. It is hardy in zones 3 to 8.

Mentor barberry (*Berberis* x *mentorensis*) grows to 5 feet tall and may be more than 7 feet wide. Its leaves are semievergreen or retained well into fall, and the stems are spiny. Mentor barberry is a hybrid that seemingly does not produce fruit. It is hardy in zones 5 to 8.

Plant either species in light shade to full sun; mentor barberry will tolerate up to half shade. Barberries will grow in just about any average soil, as long as it is well drained.

Because of their thorns, barberries make good barrier hedges. You also can include them in mixed beds or borders if you prune regularly to keep them neat and compact.

Betula

Birches (*Betula* species) are lovely, graceful trees that are, unfortunately, often troubled by borers. The **river birch** (*Betula nigra*) is among the most trouble-free birches, resisting both borers and disease, and is adapted to a range of growing conditions. The cultivar 'Heritage' is especially handsome. River birch grows to 70 feet or occasionally taller, with a spread of between 30 and 70 feet. Pyramidal to round in form, it has arching branches and triangular glossy green leaves

Serviceberry (*Amelanchier canadensis*)

Red chokeberry (*Aronia arbutifolia*)

Korean barberry (*Berberis koreana*)

River birch (*Betula nigra*)

Buxus

Boxwoods (*Buxus* species) are slow-growing, small-leaved evergreen shrubs noted for their aromatic foliage. **Littleleaf boxwood** (*Buxus microphylla*) grows to 4 feet high and 4 feet across, with small, oval, deep green leaves that turn yellowish in winter. It is hardy in zones 5 to 9. **Common** or **English boxwood** (*Buxus sempervirens*) reaches 15 to 20 feet in height and grows as wide or wider than it is tall. This species has glossy, oval, dark green leaves to 1 inch long and is hardy in zones 5 or 6 to 8, depending on the variety.

Plant boxwood in light shade to full sun, in moist but well-drained soil with a slightly acid pH. Site plants where they will not be exposed to drying winds, or set up burlap shelters or windbreaks in winter. Mulch to protect the shallow roots.

Use boxwood as a hedge for a formal garden or as a foundation plant. It takes pruning and shearing well and can be trained as a topiary.

Calycanthus

Carolina allspice or **sweetshrub** (*Calycanthus floridus*) is a bushy shrub native to the Southeast. It grows to 9 feet high and about 7 to 10 feet across. The rough-textured, dark grayish-green leaves are deciduous and more or less oval in shape. Carolina allspice is named for its unusual deep reddish-

Carolina allspice/Sweetshrub
(*Calycanthus floridus*)

Common boxwood/English boxwood
(*Buxus sempervirens*)

brown flowers, which are pleasantly sweet scented. The plant is hardy in zones 4 to 9, and requires little in the way of maintenance.

Carolina allspice grows well in light shade to full sun, in moist but well-drained soil rich in organic matter. It will adapt to a range of soil types. Prune plants when necessary after they bloom.

An excellent specimen plant or addition to a shrub border, Carolina allspice also is appealing along a path or next to a deck or patio, where you can enjoy the fragrant flowers.

Camellia

The elegant **camellias** (*Camellia* species) are broad-leaved evergreens with glossy, dark green, oval leaves and large single or double flowers.

Japanese camellia (*Camellia japonica*) grows to about 15 feet tall and 10 feet wide. Its lovely, full blossoms appear from late autumn to early spring, in red, pink, and white. They can be up to 5 inches wide.

with toothed edges. The leaves turn glowing yellow in autumn. 'Heritage' has reddish-brown bark when young that peels as the tree grows older to reveal gray or pinkish inner bark. It is hardy in zones 4 to 9.

Plant river birch in partial shade to full sun, in moist soil rich in organic matter with an acid pH. The tree will not thrive in dry or alkaline soils. If you need to prune river birch to remove dead or damaged wood, do so in summer. Pruning in spring when the sap is flowing will cause the tree to bleed.

River birch is an excellent specimen tree to plant by itself in the middle of a lawn, and also works well in groups or masses.

Camellia (*Camellia japonica*)

Sasanqua camellia (*Camellia sasanqua*) is a bit smaller, to 10 feet tall and 8 feet across. This species blooms in autumn, and has somewhat smaller flowers (to 2 to 3 inches across), single or double, in shades of red, pink, and white.

Both species of camellia are hardy in zones 7 to 9.

Camellias grow best in partial shade and fertile, humusy soil that is moist but well drained with an acid pH. Because they are extremely sensitive to cold, camellias benefit from a protected location.

In southern gardens camellias are well loved as specimen plants. They also are excellent additions to mixed borders, and are beautiful planted in groups or masses.

Cercis

Redbuds (*Cercis* species) are rather small, handsome trees known for their rosy pink spring flowers. **Eastern redbud** (*Cercis canadensis*) grows to 30 feet high, with a spread of about 30 feet. It has broadly oval to heart-shaped deciduous leaves of rich green. The clusters of small, rose-pink flowers last for up to three weeks in early spring. Redbud is hardy in zones 4 to 9 and may even survive in zone 3.

A similar species for western gardens is the **western redbud** (*Cercis occidentalis*), which is a large shrub or small tree growing to 12 feet tall and hardy only to zone 7.

Give redbuds a location in light shade to full sun, in moist but well-drained soil of good fertility. The trees need water during dry spells, but they do not thrive in soil that is constantly soggy. Prune as needed to remove deadwood and to lighten the tree's canopy if it becomes very dense.

Redbuds make lovely specimen trees, and are good choices for a mixed border or the edge of a woodland garden. Because of their compact size, they are well suited to small yards and other limited spaces.

Clethra

Sweet pepperbush or **summersweet** (*Clethra alnifolia*) is a delightful shrub for shady gardens, producing its sweet-scented flowers late in the season when they are especially welcome. Sweet pepperbush grows to 8 feet high and 4 to 6 feet wide, and has deciduous, oval green leaves with toothed edges. In late summer the plant produces spires of small white flowers with a wonderfully light, never cloying, fragrance. The flowers bloom for a month or more, and bees

Sweet pepperbush/Summersweet (*Clethra alnifolia*)

Eastern redbud (*Cercis canadensis*)

love them. Pink-flowered cultivars also are available. Sweet pepperbush is hardy in zones 3 to 9.

Sweet pepperbush will thrive in medium shade to full sun, in soil that is moist and humusy with an acid pH. The plant will tolerate a range of soil conditions, as long as the soil does not dry out. It is easy to grow and requires little in the way of maintenance.

Plant sweet pepperbush in a mixed border along with other shrubs and flowers, or in a wet location.

Cornus

Dogwoods (*Cornus* species) are among our best-loved trees, their spring flowers a familiar sight in woodlands across the eastern U.S.

The **flowering dogwood** (*Cornus florida*) is the classic eastern species, reaching 20 to 30 feet in height. Its dark green, oval leaves turn rich shades of red and purplish red in fall. The spring flowers (actually ornamental bracts surrounding the tiny true

Kousa dogwood (*Cornus kousa*)

Cornelian cherry (*Cornus mas*)

Flowering dogwood (*Cornus florida*)

flowers) are white or pink, depending on the variety. They are followed by small red fruits that birds like to eat. Flowering dogwood is hardy in zones 5 to 9. Unfortunately, it is falling prey to anthracnose disease in many locations. Gardeners often can fight off the disease by combating it at the first sign of infection, but if anthracnose is a problem in your area, you should consider planting kousa dogwood or one of the new hybrid dogwoods instead.

Kousa dogwood (*Cornus kousa*) is similar to flowering dogwood, often growing a bit larger, and with white flowers that tend to face upward and are especially lovely when viewed from an upstairs window. This species blooms a few weeks later than flowering dogwood and is hardy in zones 5 to 8. Pink cultivars are available. Like flowering dogwood, kousa dogwood has colorful autumn foliage.

A number of new cultivars have been introduced under the species *Cornus x rutgersensis*, a cross between *Cornus florida* and *Cornus kousa*. Like the kousa dogwood, these hybrids are resistant to the anthracnose that is so troublesome to flowering dogwood. The hybrids grow to 30 feet tall, are hardy in zones 5 to 8, and have pink or white flowers.

West Coast gardeners can grow the **Pacific dogwood** (*Cornus nuttallii*). Like other dogwoods, the Pacific dogwood has oval leaves and decorative bracts in spring that are creamy white or flushed with pink, and colorful leaves in fall. But it is taller, reaching a height of up to 75 feet. Pacific dogwood is hardy in zones 7 to 9. Like flowering dogwood, it has been troubled by disease.

Plant dogwoods in partial shade to full sun, in soil that is moist but well drained, is rich in organic matter, and has an acid pH. They don't like hot, dry conditions. A layer of loose mulch will keep the roots cool in summer.

Dogwoods are beautiful specimen trees that are suited to small spaces. They are lovely planted in a lawn, in groups, or along the edge of a woodland garden. Dogwoods also are good additions to gardens designed to attract birds.

Cornus

Cornelian cherry (*Cornus mas*) is a large, bushy shrub with a rounded shape. You can grow it as a small tree by removing the lower branches. Cornelian cherry grows to 20 or 25 feet high and to 20 feet across. It is among the earliest spring bloomers, sending out clusters of small yellow flowers as early as February in the southern part of its range. The leaves are oval, and the plant is hardy in zones 4 to 8. In summer cornelian cherry produces red cherrylike fruits that can be used to make jelly or jam.

Plant cornelian cherry in partial shade to full sun, in fertile, well-drained soil.

Use it as a hedge or screen, as a foundation planting, or in a border or hedgerow of mixed shrubs.

Corylopsis

Winter hazels (*Corylopsis* species) are related to witch hazels and, like witch hazels, bloom in spring.

Fragrant winter hazel (*Corylopsis glabrescens*) grows up to 18 feet high and about as wide. Its deciduous, broadly oval leaves turn yellow in fall. In early spring the plant bears drooping clusters of fragrant light yellow flowers. It is hardy in zones 5 to 8.

Buttercup winter hazel (*Corylopsis pauciflora*) is smaller, reaching a height of about 6 feet. It has broadly oval leaves, and pretty yellow, fragrant flowers in spring. Buttercup winter hazel is hardy in zones 6 to 9.

Spike winter hazel (*Corylopsis spicata*) is similar but a bit taller and wider. It is hardy in zones 5 to 8.

Spike winter hazel (*Corylopsis spicata*)

Plant winter hazels in light to partial shade (fragrant winter hazel also will tolerate full sun), in soil that is moist but well drained, is rich in organic matter, and has an acid pH. Because the plants bloom early, the buds are at risk from late spring frosts. Plant in a sheltered location, and protect the plants from cold winds.

Winter hazels are attractive in mixed borders or woodland gardens. Their yellow blossoms are especially welcome in the bleak landscape of very early spring.

Enkianthus

Redvein enkianthus (*Enkianthus campanulatus*) is a tall, narrow shrub in the heath family that grows from 8 to more than 20 feet tall, depending on the climate and growing conditions. It grows taller in mild climates. The plant has oval leaves that turn bright shades of red, orange, and yellow in fall, and clusters of small yellow or pale orange bell-shaped flowers with red veins in late spring. There are cul-

Redvein enkianthus
(*Enkianthus campanulatus*)

tivars with red, pink, and white flowers as well. The stems are red when young. Redvein enkianthus is hardy in zones 4 to 8.

Plant enkianthus in medium or light shade to full sun, in moist but well-drained soil rich in organic matter and with an acid pH.

Enkianthus is a good specimen plant and combines well with other acid-loving plants in beds and borders.

Fatsia

Japanese aralia (*Fatsia japonica*) is a handsome foliage plant that is hardy outdoors in zones 8 to 11 and grown as a houseplant farther north. The large, glossy, dark green leaves are deeply lobed, with the segments splayed out from a central point, and may be a foot or more across. Japanese aralia grows up to 10 feet tall and 10 feet wide outdoors. In fall it produces clusters of white flowers.

Japanese aralia needs full to medium shade, and moist, fertile soil rich in organic matter with an acid pH. Protect the plant from strong winds and winter sun.

Japanese aralia (*Fatsia japonica*)

Fatsia's bold leaves provide mass and foliage interest in the garden, giving a lush, tropical feeling to a shady bed or border.

Hamamelis

Witch hazels (*Hamamelis* species) are joys in the autumn or early spring garden, when their bright flowers glow like beacons against a cloudy sky.

Hybrid witch hazel (*Hamamelis* x *intermedia*) is a cross between Japanese

Witch hazel (*Hamamelis* species)

(*Hamamelis japonica*) and Chinese (*Hamamelis mollis*) witch hazels. An upright shrub with a spreading habit, hybrid witch hazel grows to 15 to 20 feet tall and about 15 feet across. In late winter or early spring it produces fragrant yellow, orange, or red flowers that look like clusters of little ribbons. Its broadly oval leaves turn yellow or red in fall. Hybrid witch hazel is hardy in zones 5 to 9.

Common witch hazel (*Hamamelis virginiana*), native to the eastern U.S., can reach 30 feet high by 25 feet across. Its ribbony yellow flowers are fragrant and bloom in late autumn to early winter. The ovate leaves turn magnificent yellow in fall. This species is hardy in zones 3 to 8.

Plant witch hazel in medium to light shade to full sun, in moist but well-drained, humusy soil with a mildly acid pH.

Witch hazels make nice additions to informal mixed beds and borders and bright woodland gardens. Because of their large size, these shrubs need lots of space to look their best.

Hydrangea

Hydrangeas are among the best shrubs for shady gardens. Their large flower clusters and handsome foliage earn them a place of honor in gardens large and small.

Bigleaf hydrangea (*Hydrangea macrophylla*) is the species most familiar to most gardeners. A rounded shrub, it grows from 3 to 6 feet tall and as much as 10 feet wide. The large oval leaves are glossy green and have toothed edges. In summer the large flower clusters bloom for a month or more in shades of pink or blue, with the deepest blue color appearing on plants grown in acid soils. Flowers on plants in alkaline soil are likely to be pink. The flower heads consist of tiny fertile flowers surrounded by larger sterile flowers that have petallike sepals. Hortensia cultivars have round, balloonlike flower heads containing mostly sterile flowers. Lacecap cultivars have a central disk of the tiny fertile flowers edged in a ring of fluttery sterile flowers. Bigleaf hydrangea is hardy in zones 5 to 9.

Peegee hydrangea (*Hydrangea paniculata* 'Grandiflora') is more tree-like, growing up to 25 feet tall and 10 or more feet across. It has oval leaves and woody stems with grayish-brown bark. From mid- to late summer the plant produces large, pyramid-shaped clusters of white flowers. The flowers stay on the plant through fall and into winter, slowly changing from white to pink to purplish to beige and, finally, to brown. This hydrangea is hardy in zones 3 to 8.

Oakleaf hydrangea (*Hydrangea quercifolia*) grows to about 6 feet tall and equally wide, with large lobed leaves that resemble the leaves of oak trees. In fall the leaves turn a purplish-bronze color. In early to midsummer the plant sends out huge pyramidal clusters of white flowers that linger like those of peegee hydrangea. Oakleaf hydrangea is hardy in zones 5 to 9.

Plant hydrangeas in partial shade to full sun, in moist but well-drained, fertile soil that is rich in organic matter. Mulch to keep the root zone cool.

Bigleaf hydrangea
(*Hydrangea macrophylla*)

Oakleaf hydrangea
(*Hydrangea quercifolia*)

Hydrangeas are lovely plants for beds and borders. A row of oakleaf hydrangeas can be used to divide space or define a boundary. Peegee hydrangea makes a fine specimen plant. Bigleaf hydrangeas are attractive planted in groups or masses.

Ilex

Hollies (*Ilex* species) are elegant evergreens with many uses in the garden.

Japanese holly (*Ilex crenata*) grows 5 to 10 feet high but can be kept smaller with regular pruning. It has small, oval, dark green leaves and small black berries in fall that are hidden by the leaves. Japanese holly is hardy in zones 5 to 8. A similar species is **inkberry** (*Ilex glabra*), which has larger oval leaves and grows to 8 feet tall and 8 to 10 feet across. Inkberry also has dark-colored fruits, somewhat larger and more visible than those of Japanese holly. It is hardy in zones 5 to 8.

A noteworthy group of hybrid hollies is the **Meserve hybrids** (*Ilex x meserveae*), which were developed by an amateur breeder in New York. Most grow between 8 and 15 feet high, and have toothed and spined leaves of lustrous dark green. Female plants bear bright red berries. The plants are hardy in zones 5 to 8.

American holly (*Ilex opaca*) is a tall native species that reaches 20 to 30 feet tall and is irregularly pyramidal in shape. The oval leaves have the spiny teeth so often associated with hollies, and are dark green, but not especially glossy. In fall female plants produce red berries. This species is hardy in zones 5 or 6 to 9.

American holly (*Ilex opaca*)

Hollies need moist but well-drained soil that is fertile and rich in organic matter and has an acid pH. Some will tolerate sandy soil, but they cannot stand poor drainage. Hollies also suffer when exposed to cold, drying winter winds, so choose a protect-ed spot if you live where it often is windy. Hollies will grow in medium shade to full sun. Inkberry likes a brighter location; give it partial shade to full sun.

Hollies are at home in woodland gardens or formal mixed borders. You can plant them as screens or dividers. Japanese holly makes an excellent formal hedge. Meserve hybrids are beautiful specimen plants. Holly berries are attractive to birds, and the plants are excellent additions to wildlife gardens. You must plant both male and female plants to get berries.

Ilex

Winterberry (*Ilex verticillata*) is a hardy shrub growing to 10 feet tall with an equal spread. It is bushy and twiggy, tending to spread by suckers to form clumps, and more or less rounded in form. Winterberry gets its name from the bright red fruits—loved by birds—that cover the female plant from early autumn into winter. The plant has oval, dark green leaves with finely toothed edges. Winterberry is hardy in zones 3 to 9.

Winterberry thrives in partial shade to full sun, and prefers soil that is moist and humusy and has an acid pH. It will adapt to a range of soil, as long as it is not alkaline, and also does well in wet locations. Both male and female winterberry plants are necessary to produce berries.

Winterberry is effective in informal mixed borders or hedgerows, near a stream or pond, or along the edge of a woodland. The red berries are striking in a winter landscape.

Kalmia

Mountain laurel (*Kalmia latifolia*) is native to the eastern U.S. It can grow anywhere from 6 to 15 feet high and equally wide. It has oval, dark green, evergreen leaves, and clusters of cup-shaped flowers in shades of pink, rose,

Winterberry (*Ilex verticillata*)

Mountain laurel (*Kalmia latifolia*)

red, or white in late spring. Plants are hardy in zones 4 or 5 to 9.

Plant mountain laurel in full shade to full sun; it will not flower as well in full shade as in brighter locations. Give the plant moist but well-drained soil with an acid pH. Mulch to keep the roots cool.

Mountain laurel is a lovely addition to a woodland garden or an informal border. It is especially effective planted in masses.

Japanese kerria (*Kerria japonica*)

Kerria

Japanese kerria (*Kerria japonica*) is a fairly compact shrub, growing to about 6 or 8 feet high and up to 10 feet across. It has many-petaled bright yellow flowers, about 1½ inches across, which bloom in spring. The deciduous leaves are oval and point-

Fetterbush/Drooping leucothoe
(*Leucothoe fontanesiana*)

ed, with toothed edges. The stems arch and form a dense mass on mature plants. Kerria is hardy in zones 4 to 9.

Plant kerria in full to partial shade, in moist but well-drained soil of average fertility. In rich soil the plant will not flower as well, but it cannot tolerate poor soils, either.

Japanese kerria makes an attractive specimen plant, and also is effective planted in masses.

Leucothoe

Fetterbush or **drooping leucothoe** (*Leucothoe fontanesiana*) is a broad-leaved evergreen that grows to 6 feet high by 6 feet wide, with gracefully arching branches that give it a fountainlike form. In spring plants bear elongated clusters of small, fragrant, white flowers. The oval evergreen leaves are glossy green in summer and turn purplish in winter. Fetterbush is hardy in zones 4 to 8.

Plant drooping leucothoe in full to partial shade, in moist but well-drained soil with an acid pH. In the southern part of its range the plant needs the greater degree of shade. Leucothoe cannot tolerate drought or frequent strong wind.

Fetterbush is wonderful in a woodland garden or massed on a slope or hillside. It also makes a good addition to an informal mixed border or to a shrub border.

Lindera

Spicebush (*Lindera benzoin*) gets its name from the fragrance emitted by the stems, leaves, and flowers when they are bruised or broken. A shrub with a rounded shape, spicebush grows to 10 or 12 feet tall and equally wide. It has oval green leaves that

Spicebush (*Lindera benzoin*)

turn yellow in autumn, and clusters of greenish-yellow flowers in early spring. Spicebush is hardy in zones 4 to 9.

Give spicebush a location in medium shade to full sun, in moist but well-drained soil.

Spicebush is an excellent butterfly plant. Plant it along the edge of a woodland, in an informal mixed border, or along a stream or pond.

Leatherleaf mahonia
(*Mahonia bealei*)

Heavenly bamboo
(*Nandina domestica*)

Sweet mock orange
(*Philadelphus coronarius*)

Mahonia

Mahonias are evergreen shrubs with glossy green, spiny leaves resembling those of holly. In spring plants bear clusters of small, bright yellow flowers. In midsummer to autumn they produce clusters of dark blue fruits that look like grapes.

Oregon holly grape (*Mahonia aquifolium*) grows to 6 feet high and about 5 feet across. It is hardy in zones 5 to 9.

Leatherleaf mahonia (*Mahonia bealei*) is larger, growing up to 12 feet high and 10 feet across. Its flowers are fragrant. It is hardy in zones 7 to 9.

Plant mahonias in light to full shade, in moist but well-drained soil rich in organic matter with an acid pH. The plants will not thrive if exposed to hot sun or drying winds.

Mahonias are good plants for woodland gardens. You also can use them as foundation plants or in mixed beds and borders.

Nandina

Heavenly bamboo (*Nandina domestica*) is a versatile plant for the temperate to warm climates of zones 6 to 9. An upright plant with canelike stems, it grows to about 8 feet tall and spreads by suckers to form clumps. The leathery blue-green leaves are long and lance shaped, similar to those of bamboo. In late spring plants bear long clusters of tiny flowers that are pink in bud and open to white.

Heavenly bamboo is adapable, growing in full shade to full sun. It prefers moist, fertile soil.

Heavenly bamboo adds vertical lines to the garden. You can plant it in shady beds and borders, along the foundation of the house, or as a screen or divider.

Philadelphus

Sweet mock orange (*Philadelphus coronarius*) is a delightful old-fashioned shrub for shady gardens. It grows to 12 feet tall and equally wide, with upright stems that tend to arch as the plants age. The oval leaves are dark green, and in late spring the plants bear wonderfully fragrant white flowers with four petals. On older plants the bark peels to expose reddish-brown to orangy-tan highlights. Sweet mock orange is hardy in zones 4 to 8.

Plant mock orange in light shade to full sun, in fertile, humusy, moist but well-drained soil. Plants grow quickly and can be pruned after they bloom to keep them under control and to encourage more profuse bloom. To rejuvenate an old plant, cut it back to the ground.

Plant mock orange along a path or near a porch, deck, or patio where you can enjoy its perfumed flowers. It is most at home in an informal garden.

Pieris

Often mistakenly called andromeda, pieris is grown for its sprays of little white flowers.

Mountain pieris (*Pieris floribunda*) is a bushy evergreen shrub of modest size, growing up to 6 feet high and 6 or more feet across. In spring it bears slender upright clusters of small, bell-shaped, fragrant white flowers. It is hardy in zones 4 to 6.

A more familiar species is **Japanese pieris** (*Pieris japonica*), which grows to 12 feet high with a spread of 6 to 8 feet. The leaves are lustrous and dark

Japanese pieris
(*Pieris japonica*)

green, and the slightly scented white flowers are borne in drooping clusters in early spring. This species is hardy in zones 5 to 8.

Japanese pieris grows in partial shade to full sun; mountain pieris tolerates light shade as well. Both species need soil that is moist but well drained and rich in organic matter with an acid pH, although mountain pieris also will tolerate a pH closer to neutral. Neither species does well in a windy location.

Pieris are good plants for the edge of a woodland, or for use in a mixed bed or border, or as specimen plants. Mountain pieris is an excellent choice where space is limited. It also works well in a rock garden.

Pittosporum

Japanese pittosporum (*Pittosporum tobira*) is a durable, versatile plant for shady gardens in warm climates. A dense, spreading shrub usually growing 10 to 12 feet high and 20 or more feet across, Japanese pittosporum has glossy, dark green, oval leaves. In spring it bears clusters of small, ivory-colored, sweetly fragrant flowers. The plant is hardy from the warmer parts of Zone 8 to Zone 11.

Pittosporum will grow in full shade to full sun and tolerates a broad range of soil from sandy to clay and acid to alkaline, as long as it is well drained. The plant withstands salt air and drought, making it a good choice for seashore gardens.

Plant pittosporum as a hedge, screen, or divider, in groups or masses, or as a foundation plant. It also flourishes in a container, and is a good plant for a deck, patio, or courtyard.

Quercus

Oaks (*Quercus* species) are among the most widespread and well-known of American trees. They can be useful in shade gardens, because many have deep roots and high canopies, allowing other, smaller plants to thrive beneath their branches.

Pin oak or **swamp oak** (*Quercus palustris*) grows to 70 feet or taller with a spread of up to 40 feet. It is pyramidal in form, with narrow, deeply lobed leaves with pointed tips. The leaves turn bronze, red, or rust colored in autumn. Swamp oak is hardy in zones 4 to 8 and in the northern parts of Zone 9.

Willow oak (*Quercus phellos*) grows up to 80 feet high with a spread of 30 to 40 feet. Its narrow, willowlike leaves cast a dappled shade that is pleasant for people and hospitable to other plants. The leaves turn yellow in fall. It is hardy in zones 5 to 9.

Red oak (*Quercus rubra*) grows to 80 feet tall with a spread of up to 50 feet. The lobed leaves have pointed tips and turn bright red in fall. Red oak is hardy in zones 3 or 4 to 9.

Pin oak and red oak like soil that is fertile and moist but well drained. Willow oak likes a wetter location, and pin oak, too, will tolerate wet soil. Red oak tolerates sandy soil. All three species need soil with an acid pH.

Any of these oaks would make a good shade tree to plant in a lawn or anchor a shady bed or border. Willow oak is a good choice to plant near a stream or pond.

Oak (*Quercus* species)

Japanese pittosporum
(*Pittosporum tobira*)

Rhododendron

Azaleas (*Rhododendron* species and hybrids) are among the most popular flowering shrubs with American gardeners and homeowners. There are both evergreen and deciduous azaleas available in hundreds of varieties suited to a range of different climates. Colors range from lavender and magenta through many shades of red and pink, as well as orange, yellow, and white. Some azaleas are fragrant; others are not. What all azaleas share is a need for shade, especially in the South, and moist, acid soil. They have funnel-shaped flowers and small oval leaves. Here are just a few of the many azaleas available to gardeners.

Flame azalea (*Rhododendron calendulaceum*) blooms in May or June in shades of yellow, salmon, coral, orange, and red-orange. They grow 4 to 8 feet tall and about 10 feet wide, and are best suited to zones 5 to 7.

Knap Hill and **Exbury hybrid azaleas** grow to 12 feet tall and about 8 feet wide, with May flowers in shades of red, rose, pink, orange, yellow, cream, and white. Their deciduous leaves turn red, orange, or yellow in autumn. These azaleas generally are hardy from Zone 5 to the cooler parts of Zone 8.

Ghent hybrid azaleas (*Rhododendron* x *gandavense*) reach a height of about 10 feet and a spread of 6 to 8 feet. Their fragrant flowers bloom in early summer in shades of red, pink, orange, yellow, and white. Ghent hybrids are hardy in zones 5 to 7.

Two groups of hybrids for warmer climates are the **Indica** and **Southern Indica hybrids**. These grow to 10 feet high and as wide, with flowers in shades of lavender, red, rose, pink, salmon, and white. They are evergreen and suited to zones 8 and 9. Belgian Indica hybrids are even more tender, hardy outdoors only in zone 10 in climates similar to the coast of southern California. They bloom in shades of red, pink, orange, salmon, and white.

Kurume hybrid azaleas reach a height of 3 to 6 feet and grow up to 8 feet across. They are evergreen and hardy in zones 6 to 9. Flowers come in shades of red, rose, pink, coral, and salmon.

Northern Lights hybrids are extremely cold tolerant—hardy to Zone 3. Colors include lavender, pink, orange, apricot, and yellow, and some flowers are fragrant. Plants grow to 7 feet high with an equal spread and bloom in May.

Pinkshell azalea (*Rhododendron vaseyi*) is an American native that reaches 10 feet in height and bears rosy pink flowers in May. It is deciduous, and hardy in zones 4 to 8.

Plant azaleas in partial shade; in northern gardens they also can take full sun. Soil should be evenly moist but well drained, fertile, and rich in organic matter with an acid pH.

Azaleas are lovely planted along the edge of a woodland, in groups or masses, or in mixed beds and borders. Mulch the plants to help the soil stay evenly moist, and choose a location that is protected from winter winds that could desiccate the plants.

Rhododendron

Rhododendrons (*Rhododendron* species and hybrids) are closely related to azaleas, but are distinguishable in several ways. Rhododendrons generally have larger leaves, clusters of flowers that are bell shaped rather than funnel shaped, and flowers with 10 stamens (most azaleas have five). Most rhododendrons have oblong, dark green, leathery leaves. Here are a few of the many rhododendrons that are recommended for American shade gardens.

Carolina rhododendron (*Rhododendron carolinianum*) grows slowly to a height of 6 feet, with a spread of about 6 feet. It blooms in May in shades of rose, pink, lilac, and white, and is hardy in zones 5 to 8.

Catawba rhododendron (*Rhododendron catawbiense*) grows about 10 feet tall and 8 feet across. Flowers bloom in April or May, depending on the location, and come in shades of lavender, rose, pink, red, yellow, peach, and white. It is hardy in zones 4 to 8.

Azalea (*Rhododendron* hybrid)

Rhododendron (*Rhododendron species*)

Dexter hybrid rhododendrons attain a height of about 10 feet and a spread of 5 to 8 feet. In late spring they produce dense clusters of fragrant blossoms in shades of lavender, rose, pink, or yellow. They are hardy in zones 5 to 8.

Rosebay rhododendron (*Rhododendron maximum*) is a large shrub that can grow to 20 feet high and 30 feet across. It is hardy in zones 4 to 7 and blooms in shades of lavender, rose, pink, and white.

P.J.M. hybrids grow to 6 feet tall and are hardy to Zone 4. The flowers are a bright shade of lavender-pink.

Plant rhododendrons in partial to full shade, giving them partial to light shade in the North and medium to full shade in the South. They need moist but well-drained soil rich in organic matter with an acid pH.

Rhododendrons are outstanding in woodland gardens, as specimen plants, in mixed beds and borders, or planted in groups or masses. They often are planted as foundation shrubs, and can work well in that situation, but taller species and varieties will grow to obscure windows. Choose one of the smaller varieties for foundation plantings.

Rhus

Sumacs (*Rhus* species) are familiar roadside plants in the eastern U.S. **Fragrant sumac** (*Rhus aromatica*) tolerates more shade than most sumacs and has a variety of landscape uses. A low, spreading shrub, it grows to 6 feet tall with a spread of 6 to 10 feet. The toothed leaves are borne in groups of three, and turn orange, red, or purplish red in autumn. The spring flowers are catkins on male plants and in small clusters on female plants. The stems are aromatic when bruised or broken, giving rise to the common name. Fragrant sumac is hardy in zones 3 to 9.

Plant fragrant sumac in half shade to full sun. It will grow in many types of soil but prefers those with an acid pH.

Fragrant sumac roots quickly and is excellent for controlling erosion on a slope or bank. It is a good plant for filling space, and can be planted as a tall ground cover or wherever you need a group of plants to fill an empty corner.

Fragrant sumac (*Rhus aromatica*)

Skimmia

Skimmia (*Skimmia japonica*) is a compact evergreen shrub with a variety of landscape uses. It grows to 4 feet tall and 4 feet across and has a neat, rounded form. The oblong leaves are medium green and clustered around the ends of the stems. In spring plants

Skimmia (*Skimmia japonica*)

produce upright clusters of fragrant white flowers. Female plants bear small red fruits that ripen in fall. Skimmia grows best in zones 7 and 8.

Plant skimmia in partial to full shade, in moist but well-drained, fertile soil that is rich in organic matter and has an acid pH. Both male and female plants are necessary to produce fruit.

Skimmia is an excellent plant for small, shady gardens. You can use it in a mixed border, plant it in groups or masses, grow it in a container in a courtyard or on a patio, or use it as a foundation plant.

Snowberry (*Symphoricarpos albus*)

Symphoricarpos

Snowberry (*Symphoricarpos albus*) gets its name from the white berrylike fruits the plant produces in fall. A dense, bushy shrub, snowberry grows to 6 feet tall and equally wide, and tends to spread by suckers to form a clump. It has oval, bluish-green leaves and in late spring has clusters of pinkish-white flowers. The plant is hardy in zones 3 to 7.

Give snowberry a location in medium shade to full sun in any average garden soil. It tolerates a wide range of soil conditions. Do any necessary pruning in early spring; the plant blooms on new growth.

Plant snowberry in a woodland garden, an informal mixed border or hedgerow, or on a shady slope or bank to control erosion.

Taxus

Yews (*Taxus* species) are handsome, soft-needled evergreens that have many landscape uses. They are among the best needled evergreens for shady locations.

Common or **English yew** (*Taxus baccata*) grows to 30 feet or taller with a spread of 10 to 20 feet; regular pruning will keep it smaller. The flat needles are rich, deep green on top and lighter yellowish green on the underside. Female trees produce red, soft-skinned, berrylike fruits. English yew grows best in zones 6 and 7.

Japanese yew (*Taxus cuspidata*) is hardier, thriving in zones 4 to 7. It can grow to 40 feet tall and as wide, but most cultivars do not exceed 20 feet. Like English yew, its needles are dark green on top and lighter underneath. Female plants bear red fruits.

Yews will grow in full shade to full sun. They prefer moist but well-drained, fertile soil with an acid pH, but will adapt to other soils, including those with a neutral to mildly alkaline pH. Yews hold up reasonably well in city conditions, but they cannot tolerate drying winter winds. Deer usually love them.

Yews are lovely specimen plants, and work well in formal landscapes. They tolerate frequent pruning and shearing, and can be clipped as hedges. You also can plant them in a row as a screen or divider and let them assume their natural form. Although yews have been overused as foundation plants they serve that purpose admirably.

Tsuga

The **Canada hemlock** or **eastern hemlock** (*Tsuga canadensis*) is a beautiful, fine-textured conifer native to the eastern U.S. It usually reaches a mature height of 50 to 75 feet with a spread of 25 to 35 feet and a pyrami-

Yew (*Taxus* species)

dal form. The branches of older trees tend to droop a bit. The flat, soft needles are rich dark green in color. The tree is hardy in zones 3 to 7.

Eastern hemlock tolerates more shade than most other conifers; you can site it in full shade to full sun. It prefers moist but well-drained soil rich in organic matter with an acid pH, but has been known to tolerate neutral to mildly alkaline soils as well. It cannot survive long in a very dry soil or an exposed, windy location. It

Canada hemlock/Eastern hemlock (*Tsuga canadensis*)

also can suffer scorched foliage in sunny locations and temperatures above 95° F.

Unfortunately, hemlocks are being attacked by an insect called the woolly adelgid, which is killing the trees in some parts of the country. Your county extension agent can tell you if the adelgid is a problem where you live; if it is, avoid planting hemlocks. The insect is recognizable as a white, cottony mass on the branches and foliage. Dormant oil sprays afford a means of control.

Despite its problems, eastern hemlock is worth the effort involved in growing it. It makes a lovely specimen tree and a good addition to a woodland garden or a shady bed or border. You also can plant a row of trees as a hedge or screen.

Vaccinium

Blueberries (*Vaccinium* species) are good choices for naturalistic shade gardens, offering the dual benefits of edible fruit and colorful fall foliage.

Highbush blueberry (*Vaccinium corymbosum*) grows up to 12 feet high and wide, has oval leaves, and is hardy in zones 3 to 7. In fall the leaves turn vivid shades of yellow, orange, and red. **Rabbiteye blueberry** (*Vaccinium ashei*) is very similar but suited to zones 7 to 9. To produce fruit you must plant two or three different vari-

Highbush blueberry
(*Vaccinium corymbosum*)

eties of rabbiteyes. Consult your county extension agent for advice on which blueberry cultivars (of either species) grow well in your area.

Plant blueberries in partial shade to full sun, in moist but well-drained soil rich in organic matter, with an acid pH (4.5 to 5.5). Mulch the plants to conserve soil moisture and keep the roots cool. Cover the plants with cheesecloth or bird netting as the fruit ripens to keep birds from getting the blueberries.

Blueberries are good plants for the edge of a woodland garden or a hedgerow or border of acid-loving shrubs and trees.

Viburnum

Viburnums are among the best flowering shrubs for American gardens. Their handsome foliage and clusters of white or pink flowers are exceptionally decorative, and their fruit is attractive to birds. There are many viburnum species and varieties available; here are just a few.

Mapleleaf viburnum (*Viburnum acerfiolium*) is more shade tolerant than most and is a good choice for woodland gardens. It grows to about 6 feet tall and to 4 feet across, and spreads by suckers to form clumps. Mapleleaf viburnum has rich green, lobed leaves that resemble maple leaves and turn purple-red in fall. In late spring there are clusters of ivory flowers. It is hardy in zones 3 to 8.

Burkwood viburnum (*Viburnum* x *burkwoodii*) grows 8 to 10 feet high and 5 to 8 feet across. It has rough-textured, oval, dark green leaves and clusters of fragrant white flowers in spring. Some cultivars have colorful fall foliage. It is hardy in zones 4 to 8.

Korean spice viburnum (*Viburnum carlesii*) is noted for the fragrance of its white flowers, which come in large round clusters in spring. This species has broadly oval, dark green leaves

Viburnum
(*Viburnum plicatum* var. *tomentosum*)

with toothed edges, and is hardy in zones 4 to 8. It grows to about 6 feet high by 6 feet across.

Doublefile viburnum (*Viburnum plicatum* var. *tomentosum*) grows to about 10 feet high and 10 to 12 feet across. It has broadly oval leaves with toothed edges, and in spring is practically covered with long, flat-topped clusters of white flowers. The branches tend to droop slightly. In fall the leaves turn reddish purple. This elegant plant is hardy in zones 5 to 8, and many cultivars are available.

Other viburnums recommended for American gardens include **arrowwood viburnum** (*Viburnum dentatum*), **fragrant viburnum** (*Viburnum* x *carlcephalum*), **Judd viburnum** (*Viburnum* x *juddii*), **linden viburnum** (*Viburnum dilatatum*), and **witherod viburnum** (*Viburnum cassinoides*).

Most viburnums grow best in partial shade to full sun; mapleleaf viburnum can tolerate medium shade. Give plants moist but well-drained, mildly acid soil of average to good fertility.

Viburnums are ideal plants for mixed beds and borders, for screening, or to feature as specimen plants. The more shade-tolerant species, such as mapleleaf viburnum, work well in woodland gardens.

Perennials

Perennials are herbaceous plants whose tops usually die back to the ground in winter while the roots live on underground. Some perennials are evergreen.

With a little effort, perennials reward the gardener year after year. They do need dividing when they become crowded, and other maintenance is necessary to keep them looking and blooming their best, but perennials are excellent sources of color and mass for gardens. Shade gardeners can choose from a surprisingly large assortment of perennials, from native plants and wildflowers best suited to naturalistic gardens to garden plants and hybrids that excel in more traditional beds and borders.

Acanthus

Bear's breeches (*Acanthus mollis*) is a large, bold, sculptural plant that grows 4 to 5 feet tall. It has large, prickly, dark green leaves that are lobed or deeply cut and can be 2 feet long. In mid- to late summer, plants produce stiff spikes 2 to 3 feet tall of tubular white or violet flowers. A purple-pink bract with a spine at the tip surrounds each flower. Bear's breeches is hardy in zones 6 to 10.

Plant bear's breeches in partial shade to full sun; in Zone 8 and south it needs some shade in the afternoon. It grows best in well-drained soil; good drainage is especially important in winter. Space plants 3 to 4 feet apart. Winter mulch is a good idea in the northern part of the growing range. Propagate by division or seed.

Bear's breeches is a striking plant for the back of a shady bed or border.

Aconitum

Monkshood has spikes of helmut-shaped, dark blue-violet or white flowers on tall stems. Its leaves are decorative, dark green, and deeply lobed. The roots and other parts of the plant are poisonous.

Azure monkshood (*Aconitum carmichaelii*) blooms in late summer to

Bear's breeches (*Acanthus mollis*)

Azure monkshood
(*Aconitum carmichaelii*)

mid-autumn. It grows 3 to 6 feet tall and spreads 1 to 2 feet. **Common monkshood** (*Aconitum napellus*) blooms in early to midsummer. It grows 3 to 4 feet tall and spreads 1 to 2 feet. Both species are hardy in zones 4 to 8.

Monkshood grows best in cool climates. Plant both species in sun to partial shade, in soil that is deep, rich, moist, and well drained. Divide monkshood every several years after the plants have reached maturity.

Monkshood is an ideal plant for a semishady border.

Red baneberry (*Actaea rubra*)

Actaea

Red baneberry (*Actaea rubra*) is a bushy plant with divided, fernlike leaves. It produces small spikes of tiny white flowers followed, in summer, by shiny red berries that are poisonous. The plant grows about 18 inches tall and is hardy in zones 2 to 9. Another species, *Actaea pachypoda*, has white berries.

Plant baneberry in medium to full shade, in moist but well-drained soil. Mulch in summer to help keep the roots cool. Space plants about 1 foot apart. Propagate by division or seed.

Red baneberry is a good plant for a woodland garden. It is not recommended for households with young children or curious pets that might be tempted to eat the berries.

Alchemilla

Lady's mantle is a compact plant whose classification is confusing. Two species are generally identified: *Alchemilla mollis*, found in English gardens, and *Alchemilla vulgaris*, an American form. The plants are so similar, however, that it's debatable whether they are different species.

Plants have round, grayish-green, lobed leaves with scalloped edges. The leaves are somewhat fluted and are covered with soft hairs. They collect drops of dew and rain in a beguiling way. In late spring to early summer the plants send out small sprays of little chartreuse flowers. Lady's mantle grows 1½ to 2 feet high. It is hardy in zones 3 to 9.

Plant lady's mantle in light shade to full sun, in moist but well-drained soil of average fertility. Shade is especially important in the southern part of the growing range. Lady's mantle does not do well in dry or soggy soil. Space plants 1 to 1½ feet apart in the garden. Propagate by division or seed.

Lady's mantle is a quietly atttractive plant for the front of a shady bed or border. You also can plant it as an edging along a path or sidewalk.

Anemone

Anemones or **windflowers** are a diverse group of plants. Some must have full sun, but those described here are three that can tolerate some degree of shade.

European wood anemone
(*Anemone nemorosa*)

Lady's mantle (*Alchemilla mollis*)

Meadow anemone (*Anemone canadensis*), a native wildflower, grows to 2 feet high, with compound, divided, light green leaves and white flowers in early summer. It is hardy in zones 3 to 7.

Japanese anemone (*Anemone* x *hybrida*) is a wonderful plant for beds and borders. It produces elegant wide-petaled flowers of rosy red, pink, or white with yellow centers, in late summer to early fall. The flowers are carried on slender stems above a mound of pretty, compound, three-part leaves. Japanese anemones can be up to 5 feet tall when in bloom; they are shorter and flower later when grown in more shade. Plants are hardy in zones 6 to 10.

European wood anemone (*Anemone nemorosa*) grows just 8 inches tall, with compound leaves and white or rosy-purple flowers in mid- to late spring. It is hardy in zones 3 to 8.

Anemones grow best in deep, moist but well-drained, fertile soils rich in organic matter. Mulch in summer to help retain soil moisture, and mulch in winter in the northern part of the growing range.

Meadow anemone and European wood anemone are good plants for woodland gardens. Japanese anemone belongs in a bed or border.

Aquilegia

Columbines (*Aquilegia* species) are graceful, spurred flowers that seem to dance in the breeze on their slender stems. They have been grown in gardens for hundreds of years. The flowers bloom above a low rosette of divided scalloped or slender leaves.

Rocky Mountain columbine (*Aquilegia caerulea*) grows to 2½ feet high when in bloom. The flowers are blue to lavender and white, with long blue

Wild columbine (*Aquilegia canadensis*)
Columbine (*Aquilegia* hybrid, inset)

spurs; they appear in spring or early summer. Rocky Mountain columbine is native to the Rockies and hardy in zones 3 to 7.

American or **wild columbine** (*Aquilegia canadensis*) grows 1 to 2 feet tall, with small, delicate, red and yellow flowers about 1½ inches long, with

dainty red spurs. Native to eastern North America, wild columbine is hardy in zones 3 to 9 and blooms in late spring to early summer.

Many **hybrid columbines** (*Aquilegia* x *hybrida*) have been developed by breeders. They average 2 to 3 feet in height, with larger, wider flowers in a range of colors, including blue, lavender, pink, red, yellow, salmon, and white. Some flowers combine white with another color; some have spurs, and some do not. Most hybrid columbines are hardy in zones 5 to 9 and bloom in spring or early summer.

Plant columbines in well-drained soil of average to good fertility and rich in organic matter. In northern or frequently cloudy locations they will take full sun; otherwise partial shade is best. Space plants 1 to 1½ feet apart. Columbines are prone to leaf miners; remove and destroy affected leaves. Propagate by division or from seed.

Columbines are lovely in flower beds and borders, and are classic cottage-garden plants. Rocky Mountain columbine makes a good addition to a rock garden, and American columbine is a good choice near the edge of a woodland garden.

Arum

Italian arum (*Arum italicum* 'Pictum') is noted for its long-stalked arrow-shaped leaves veined and mottled with creamy white. In late spring it produces a pale green or purplish leafy spathe that encloses a stiff vertical column of tiny yellow flowers. In late summer there is an upright cluster of bright red berries. Italian arum grows about 1½ feet high and is hardy in zones 6 to 11. It grows from tuberous roots.

Grow Italian arum in medium shade to full sun, in soil that is moist and humusy. It is a good plant for a woodland garden.

Italian arum (*Arum italicum* 'Pictum')

Goat's beard (*Aruncus dioicus*)

Aruncus

Goat's beard (*Aruncus dioicus*) is a bushy, branched plant that can reach a height of 6 or 7 feet. It has compound leaves composed of toothed oval leaflets. In early summer it produces tall, branched clusters of tiny white flowers that are feathery and fluffy like those of astilbes. Male and female flowers grow on separate plants. Goat's beard is hardy in zones 3 to 9.

Give goat's beard a location in partial shade to full sun, in fertile, moist but well-drained soil that is rich in organic matter. Propagate by division or seeds.

Plant goat's beard in the back of a flower bed or border.

Astilbe

Astilbes are among the very best flowers for shady gardens. They produce feathery plumes of tiny flowers on slender stems above a low clump of compound leaves composed of deeply toothed segments. The best-known varieties are **Astilbe hybrids** (*Astilbe* x *arendsii*). They vary from 2 to 3 feet when in bloom, and flowers come in white, red, and several shades of pink. Bloom time varies from mid-spring to late summer. Plants are hardy in zones 4 to 8. Good dwarf varieties are *Astilbe chinensis* 'Pumila' and *Astilbe* 'Sprite,' which grow to only 1 foot tall and have pink flowers in summer.

Plant astilbes in partial shade (they also tolerate full sun in the North), in soil that is fertile, moist but not soggy, and rich in organic matter. Propagate by division; astilbes are easy to divide. Space plants 1 to 2 feet apart.

Astilbes are wonderful plants for beds and borders, and also like a location near a stream or pond where the soil is moist but not waterlogged.

Bergenia

Bergenias are double-duty plants; both their flowers and their foliage are decorative in the garden. **Heart-leaf bergenia** (*Bergenia cordifolia*) is the most frequently grown species. Its thick, broad, glossy leaves are bright green and up to a foot long; in cold weather they turn a bronzy color. In spring the plants bear clusters of deep pink flowers that are carried above the leaves on sturdy stems. Plants grow about a foot tall and should be spaced 6 to 12 inches apart. Cultivars are available with red, purple, white, or rose-pink flowers. Plants are hardy in zones 3 to 10.

Plant bergenia in partial shade, in moist but well-drained soil of average fertility. The plants are, unfortunately, favorites of slugs. Propagate bergenia by division.

Bergenias are handsome plants for the front of the border. They tend to spread and are pretty growing along a path or under a tree.

Brunnera

Siberian bugloss (*Brunnera macrophylla*) is an easy-to-grow perennial with sky-blue flowers very like those of forget-me-nots. The plants produce their branched sprays of little flowers in mid-spring to early summer above a clump of broad, heart-shaped, rough-textured leaves of rich green. Plants grow about 1½ feet tall and are hardy in zones 3 to 8.

Plant Siberian bugloss in medium shade to full sun in fertile, moist but well-drained soil. Mulch in winter north of Zone 6. Space plants 1 to 2 feet apart. Propagate by division. Plants also may self-sow.

Siberian bugloss is appealing in the front of an informal bed or border.

Heart-leaf bergenia
(*Bergenia cordifolia*)

Siberian bugloss
(*Brunnera macrophylla*)

Astilbe hybrid (*Astilbe* x *arendsii*)

Marsh marigold (*Caltha palustris*)

Caltha

Marsh marigold (*Caltha palustris*) is related to buttercups, and its cheery yellow flowers brighten up boggy gardens. Plants grow to 2 feet tall, with clumps of heart-shaped, glossy green leaves. In early spring, clusters of sunny 1-inch-wide flowers are carried above the foliage on branched stems. Plants are hardy in zones 2 to 8.

Plant marsh marigold in partial shade to full sun, in soggy soil rich in organic matter. It can grow in drier soil if the soil is humusy and not allowed to dry out completely, and if the location is shady. Plants self-sow and will spread. Space them 1 to 1½ feet apart.

Marsh marigold is an ideal plant for a bog garden, a low-lying wet spot, or a location near the edge of a pool, pond, or stream.

Campanula

Bellflowers or **harebells** (*Campanula* species) are charming, old-fashioned plants for beds or borders. The two described here are good choices for shady locations.

Carpathian harebell (*Campanula carpatica*) grows 8 to 18 inches tall, with a spreading habit. The violet-blue flowers are 1 to 2 inches across and carried on slender stems above a clump of toothed, oval leaves. Some varieties have white, blue, and lavender flowers. Carpathian harebell is hardy in zones 3 to 7. Space plants 8 to 18 inches apart.

Peach-leaf bellflower (*Campanula persicifolia*) reaches a height of 2 to 3 feet, with toothed, lance-shaped leaves and in summer, loose clusters of bell-shaped purple-blue flowers. White-flowered varieties also are available. Plants are hardy in zones 4 to 9. Space plants 1 to 1½ feet apart.

These bellflowers grow best in light shade to full sun, in moist but well-drained, fertile soil with a neutral to mildly alkaline pH. They tolerate a range of pH. A winter mulch is helpful in Zone 6 and north. Propagate by division, cuttings, or seeds.

Use bellflowers in flower beds and borders. They are classic cottage-garden flowers.

Bellflower/Harebell
(*Campanula carpatica*)

Pink turtle-head
(*Chelone lyonii*)

Chelone

Turtle-head (*Chelone* species) got its name from the shape of its tubular, two-lipped flowers. **Pink turtle-head** (*Chelone lyonii*) grows to about 3 feet tall, with elongated oval leaves with toothed edges and spikes of clear pink blossoms in late summer to mid-autumn. It is hardy in zones 3 to 8.

Another species, *Chelone obliqua*, has similar oval leaves and rose-pink flowers that bloom for a long time, also in late summer and fall. This species grows 2 to 3 feet tall and is hardy in zones 4 to 9.

Plant pink turtle-head in partial shade and *Chelone obliqua* in partial shade to full sun. Turtle-heads need moist to wet soil, preferably rich in organic matter. Space plants 1½ to 2 feet apart and do not crowd them; they are prone to mildew where air circulation is poor. Propagate by division, cuttings, or seeds.

Turtle-heads are pretty along streams, pools, and ponds, in bog gardens, or in beds and borders where the soil is constantly moist.

Goldenstar/Green and gold
(*Chrysogonum virginianum*)

Chrysogonum

Goldenstar or **green and gold** (*Chrysogonum virginianum*) is a native wildflower. It grows 4 to 10 inches tall, with a mat of oval leaves of rich green. In spring and summer, starry, daisylike flowers of bright golden yellow are borne above the leaves. Plants are evergreen in the South and hardy in zones 5 to 9.

Plant goldenstar in medium shade to full sun, in moist but well-drained soil of average fertility. A winter mulch is beneficial in cooler climates, but not where soil is heavy and may be poorly drained in winter. Space plants 6 to 12 inches apart.

Goldenstar is good for edging or the front of a shady flower bed or border. Or plant it along a path in a woodland garden or in masses as a ground cover.

Cimicifuga

Black snakeroot or **bugbane** (*Cimicifuga racemosa*) is native to the Northeast. It produces long, slender wands of tiny white flowers atop tall (to 6 feet) stems in midsummer to early autumn. Plants have large, compound, dark green leaves composed of three oval leaflets with toothed edges. A related species, **Kamchatka bugbane** (*Cimicifuga simplex*), grows to 4 or 5 feet tall and blooms in autumn. Both species are hardy in zones 3 to 8 or 9. Propagate by division or seed.

Give black snakeroot a location in partial shade to full sun; plants appreciate afternoon shade in the warmer parts of the growing range. The ideal soil is moist but well drained, rich in organic matter, and mildly acidic. Space plants 1 to 1½ feet apart.

Cimicifuga is a wonderful plant for the back of a shady border or a bright, open woodland garden.

Clivia

A relative of amaryllis, **clivia** or **Kaffir lily** (*Clivia miniata*) brings a bright flash of color to shady gardens in warm climates. Plants grow 1½ to 2½ feet tall, with straplike green leaves and, in late winter to early spring, clusters of orange or red trumpet-shaped flowers, each about 3 inches long. The flowers are followed by red berries. Kaffir lily is hardy outdoors only in zones 9 to 11; farther north it is grown as a houseplant.

Plant clivia in partial to full shade, in light, well-drained fertile soil rich in organic matter. Plants need even moisture when in active growth; in autumn let the soil dry out between waterings to give plants a rest. Water only enough to keep the soil from completely drying out. Propagate by dividing the thick, fleshy roots.

Grow Kaffir lily in beds and borders or in containers.

Black snakeroot/Bugbane
(*Cimicifuga racemosa*)

Clivia/Kaffir lily (*Clivia miniata*)

Elephant ears/Taro
(*Colocasia esculenta*)

Colocasia

Elephant ears or **taro** (*Colocasia esculenta*) is grown as a food plant in the South Pacific and for its huge ornamental leaves in the warmest parts of the U.S. The thick, arrow-shaped leaves grow to 4 feet long, on stems up to 6 feet high, and form dramatic clumps. Plants are hardy outdoors only in frost-free gardens in zones 10 and 11.

Plant elephant ears in partial to full shade, in moist but well-drained, humusy soil.

Use these bold plants as specimens, or as part of a tropical bed or border.

Yellow corydalis (*Corydalis lutea*)

Corydalis

Yellow corydalis (*Corydalis lutea*) is related to bleeding heart. It produces a neat mound of delicate, compound, ferny leaves of soft grayish green. From spring through much of the summer the plants bear clusters of small, bright yellow flowers. Corydalis is hardy in zones 5 to 8.

Plant corydalis in light shade to full sun, in moist but well-drained soil rich in organic matter. Space plants 6 to 12 inches apart. Yellow corydalis is difficult to grow from seed and is best propagated by division.

Corydalis is attractive in the front of a bed or border, in a rock garden, or tucked into a pocket in a wall.

Dicentra

This genus includes a number of lovely wildflowers that are favorites for shady gardens.

Dutchman's breeches (*Dicentra cucullaria*) grows no higher than 1 foot, with a mound of compound foliage that dies back in summer. In early spring the plants send out clusters of dangling white flowers that look like pairs of pantaloons hung out to dry. Dutchman's breeches are hardy in zones 3 to 9. Space plants 1 foot apart.

Fringed bleeding heart (*Dicentra eximia*), another native of the eastern U.S., produces a mound of lacy, finely cut leaves. From late spring through much of the summer it bears loose clusters of slender, heart-shaped flowers of deep reddish pink. A nearly identical species of western gardens is the **western bleeding heart** (*Dicentra formosa*). Both of these bleeding hearts grow to about 1½ feet tall and are hardy in zones 3 to 9. Space plants 1 foot apart.

Common bleeding heart (*Dicentra spectabilis*) is an old-fashioned plant with larger, less finely divided leaves.

Common bleeding heart
(*Dicentra spectabilis*)

The pendent, heart-shaped flowers are broader than those of fringed bleeding heart, with narrow white petals projecting down from the center, between the two "halves" of the heart. Flowers bloom in mid- to late spring, and the plants die back to the ground in midsummer. This species reaches a height of about 3 feet and is hardy in zones 3 to 9. Space plants 2 to 2½ feet apart.

Plant Dutchman's breeches in partial to full shade, fringed and western bleeding hearts in full sun to full shade, and common bleeding heart in light shade to full sun. They all like moist but well-drained, humusy soil. Drainage is important; none of these plants will last long in soggy ground. Give plants a winter mulch in the northern parts of the growing range. Dutchman's breeches is best in woodland and wildflower gardens. The bleeding hearts are at home in beds and borders or woodland gardens. Common bleeding heart is a charming addition to a cottage garden.

Digitalis

Foxgloves are classic garden flowers. The best-known species, *Digitalis purpurea*, is a biennial that is included in the section on annuals and biennials

Yellow foxglove
(*Digitalis grandiflora*)

later in this chapter. There also are several perennial species, one of the best of which is **yellow foxglove** (*Digitalis grandiflora*). Yellow foxglove grows to about 2 feet tall, with a vertical spike of light yellow, tubular, 2-inch flowers in late spring or summer. The flowers are carried above a rosette of glossy oval leaves with prominent veins. Yellow foxglove is hardy in zones 4 to 9. It often will rebloom in fall if you cut it back when the flowers fade. A winter mulch is beneficial.

Plant yellow foxglove in partial shade to full sun, in moist but well-drained soil rich in organic matter. Space plants 1 to 1½ feet apart.

Yellow foxglove is attractive in beds and borders.

Dodecatheon

Shooting-star (*Dodecatheon meadia*) is a native wildflower that is showing up in more and more gardens. Hardy in zones 4 to 8, it has a basal cluster of smooth, oblong leaves. In late spring it bears clusters of pale pinkish-white to deep pink flowers with reflexed petals atop slender stems that grow 1½ to 2 feet tall. A similar species for western gardens, *Dodecatheon clevelandii* has rose-pink flowers and is

hardy in zones 8 to 11. Plants die back to the ground in midsummer.

Plant shooting-stars in medium shade to full sun, in moist but well-drained soil rich in organic matter. Moisture is especially important when the plants are growing actively. Space plants about 1 foot apart.

Shooting-stars are lovely in wildflower gardens as well as more traditional beds and borders.

Doronicum

Leopard's bane (*Doronicum* species) brings yellow daisy flowers to shady gardens in spring.

Caucasian leopard's bane (*Doronicum orientale*, also listed as *Doronicum cordatum*) grows to 2 feet high, with a basal clump of toothed, heart-shaped to kidney-shaped leaves and yellow daisy flowers to 2 inches across. It is hardy in zones 3 to 8.

Another species, *Doronicum pardalinum*, is taller, growing up to 4 feet, with a low clump of heart-shaped leaves and bright yellow flowers in late spring. It is hardy in zones 3 to 8.

Plant leopard's bane in partial to light shade (it also can take full sun in the North), in humusy, moist but well-drained soil. Space *Doronicum*

Leopard's bane
(*Doronicum* species)

Shooting-star (*Dodecatheon meadia*)

orientale 1 foot apart and *Doronicum pardalinum* 2 feet apart.

Leopard's bane is a good companion for spring bulbs in beds and borders. Use it also in woodland gardens.

Echinacea

Purple coneflower (*Echinacea purpurea*) is a prairie plant that's becoming popular in beds and borders in many locations. The plants have elongated leaves with toothed edges, and purple-pink daisy flowers with drooping petals (actually rays) and orange to brown centers. They are hardy in zones 3 to 9.

Purple coneflower
(*Echinacea purpurea*)

Although in its native habitat purple coneflower grows in full sun, it also does well in partial to light shade. The ideal soil is light and well drained. Purple coneflower is drought tolerant and easy to grow. Its flowers attract butterflies. Space plants 1½ to 2 feet apart; they are prone to mildew if crowded too closely together.

Purple coneflower is an excellent plant for flower beds and borders or shady meadows.

Eupatorium

This genus contains several plants of interest for naturalistic gardens. **Mist flower** or **hardy ageratum** (*Eupatorium coelestinum*) grows to 2 or 3 feet tall. The branched, bushy plant has triangular leaves with toothed edges, and from midsummer to frost bears flat-topped clusters of pale blue to blue-violet flowers that somewhat resemble

a large version of the annual garden ageratum grown in flower beds. Plants are hardy in zones 6 to 10.

Joe-Pye weed (*Eupatorium purpureum*) is a large plant that can be 6 feet tall. It has lance-shaped leaves with toothed edges on sturdy stems. In summer and early fall, the plant has large rounded clusters of rosy-pink to purplish-pink flowers. It is hardy in zones 3 to 11.

Both plants grow in light shade to full sun. Mist flower likes well-drained soil. Joe-Pye weed prefers wetter conditions. Space mist flower about 1 foot apart and Joe-Pye weed 2 to 3 feet apart. Propagate by division or seed.

Mist flower is useful in informal flower beds and borders or meadow gardens. Joe-Pye weed is a good choice for a bog garden or alongside a stream or pond.

Galax

Wandflower (*Galax urceolata*) is a lovely woodland plant native to the Southeast. It produces a low cluster of glossy green, heart-shaped leaves with toothed edges. In late spring to early summer plants bear slender, 1-foot-tall vertical wands of tiny white flowers. It is hardy in zones 4 to 8.

Plant wandflower in light to full shade, in light, moist but well-drained soil rich in organic matter. Space plants a foot apart.

Wandflower is at home in a woodland garden, in a shady bed or border, or along a path. You also can mass the plants under shrubs and trees.

Gentiana

Gentians have lovely blue flowers, but they are notoriously finicky and difficult to grow. Some species are less persnickety than others, however, and the ones described here are worth a try.

Willow gentian (*Gentiana asclepiadea*) grows 1 to 3 feet tall, with arch-

Wandflower (*Galax urceolata*)

ing stems and narrow, willowlike leaves. Its deep blue, bell-shaped flowers appear in summer to early fall. It is hardy in zones 5 to 8.

Bottle gentian or **closed gentian** (*Gentiana andrewsii*) is 1 to 2 feet tall, with straight stems and pairs of lance-shaped leaves. The clustered deep blue to violet flowers never open—they look like swollen buds. Plants

Mist flower/Hardy ageratum
(*Eupatorium coelestinum*)

Bottle gentian/Closed gentian
(*Gentiana andrewsii*)

bloom in late summer to early fall and are hardy in zones 3 to 8.

Crested gentian (*Gentiana septemfida*) grows to 1 foot tall and may stand erect or droop. Plants bear small, oval leaves, and clusters of slender, dark blue, bell-shaped flowers in late summer. Crested gentian is hardy in zones 3 to 8.

Gentians grow well in partial to full shade; bottle gentian also will take full sun in cooler climates. Give willow and crested gentians soil that is moist but well drained and rich in organic matter, with a mildly acid pH. Bottle gentian likes soil that is constantly moist, even soggy. Space bottle and crested gentians 1 foot apart, willow gentians 2 feet apart.

Grow bottle gentian alongside a stream, pool, or pond. Willow and crested gentians are good choices for flower beds and borders or woodland gardens.

Geranium

Hardy geraniums or **cranesbills** (*Geranium* species) are different from the bedding geraniums belonging to the genus *Pelargonium* that are so ubiquitous in summer. Hardy geraniums are smaller plants with single flowers in shades of pink, violet, or white. Most of them grow well in partial or light shade to full sun. Here are a few choice ones.

The hybrid cultivar **'Johnson's Blue'** is larger than most, growing in a loose sprawl up to 2 feet tall, with 2-inch-wide flowers of a slightly purplish blue for several weeks in early summer. Flowers bloom above a mound of lobed and divided leaves. Plants are hardy in zones 5 to 9. Space them 1½ to 2 feet apart.

Bigroot geranium (*Geranium macrorrhizum*) reaches a height of 1 to 1½ feet tall and has aromatic leaves that are lobed and divided. In mid- to late spring there are clusters of small flow-

ers that are pink, magenta, or white, depending on the variety. This species is hardy in zones 3 to 9. Space plants about 1½ feet apart.

Wild geranium (*Geranium maculatum*) is a wildflower native to central and eastern North America. It has deeply divided leaves with pointed lobes, and clusters of deep pink flowers in spring or early summer. Wild geranium is hardy in zones 3 to 9.

The unfortunately named **bloody cranesbill** (*Geranium sanguineum*) has flowers that are actually rose-pink with darker pink veins. They bloom in late spring and summer above a mat of lobed and divided leaves. The variety 'Striatum,' known as the **Lancaster geranium**, has clear pink flowers with darker veins carried above a mat of delicate, deeply divided foliage. It blooms lavishly in late spring to early summer, and sporadically until fall. Both plants are hardy in zones 4 to 9. Space the geraniums 1½ feet apart.

Cranesbills grow best in moist but well-drained soil rich in organic matter. Average fertility suits them just fine. Give them afternoon shade if you live in a southern location.

Plant wild geranium in a bright woodland or wildflower garden. The other geraniums are excellent for flower beds and borders.

Gunnera

A dramatic foliage plant for mild to warm climates, *Gunnera manicata* produces broad clumps of huge, lobed, toothed leaves up to 6 feet across. The leaf segments are arranged like fingers on a hand, and are covered with soft hairs. The leaves are carried on tall, sturdy stems that can grow as tall as 8 feet. Gunnera are hardy in zones 7 to 11, and bring a bold, tropical look to the garden.

Gunnera does well in light shade to full sun, and needs soil that is moist

Hardy geranium/Cranesbill
(*Geranium* species)

and fertile. Space plants about 8 feet apart, and mulch over winter in the northern part of the growing range.

Use gunnera as a specimen plant or along the edge of a stream or pond.

Gunnera (*Gunnera manicata*)

Helleborus

Hellebores are subtly lovely plants for shady gardens. There are several species, the best-known of which are Christmas rose and Lenten rose.

Christmas rose (*Helleborus niger*) grows from 9 inches to about 1½ feet high, with a basal clump of glossy evergreen leaves that are deeply divided. The cup-shaped flowers are white tinged with pink, and turn pinker as they age. Christmas rose blooms in late winter or early spring, depending on location, and is hardy

Christmas rose (*Helleborus niger*)

in zones 4 to 8. Space plants 1 to 1½ feet apart.

Lenten rose (*Helleborus orientalis*) is similar in size, with leaves much like those of Christmas rose. The nodding flowers appear in spring and can range in color from pinkish white to pink to maroon. Plants are hardy in zones 4 to 9.

Give Christmas and Lenten roses partial to medium shade, and soil that is moist but well drained and fertile, with a neutral to alkaline pH. Plants appreciate some lime worked into the soil. Space them 1 to 2 feet apart. Propagate by division.

Christmas and Lenten roses are not easy to grow, but they are very rewarding when you succeed. They are charming in woodland gardens or in informal beds and borders.

Hemerocallis

Daylilies (*Hemerocallis* species and cultivars) are among the most versatile, easy-to-grow perennials for home gardens. They thrive in partial or even light shade as well as full sun, and you can use them in lots of different ways. The many hybrids available come in a host of warm colors from deep reds to tawny oranges and pinks from vibrant rose to pale blush. There are mellow golds and butter yellows, soft salmons, vibrant melons, and rich russets.

Daylilies bear their trumpet-shaped flowers in clusters atop tall stems that rise above mounds of arching, strap-shaped leaves. They range in height from 1 to 6 feet and are hardy in zones 3 to 9.

Daylilies tolerate a range of soils but bloom best in soil of average fertility that contains substantial amounts of organic matter. Space plants 1½ to 2 feet apart. The fleshy roots are easily divided when plants become crowded.

Grow daylilies in beds and borders, or along a driveway or sidewalk. Or plant them in masses as a tall ground cover to fill a large area.

Heuchera

Heuchera is grown more for its mounds of foliage than for its small, greenish-white flowers. The rounded leaves of **alumroot** (*Heuchera americana*) emerge mottled, turn uniform green, then redden in winter. **Rock geranium** (*Heuchera villosa*) has triangular green leaves. Alumroot blooms in late spring to early summer. It is hardy in zones 4 to 6. Rock geranium blooms in midsummer to early autumn. It is hardy in zones 5 to 7.

Daylilies (*Hemerocallis* species)

Alumroot (*Heuchera americana*)

Both plants grow 2 to 3 feet tall and spread 1 to 2 feet.

Plant both species in light shade, in sandy, humus-rich, well-drained soil. The plants tolerate dry conditions once established. Divide them every three or four years.

Use alumroot and rock geranium as a ground cover for woodlands.

Hosta

Hostas or **plantain lilies** (*Hosta* species and cultivars) are shade garden favorites, and many species and varieties are available in a range of sizes. You could easily create an entire garden of nothing but hostas.

The plants produce clumps of leaves—each growing from the ground on its own stalk—that range from narrow and lance shaped to broad and rounded. They may be smooth, deeply veined, or puckery, dull or glossy, in shades of green ranging from blue-green to chartreuse. Some are edged, striped, or flushed with creamy white, golden yellow, or a lighter or darker shade of green than the rest of the leaf. Sometime in early to late summer plants send up tall spikes of bell-shaped white or lilac flowers that are fragrant in some species; blooming time varies with the species and variety. Hostas can be as small as 4 inches high and barely a foot across to 3 feet tall and 4 feet wide. The flowering stems may be up to 5 feet tall. Most hostas are hardy in zones 3 to 8 or 9.

Hostas thrive in partial to full shade, or even full sun in the North, in moist but well-drained soil of average fertility. Spacing distance depends on the size of the species or variety you are planting but usually ranges from 1 to 3 feet. Slugs love hostas, so take appropriate measures if they are a problem in your garden. Propagate by division.

Hostas are versatile, handsome plants in beds and borders, in masses, or as edgings along a driveway, path, or sidewalk.

Iris

Irises are among our most treasured garden perennials. The familiar bearded iris grows best in full sun, but some of the others do just fine in partial shade.

Japanese iris (*Iris ensata*) has flowers that are larger and flatter than most other irises. They come in shades of purple, blue, pink, burgundy, yellow, and white, and bloom in midsummer. Like other irises, Japanese iris has flat, sword-shaped leaves. Plants grow 2 to 3 feet tall and are hardy in zones 5 to 10.

Siberian iris (*Iris sibirica*) grows 2 to 4 feet tall, with slender, grassy leaves and elegant, narrow flowers of purple, blue, lavender, white, yellow, or purple-red. They flower in early summer and are hardy in zones 4 to 9.

Hosta (*Hosta* species) above and inset

Iris (*Iris sibirica*)

Both species thrive in partial shade or full sun. Japanese iris needs moist to wet soil with a neutral to mildly acid pH; it also will do well in shallow water. Give Siberian iris moist but well-drained soil of average to good fertility. Space Japanese iris 1½ feet apart and Siberian iris about 2 feet apart.

Japanese iris is stunning planted around the edge of a pool or in a bog garden. Two other species for naturalistic plantings in wet places are blue flag (*Iris versicolor*) and yellow flag (*Iris pseudacorus*). Plant Siberian iris in either formal or informal flower beds and borders.

Lobelia

Most gardeners are familiar with the dainty annual edging lobelia, but this varied genus contains larger plants as well.

Cardinal flower (*Lobelia cardinalis*) is a wildflower native to the eastern and midwestern U.S. It grows from 1 to 4 feet tall, with lance-shaped leaves. In late summer vertical spikes of remarkable scarlet flowers appear, their structure and color truly reminiscent of their namesake. Hummingbirds and butterflies find them attractive. Cardinal flower is very hardy, flourishing in zones 2 to 8.

Great blue lobelia (*Lobelia siphilitica*), another American native, reaches a height of 2 to 3 feet. It has oblong leaves with toothed edges, and in late summer bears spikes of rather small, blue to purplish, two-lipped flowers. There also is a white-flowered form. It is hardy in zones 4 to 8.

Cardinal flower (*Lobelia cardinalis*)

Plant cardinal flower in medium shade to full sun, in moist to wet, humusy soil. Give great blue lobelia a location in light shade to full sun, with moist but well-drained, fertile soil rich in organic matter. Space both species about 1 foot apart. Mulch in winter in northern locations.

Cardinal flower is striking in a bog garden or along a stream or pond. Great blue lobelia is effective in a wildflower garden, informal or naturalistic bed or border, or meadow, as long as the soil is evenly moist.

Mertensia

Virginia bluebells (*Mertensia virginica*) is a lovely native wildflower. It grows to 2 feet tall and has oblong leaves. In late spring it produces loose clusters of small trumpet-shaped flowers that are pink when in bud, open to a lovely clear blue, and then turn pinkish as they age. The plants die back to the ground after they finish blooming. They are hardy in zones 3 to 9.

Plant Virginia bluebells in light shade to full sun, in moist but well-drained soil that is rich in organic matter and has an acid pH. Space plants 1 to 1½ feet apart.

Virginia bluebells is delightful in a woodland garden, a wildflower bed, or a meadow garden, or along the bank of a stream. Grow it with ferns or other compatible plants that will fill in the empty spots left when the bluebells die back.

Monarda

Bee-balm (*Monarda didyma*) is an eastern wildflower that is equally at home in meadows and gardens. It grows to 3 feet tall, with toothed, oval leaves that smell like mint. In summer bee-balm has round clusters of tubular flowers that are scarlet in the species of purple, pink, crimson, or white in the various cultivars. It is hardy in zones 4 to 9.

Virginia bluebells (*Mertensia virginica*)

Bergamot (*Monarda fistulosa*) has oval to lance-shaped leaves and clusters of grayish-lavender to light pink flowers surrounded by white bracts in summer. It is hardy in zones 3 to 9.

Both species grow in partial or light shade to full sun, in rich, humusy soil. Bee-balm likes moist soil; bergamot can tolerate drier conditions. Space bee-balm about 1 foot apart and bergamot 1½ feet apart.

Bee-balm is lovely in a wildflower garden, informal bed or border, or meadow garden. Bergamot is best in a meadow, prairie, or other naturalistic garden setting.

Bee-balm (*Monarda didyma*)

Myosotis

Forget-me-nots (*Myosotis scorpioides*) are diminutive woodland plants with sprays of charming little sky-blue flowers with yellow centers in spring to early summer. The plants produce mats of oval leaves close to the ground and are seldom more than 6 inches high when in bloom. Forget-me-nots are hardy almost everywhere—zones 3 to 11.

Give forget-me-nots partial to medium shade; afternoon shade is a must in warm climates. A moist but well-drained, humusy soil of average fertility suits them just fine. They do not like dry conditions and tend to turn brown in drought. Space plants 6 to 9 inches apart.

Forget-me-not (*Myosotis scorpioides*)

Plant forget-me-nots in a woodland garden or wildflower bed. They are nice along a path or trail, especially in combination with ferns and other woodland plants.

Phlox

Some of the best plants for American gardens belong to the genus *Phlox*. Some need full sun, but there are two for shady conditions.

Wild sweet William or **wild blue phlox** (*Phlox divaricata*) is semievergreen and grows about 1 foot tall. In spring clusters of lavender-blue flow-

Wild sweet William/Wild blue phlox
(*Phlox divaricata*)

ers bloom on slender stems above the low mat of 2-inch, oval leaves on creeping stems. There also is a white-flowered variety. Wild sweet William is hardy in zones 4 to 9.

Creeping phlox (*Phlox stolonifera*) grows just 6 to 8 inches high, with a low mat of oval leaves on creeping stems. In mid-spring plants bear clusters of rose-purple, lavender, pale blue, or white flowers on upright stems. Plants are hardy in zones 3 to 8.

Both species grow best in partial to light shade, but they will tolerate full sun in northern gardens. Creeping phlox tolerates more shade than wild sweet william. Give them moist but well-drained soil rich in organic matter, and space plants about 1 foot apart. The plants will spread easily to cover an area.

These phloxes are lovely in woodland gardens, planted as ground cover or close to a path. You also can plant them under shrubs, with daffodils or other spring bulbs, or as a carpet under summer perennials.

False dragonhead/Obedient plant
(*Physostegia virginiana*)

Physostegia

False dragonhead or **obedient plant** (*Physostegia virginiana*) grows to about 3 feet tall, with erect stems along which grow lance-shaped leaves with toothed edges. In late summer and often into fall, spikes of tubular, two-lipped flowers of pink, rose, lavender, or white appear at the tops of the stems. The plants are hardy in zones 3 to 11.

False dragonhead is easy to grow in partial shade. In northern gardens it also will thrive in full sun. Not especially fussy in regard to soil, the plants will grow in moist but well-drained soil of average fertility, but also tolerates heavy clay and low fertility. They will spread; divide them when they become crowded.

Plant false dragonhead in beds and borders, where it will bring vertical line to the composition.

Polemonium

Polemonium is a native perennial with pinnately divided, ladderlike leaves on the lower halves of long stems. **Jacob's ladder** or **Greek valerian** (*Polemonium caeruleum*) has bell-shaped blue—or sometimes white—five-petaled, ½-inch flowers clustered loosely at the tops of stems. Blooming in late spring to late summer, the plants grow 1 to 2½ feet tall and spread 8 to 12 inches. They are hardy in zones 2 to 7.

Creeping polemonium (*Polemonium reptans*) is a smaller plant; it grows to about 1 foot tall.

Plant both species in full sun to partial shade, in well-drained, evenly moist, humus-rich soil. Mulch during winter in cooler climates.

Jacob's-ladder/Greek valerian
(*Polemonium caeruleum*)

Polygonatum

Solomon's-seal (*Polygonatum* species) is a woodland wildflower native to the eastern U.S. There are several species, all of which are similar, and they're ften confused.

Giant Solomon's-seal (*Polygonatum commutatum*) can grow up to 6 feet tall, with arching stems lined with alternating oval leaves to about 6 inches long. In late spring greenish-white, tubular flowers dangle from the undersides of the stems. The flowers are followed by blue-black berries. This species is hardy in zones 3 to 8.

Variegated Solomon's-seal (*Polygonatum odoratum* var. *thunbergii* 'Variegatum') grows to 2 feet. Its leaves are edged in creamy white. The lightly fragrant flowers bloom in late spring. This species is hardy in zones 5 to 9.

Solomon's-seal grows in partial to full shade. The ideal soil is moist but well drained and rich in organic matter. Space giant Solomon's-seal 2 to 3 feet apart and variegated Solomon's-seal 1 foot apart.

Solomon's-seal makes a nice addition to woodland gardens and in informal beds and borders.

Primula

Primroses (*Primula* species) are appealing little plants that have turned some gardeners into collectors. Many of them are demanding and can be difficult to grow, but the two species described here are good bets for home gardens.

Japanese primrose (*Primula japonica*) is one of the easiest primroses to grow. It grows from 1 to 2½ feet tall and has a basal rosette of spatula-shaped leaves about 9 inches long with toothed edges. In late spring clusters of five-petaled, yellow-centered flowers grow atop tall, straight stems. They bloom in shades of red and pink, from burgundy and

Variegated Solomon's-seal
(*Polygonatum odoratum var. thunbergii* 'Variegatum')

crimson to pale pink, and also in white. Japanese primrose is hardy in zones 6 to 9.

Polyanthus primrose (*Primula* x *polyantha*) is a familiar sight in florist shops and supermarkets in late winter and has been grown in gardens since

Japanese primrose (*Primula japonica*)

Polyanthus primrose
(*Primula* x *polyantha*)

the 1600s. The small plants are usually no more than a foot tall, with a rosette of deep green, rough-textured, spatulate leaves with bluntly toothed edges. The flower clusters appear in spring when grown outdoors, on stems that may be just a few inches or up to 1 foot long. All the flowers have a distinct yellow eye, and may be deep violet, purple, magenta, pink, red, lavender, yellow, or white. Polyanthus primrose is hardy in zones 3 to 8.

Plant these primroses in partial shade to full sun. They prefer soil that is evenly moist and rich in organic matter. Japanese primrose also thrives in wet places and often will self-sow and spread itself about. Space Japanese primroses about 1 foot apart and polyanthus primrose 6 to 9 inches apart. Mulch plants over winter in the cooler parts of the growing range. Slugs like primroses, so take appropriate measures if slugs are a problem in your garden.

Primulas are delightful in the front of shady beds and borders. Japanese primrose is especially lovely naturalized along a stream or pond.

Sanguisorba

Bloodroot (*Sanguisorba canadensis*) is one of our most beautiful woodland wildflowers, and a harbinger of spring in wild places in the eastern part of the country. The attractive leaves are deeply lobed and somewhat grayish green. In early spring plants bear pure white flowers with pointed oblong petals. A double-flowered cultivar is available. Plants grow 6 to 8 inches tall and are hardy in zones 3 to 8.

Plant bloodroot in light to full shade, in moist but well-drained soil rich in organic matter. Space plants about 1 foot apart. They spread slowly by rhizomes to form clumps. Propagate plants by dividing the rhizomes.

Bloodroot is lovely in a woodland garden or flower bed.

Bloodroot (*Sanguisorba canadensis*)

Shortia

Oconee bells (*Shortia galacifolia*) is an evergreen wildflower native to the Carolinas. Growing to about 8 inches high, it has oval to round leaves of glossy deep green, with toothed edges. The leaves turn bronzy in winter. In spring the plants bear lovely pinkish-white bell-shaped flowers. They are hardy in zones 5 to 8.

Plant Oconee bells in light to medium shade, in fertile, moist but well-drained soil that is rich in organic matter and has an acid pH. Space plants 10 to 12 inches apart.

Oconee bells are charmers in woodland gardens. Plant them along a path or massed under shrubs and trees.

Smilacina

False Solomon's-seal (*Smilacina racemosa*), another of our North American wildflowers, got its common name from its similarity to the true Solomon's-seal (*Polygonatum*). Like Solomon's-seal, this plant produces clumps of arching stems with flat, elongated leaves. The flowers, however, are quite different. In spring plants bear branched clusters of tiny white, foamy-looking flowers at the ends of the stems. These are followed in sum-

Oconee bells (*Shortia galacifolia*)

mer by pretty red berries. Plants grow 1½ to 2½ feet high and are hardy in zones 3 to 8. A similar plant for western gardens is fat Solomon (*Smilacina racemosa* var. *amplexicaulis*).

A woodland plant in its natural habitat, false Solomon's-seal flourishes in partial to full shade, in humusy, moist but well-drained soil with a mildly acid pH. It appreciates a winter mulch in the northern parts of the growing range. Space plants about 1 foot apart.

False Solomon's-seal is an excellent choice for a woodland garden, a wildflower garden, or an informal flower bed or border.

False Solomon's-seal
(*Smilacina racemosa*)

Goldenrod (*Solidago* species)

Solidago

Goldenrod (*Solidago* species) announces the end of summer in fields and meadows, along roadsides, and even in woodlands. Contrary to a widely held belief, they don't cause hay fever. There are cultivated forms of goldenrod, too, and they grow beautifully with some shade. All have plumy clusters of tiny golden-yellow flowers.

Canada goldenrod (*Solidago canadensis*) grows from 2 to 5 feet high, with lance-shaped leaves to 6 inches long with toothed edges. Plants spread by means of rhizomes to form clumps. This species is hardy in zones 3 to 8.

Sweet goldenrod (*Solidago odora*) is similar in size, with slightly smaller, aromatic leaves and the typical yellow flower clusters. It is hardy in zones 3 to 9.

European breeders have created numerous hybrid goldenrods. Some of the best hybrids for gardens are 'Cloth of Gold,' which grows 1½ feet high; 'Crown of Rays,' with large flower clusters on 2-foot plants; 'Gold Dwarf,' which grows just 1 foot tall; and 'Goldenmosa,' which blooms early and grows 2½ to 3 feet high.

Goldenrod does well in light shade to full sun, in moist but well-drained soil of average fertility. Space plants 1 foot apart, and divide them when they become crowded.

Use goldenrod to bring a flash of late-season color to the edge of a woodland garden, in a meadow, or in an informal flower bed or border. Goldenrods are marvelous companions for asters.

Thalictrum

Meadow-rues are tall, stately plants that are lovely in the back of flower beds and borders.

Columbine meadow-rue (*Thalictrum aquilegifolium*) grows to 3 feet high, with compound, lobed leaves similar to columbines. In early summer plants bear fluffy clusters of tiny lavender-pink, purple, or white flowers. It is hardy in zones 4 to 8.

Lavender mist meadow-rue (*Thalictrum rochebrunianum*) grows to 5 feet or taller, with blue-green, lobed leaves and, in late summer, branched clusters of light purple flowers on tall, canelike stems. It is hardy in zones 5 to 8.

Plant meadow-rue in light shade to full sun, in moist but well-drained soil rich in organic matter. Space columbine meadow-rue 1 foot apart and lavender mist meadow-rue 1½ to 2 feet apart.

Meadow-rues are lovely plants for beds and borders or meadow gardens.

Tiarella

Foamflower or **Allegheny foamflower** (*Tiarella cordifolia*) is a delightful little plant for shady gardens. It grows 6 to 12 inches high, with a mat of heart-shaped to triangular-lobed leaves to about 4 inches across. In mild climates the leaves are evergreen and

Lavender mist meadow-rue (*Thalictrum rochebrunianum*)

turn reddish bronze in winter. In late spring to early summer the plants send out slender, erect clusters of tiny, foamy white flowers. The plants spread by means of stolons (runners). They are hardy in zones 3 to 8.

Plant foamflower in partial to full shade, in moist, humusy soil with a mildly acid pH. Space the plants 1 to 1½ feet apart.

Foamflower spreads rapidly and makes a handsome ground cover for an area that does not receive foot traffic. It makes a wonderful carpet in a

Foamflower/Allegheny foamflower (*Tiarella cordifolia*)

woodland garden and can be planted in the front of an informal bed or border. Dig new plants that form where the runners take root if you want to keep foamflower from spreading.

Tradescantia

Spiderwort (*Tradescantia* species) is a long-blooming wildflower. The garden form (*Tradescantia* x *andersoniana*) was hybridized from several wild species, including Virginia spiderwort (*Tradescantia virginiana*). Hardy in zones 3 to 9, spiderwort has a clump of narrow, grassy leaves and three-petaled flowers of violet, blue, purple, magenta, or white in early to midsummer. Virginia spiderwort has violet flowers. The flowers come in clusters; each flower lasts only a day, but the clusters open gradually over a period of weeks. Plants grow 1 to 2 feet tall.

Plant spiderwort in full sun to light shade (Virginia spiderwort will tolerate medium shade), in moist but well-drained soil rich in organic matter. Plants will tolerate a range of soils and will tend to become unruly in rich soil—average to poor fertility is best for them. Space plants 1½ to 2 feet apart, and divide them every few years to maintain vigor and bloom quality.

Spiderworts are suited to informal flower beds and borders and to wildflower gardens.

Spiderwort
(*Tradescantia* x *andersoniana*)

Big merrybells (*Uvularia grandiflora*)

Uvularia

An attractive plant with a clownish name, **big merrybells** (*Uvularia grandiflora*) is native to woodlands in eastern and central North America and is closely related to another good shade garden plant, **fairy bells** (*Disporum*). Big merrybells grows to about 2 feet tall, with long, narrow leaves and nodding, light yellow, bell-shaped flowers in early spring. The leaves often go limp when the flowers bloom, but after they finish, the foliage perks up and spreads out to become an attractive ground cover. Big merrybells are hardy in zones 3 to 8. A similar but smaller species also recommended for gardens is *Uvularia perfoliata*.

Plant big merrybells in partial to full shade, in soil that is moist, humusy, and neutral to alkaline, rather than acid, in pH. Space plants about 1 foot apart.

Merrybells is a pretty plant to grow in a woodland garden or a wildflower bed or border.

Viola

Violets and **violas** (*Viola* species) are charming little plants with a variety of uses in the garden. There are native violets for all the temperate regions of the U.S., and they are ideal for wildflower gardens. The two mentioned here have been bred for more widespread garden use.

The **horned violet** or **tufted pansy** (*Viola cornuta*) grows 6 to 12 inches high, with five-petaled flowers on slender stems above a neat mound of oval to rounded, toothed leaves that are evergreen. The flowers are larger than violets but smaller than pansies, and they may be purple-red, orange, apricot, violet, or white. The plants bloom in spring. They are hardy in zones 6 to 9.

Sweet violet (*Viola odorata*) is an old-fashioned plant with a low mound of heart-shaped leaves and fragrant five-petaled flowers of purple, pink, or white on slender stems in spring. It grows 8 to 10 inches tall and is hardy in zones 6 to 9.

Violet (*Viola* species)

Plant violas and violets in partial to full shade, in soil that is moist and humusy. Violets spread by rhizomes and some species can become a nuisance over time. Space plants 8 to 12 inches apart.

Violas and violets are pretty in the front of a bed or border, as edging along a path or sidewalk, or as a carpet under trees and shrubs.

Annuals

Annuals are wonderful additions to beds and borders, and most of them also are excellent in containers. Although you have to plant them every year, annuals reward you with color from spring to fall, and many of them are a snap to grow. They expand the shade-garden palette and offer a variety of forms and textures as well. Spiky plants such as Victoria salvia and foxgloves provide a welcome source of vertical lines. Petite, low growers like polka-dot plant and sweet alyssum make pretty carpets or ground covers when planted around and between other, taller plants.

Anchusa

Bugloss or **summer forget-me-not** (*Anchusa capensis*) is a biennial usually grown as an annual. It will bloom the first year from seed. Plants grow to 16 inches high, with lance-shaped leaves and clusters of little blue flowers at the tips of the stems. You also can get pink and white cultivars.

Plant bugloss in partial shade to full sun, in moist but well-drained soil of average fertility. Start seeds early indoors or direct-sow in early spring. Set out plants around the last frost date; they are considered half-hardy. Space the plants 1 foot apart. Cut back the stems when plants finish blooming and they will rebloom.

Bugloss is pretty in drifts or masses in informal beds and borders.

Bugloss/Summer forget-me-not
(*Anchusa capensis*)

Begonia

The ubiquitous **wax begonia** (*Begonia* x *semperflorens-cultorum*) is actually a tender perennial grown as an annual because it cannot survive cold winters. The bushy plants grow 6 to 12

Wax begonia (*Begonia* x *semperflorens-cultorum*)

inches tall and produce neat mounds of fleshy, glossy, broadly oval leaves of green, variegated green and white, or bronze, with irregular edges. All summer long plants bear clusters of red, pink, or white flowers. Tuberous begonias, which also are grown as annuals, are discussed in the section on bulbs.

Plant wax begonias in light shade to full sun. In Zone 7 and south, afternoon shade is essential. Begonias like moist but well-drained, fertile soil rich in organic matter. Space plants 8 to 12 inches apart, and do not set them in the garden until all danger of frost is past. Choose green-leaved varieties for shady locations; bronze-leaved varieties are better in the sun.

Wax begonias are attractive in formal beds and borders, and their compact habit makes them good for edging. They also are excellent choices for pots, planters, and window boxes.

Browallia

Sometimes called **bush violet**, *Browallia speciosa* deserves to be more widely grown in shady gardens. The neat, bushy plants have rich green, lance-shaped leaves and violet-blue or

Bush violet (*Browallia speciosa*)

white, five-petaled flowers with tubular throats. Plants grow to about 1 foot tall and bloom until frost.

Browallia thrives in partial to full shade, in moist but well-drained soil of average to good fertility. Plants are tender and should not go into the garden until all danger of frost is past. Space them 1 to 1½ feet apart.

Browallia is pretty massed near the front of a bed or border and also is a good choice for containers. You can pot them up and bring them indoors to use as winter houseplants at the end of the outdoor growing season, before the first fall frost arrives.

Calendula

Pot marigold (*Calendula officinalis*) has been grown since the Middle Ages and figures in the great medieval herbals of Gerard and others. It grows to 2 feet high, with 2- to 4-inch, full, many-petaled, daisylike flowers of golden yellow, orange, or creamy white. The coarse leaves are light grayish green and have a strong smell. Calendula is a true annual and blooms from spring to fall where summers are not too hot. Warm-climate gardeners can grow calendula for winter flowers.

Plant calendulas in light shade to full sun, in moist but well-drained soil of average or even poor fertility. The plants are hardy and grow best in cool weather. You can sow seeds in fall for bloom the following spring, or in spring as soon as the soil can be worked. Or set out plants in spring when the soil can be worked and the danger of heavy frost is past. Space plants 1 to 1½ feet apart. Deadhead regularly to keep them blooming.

Calendulas are cheerful plants for informal beds and borders and also do well in containers. The petals are edible, sometimes dried and used as a substitute for saffron, and the plants also can be included in herb and vegetable gardens.

Pot marigold (*Calendula officinalis*)

Farewell-to-spring/Satin flower (*Clarkia amoena*)

Clarkia

Farewell-to-spring or **satin flower** (*Clarkia amoena*) is a West Coast native that bursts into bloom as spring turns to summer, and continues flowering through much of the summer. Plants grow 2 or 2½ feet high, with lance-shaped leaves and four-petaled flowers in shades of red, rose, pink, lavender, yellow, and white, some in bicolored combinations.

Plant clarkia in light shade to full sun, in well-drained soil of average fertility. It needs regular moisture when young but tolerates dry conditions in summer when it blooms. It is hardy and grows best in cool weather. Direct-sow in early spring when danger of heavy frost is past. Gardeners in Zone 9 and south can sow in autumn. Space plants 6 to 9 inches apart. They may need staking.

Clarkia is lovely in flower beds and borders.

Coleus (*Coleus* x *hybridus*)

Chinese forget-me-not
(*Cynoglossum amabile*)

Chinese houses (*Collinsia heterophylla*)

Coleus

This member of the mint family is treasured for its colorful leaves. Sometimes called flame nettle, **coleus** (*Coleus* x *hybridus*) grows 1 to 2 feet high, with heart-shaped or elongated leaves with scalloped, fringed, or notched edges. There are many cultivars with leaves in various combinations of maroon, red, green, chartreuse, orange, and creamy white. Plants bear slender, upright spikes of small lavender or white flowers, but many gardeners feel they detract from the foliage and prefer to pinch them off. Coleus is a tender perennial grown as an annual.

Plant coleus in partial to full shade, in moist, fertile soil rich in organic matter. Do not plant out until all danger of frost is past in fall. Space plants 8 to 12 inches apart. Pinch back the plants when they are young to encourage bushier growth. In fall, before frost, you can take cuttings to root for winter houseplants; coleus roots easily in water.

Grow coleus in flower beds and borders or in containers.

Collinsia

Chinese houses (*Collinsia heterophylla*), native to California, got its nickname from the structure of its flowers. They are two-lipped, purple and white, and grow one above another around the tips of the slender stems, apparently reminding someone of the stories of a pagoda. The bright green leaves are 1 to 2 inches long. Leaves, stems, and flowers are covered with soft fuzz. Plants are hardy and grow to 2 feet high.

Plant Chinese houses in partial to light shade, in moist but well-drained soil rich in organic matter. Direct-sow in fall or in early spring as soon as the soil can be worked. Space plants about 6 inches apart. Plants will bloom through most of the summer if you deadhead regularly.

Chinese houses is a good choice for a wildflower garden or a rock garden.

Cynoglossum

Chinese forget-me-not (*Cynoglossum amabile*) is a hardy biennial that blooms the first year from seed and is often grown as an annual. The branched plants grow to 2 feet high, with clusters of small, blue, forget-me-not flowers.

Plant Chinese forget-me-not in light shade to full sun, in moist but well-drained soil of average to good fertility. Start seeds early indoors or direct-sow as soon as the soil can be worked in spring. Set out plants on or a few weeks before your last frost date. Space them about 9 inches apart. Plants tend to self-sow and spread.

Chinese forget-me-not is an attractive plant for informal beds and borders, and is most effective when planted in drifts or masses.

Digitalis

The best-known species of **foxglove,** *Digitalis purpurea*, is a biennial. It's an old-fashioned cottage-garden favorite, and a charming, easy-to-grow plant. The cultivar 'Foxy' will bloom the first year from seed and can be grown as an annual. Foxglove can grow as tall as 5 feet, but 3 to 4 feet is more common. It has a rosette of large, oblong, rough-textured leaves, and in summer spikes of tubular flowers in shades of lavender-pink, rose, pink, white, and peach with spots on the inside. Foxgloves are hardy to Zone 4.

Plant foxglove in partial to light shade, in moist but well-drained, fertile soil. Set plants about 2 feet apart.

Foxglove (*Digitalis purpurea*)

Persian violet (*Exacum affine*)

Plants often rebloom if you cut down the old flower stalks. Or you can let the plants self-sow and spread.

Foxglove is delightful in the back of a flower bed or border, in a cottage garden, or in front of a picket fence, wall, or hedge.

Exacum

Persian violet (*Exacum affine*) is a tender biennial that makes a lovely garden annual. All summer long, its neat mound of small, oval, glossy green leaves is covered with star-shaped purple flowers with bright yellow centers. Plants grow 8 to 12 inches high.

Persian violet needs partial to medium shade and moist but well-drained soil of average fertility. You can start plants early indoors and move them out to the garden after all danger of frost is past. The seeds need light to germinate, so press them lightly into the soil but do not cover them. Space plants 8 to 15 inches apart in the garden.

Persian violet is a pretty plant for the front of a bed or border and also grows well in containers.

Fuchsia

Hybrid fuchsias (*Fuchsia* x *hybrida*) are tender shrubs that most of us grow as annuals in hanging baskets. In mild-winter climates where summers are

Hybrid fuchsia (*Fuchsia* x *hybrida*)

not too hot, such as along the West Coast, the plants will winter over and can be grown as shrubs. Fuchsias can grow to 3 feet or more, but the ones grown in baskets are generally cascading in habit. They have oval leaves and flowers with back-turned sepals surrounding bell-shaped to tubular petals. There are many varieties of fuchsia with single or double flowers in shades of purple, rose, pink, red, and white; many are bicolors. There also is a hardy species, *Fuchsia magellanica*, that survives winters as far north as Zone 7.

Plant fuchsias in partial to medium shade, in moist, humusy, fertile soil. They do not do well in dry conditions. Pinch back the tips of the stems to encourage bushier growth. Plants can go outdoors when most danger of frost is past. In the garden, space them 1½ to 2 feet apart, 3 feet apart where they are perennial.

Fuchsias are best known as plants for hanging baskets, but they are equally effective in tubs and planter boxes. The more upright kinds are attractive and unusual in shady flower beds and borders.

Polka-dot plant
(*Hypoestes phyllostachya*)

Hypoestes

Polka-dot plant (*Hypoestes phyllostachya*) used to be known only as a houseplant, but it is proving to be a good choice for outdoor gardens, too. A tender perennial grown as an annual, polka-dot plant grows about 1 foot high or less, with pointed oval green leaves splashed and dotted with pink.

Grow plants in light shade to full sun, in moist but well-drained, fertile soil containing plenty of organic matter. Set out plants when all danger of frost is past, and space them 1 foot apart. Start seeds early indoors if you like. Pinch back the tips of the stems to encourage bushier growth.

Mass polka-dot plants in the front of beds and borders or under deep-rooted trees, or grow them in containers along with taller plants.

Impatiens

The most popular bedding plant for shady places, **impatiens** is so widely used that it's now considered a cliche in some horticultural circles. Still, it is so easy to grow and free-blooming that it's a hard plant to dislike.

The **common bedding impatiens** (*Impatiens* hybrids) grows 6 to 18

Impatiens (*Impatiens* hybrid)

inches tall, with a spreading, mounded form. It has oval leaves and single or double flowers in shades of red, orange, rose, pink, lavender, and red-violet, as well as white. Some plants are bicolored.

Balsam impatiens (*Impatiens balsamina*) is an upright plant to 2½ feet high, with lance-shaped leaves and red, orange, pink, lilac, or white flowers that grow close to the stems under the leaves. They bloom all summer.

Plant bedding impatiens in medium shade to full sun. Plant balsam impatiens in light shade or sun; in the North they can take full sun, but they need some shade farther south. Impatiens appreciate moist but well-drained, fertile soil, but will survive in poorer soils as well. Set out plants when all danger of frost is past, and space them 6 to 12 inches apart.

Bedding impatiens are good for edging, massing under trees and in shady beds and borders, planting along a sidewalk or driveway, or growing in containers and hanging bas-

kets. Balsam impatiens works best in an informal bed or border.

Lobelia

Edging lobelia (*Lobelia erinus*) is a dainty little plant that grows about 6 inches high, with two-lipped flowers of electric blue, white, or violet-red. Its small, narrow leaves have irregularly scalloped edges. Plants are half-

Edging lobelia (*Lobelia erinus*)

hardy; they bloom all summer where the weather is not too hot and will rebloom in late summer and fall in warmer locations.

Plant lobelia in light shade to full sun, in moist but well-drained soil of average fertility. Plants grow best in cool weather. Start seeds early indoors if desired. Set out plants when most danger of frost is past, and space them 6 to 9 inches apart. If flowering slows in midsummer, cut back the plants and they will rebloom.

Lobelia is a neat, pretty edging plant for flower beds and borders; for a more unusual look, plant it in masses in the front of the garden. An excellent container plant, lobelia will cascade over the edge of a window box or hanging basket.

Lobularia

Sweet alyssum (*Lobularia maritima*) is a petite, old-fashioned plant with lots of uses in the garden. It grows from 3 to 10 inches tall, with a low, spreading habit. Plants bear small, narrow leaves and cover themselves with clusters of little honey-scented white flowers from spring to fall frost. In warm climates sweet alyssum are perennial and bloom all year, or they can be planted as winter annuals.

Sweet alyssum (*Lobularia maritima*)

There also are varieties with purple, lavender, red-violet, or pink flowers.

Plant sweet alyssum in light shade to full sun, in moist but well-drained soil of average fertility. Seeds or plants can go into the garden in early spring when the danger of heavy frost is past. Space them 6 to 9 inches apart. If blooming slows in midsummer, shear back the plants to rejuvenate them. Plants may self-sow when not cut back. Sweet alyssum is considered a hardy annual except in warm climates and grows best in cool weather.

Sweet alyssum most often is used as an edging, but it also is lovely planted in masses as a carpet under taller perennials or spring bulbs. It makes a fine plant for window boxes and other containers as well.

Mimulus

Monkey flower (*Mimulus* x *hybridus*) is a tender perennial often grown as an annual. It reaches a height of 12 to 14 inches, with toothed, pointed oval leaves. The flashy flowers have petals gathered into two lips, and tubular throats. Monkey flower blooms in bright shades of red, orange, and yellow, often spotted and splashed with another of those colors. Plants bloom all summer into fall.

Monkey flower (*Mimulus* x *hybridus*)

Plant monkey flower in partial to full shade, in moist but well-drained soil rich in organic matter. Plants grow best in cool weather but should not go out into the garden until frost danger is past. Space them about 6 inches apart.

Monkey flower brightens up a flower bed or border and also grows well in containers.

Annual forget-me-not
(*Myosotis sylvatica*)

Myosotis

Annual forget-me-not (*Myosotis sylvatica*), like its perennial relative, bears clusters of small blue flowers with a contrasting yellow center above its hairy oval leaves in spring. Some cultivars have pink or white flowers. Plants grow from 8 inches to 2 feet tall, depending on the variety. Although a biennial, this species will sometimes bloom the first year from seed. The plants often self-sow and spread themselves around the garden.

Plant forget-me-nots in medium shade to full sun, in moist but well-drained, humusy soil. Plants are hardy and grow best in cool weather. Direct-sow in fall (in Zone 7 and south) or in early spring as soon as the soil can be worked (in the North). Set out plants when most danger of frost is past. Space them 6 to 12 inches apart.

Forget-me-nots are delightful in woodland gardens, wildflower beds, and informal beds and borders. They are best in a location where you can let them self-sow and wander around the garden from year to year, but you also can dig and transplant self-sown seedlings where you want them. Forget-me-nots are especially nice as a carpet under tall narcissus and other late-blooming spring bulbs.

Nicotiana

Flowering tobacco (*Nicotiana alata*) is related to the tobacco grown commercially and to petunias, tomatoes, pota-

Flowering tobacco (*Nicotiana alata*)

toes, and the rest of the nightshade family. Some species, notably *Nicotiana sylvestris*, grow to 5 feet tall, but many of the hybrids top out at around 2 feet. Plants are branched, with elliptical leaves of grayish green and tubular flowers with star-shaped petals in shades of red, rose, pink, white, and pale green. Some plants are fragrant, especially at night. The flowers are covered with soft, sticky hairs like petunias.

Plant nicotiana in partial shade to full sun, in moist but well-drained

soil of average fertility. Direct-sow or set out plants around the time you expect the last spring frost. Nicotiana is half-hardy and will not be harmed by a touch of light frost. Space plants 1½ to 2 feet apart. Pinch back the young plants to encourage bushier growth. Nicotiana will bloom all summer if you deadhead it regularly. If flowering slows in midsummer, cut back the stems.

Nicotiana is a good choice for informal beds and borders, and also does well in containers.

Nierembergia

Cupflower (*Nierembergia hippomanica*) is a delicate-looking plant with thin, wiry stems, narrow leaves, and small, cup-shaped flowers of blue or white. The plants are branched and bushy, and they form a low mound 6 to 8 inches high.

Plant cupflower in light shade to full sun, in moist but well-drained soil. It is perennial in zones 9 to 11 and treated as a half-hardy annual elsewhere. Set out plants around the time you expect the last frost, and space them 6 to 8 inches apart.

Cupflower is a good choice for the front of a flower bed or border, especially a small garden that can be viewed at close range. It also does well in containers.

Salvia

Salvias are easy-to-grow, dependable flowers that bloom heartily all summer until frost stops them.

Scarlet sage (*Salvia splendens*) grows to 2 to 3 feet high, with compact spikes of two-lipped flowers of brilliant, eye-popping scarlet and rich green leaves. The color can be difficult to combine with other flowers in the garden, and it is at its best when surrounded by lots of green foliage and white flowers that do not fight it for attention. Newer cultivars offer

Cupflower (*Nierembergia hippomanica*)

Scarlet sage (*Salvia splendens*)

flowers in white, pink, and purple that are easier on the eye.

A cultivar of **mealy-cup sage**, *Salvia farinacea* 'Victoria' is more versatile. The branched, bushy plants grow to 2 to 3 feet, with oblong leaves and many spikes of small violet-blue flowers. A care-free, vigorous plant, 'Victoria' salvia blooms all summer and needs only occasional deadheading to keep it looking neat. The lovely blue color combines beautifully with many other flowers, especially those in pinks, salmons, and yellows.

A white-flowered cultivar also is available, but in my experience it is less vigorous than the blue form. In Zone 8 and south mealy-cup sage is perennial.

Plant salvias in partial shade to full sun, in moist but well-drained soil of average fertility. Plants can go into the garden around the last frost date; they are considered half-hardy. You can, if you like, start seeds early indoors. Space scarlet sage 9 to 12 inches apart and 'Victoria' 1 to 1½ feet apart. Deadhead plants when the flowers fade to keep them blooming lavishly. The flowers of 'Victoria' last longer in good condition than those of scarlet sage. Water plants during dry weather.

Both salvias are suited to flower beds and borders, and grow beautifully in containers.

Torenia

Wishbone flower (*Torenia fournieri*) gets its nickname from the fused stamens in the throat of the flower; they resemble a tiny wishbone. The flowers have tubular throats and flared petals in deep velvety violet-purple, rose-

Wishbone flower (*Torenia fournieri*)

pink, or white, with a yellow spot on the lowest petal. The compact plants grow 6 to 12 inches high.

Plant wishbone flower in partial to light shade, in moist but well-drained, fertile soil. Direct-sow in early spring or start seeds early indoors. Set out plants when all danger of frost is past. Space plants 6 to 8 inches apart.

Wishbone flower is a pleasant change from impatiens and wax begonias and is pretty planted in drifts or masses in the front of a shady bed or border. Its small size makes it a good container plant, too.

Viola

Pansies and johnny-jump-ups are two relatives of violets that are fun to grow in annual gardens.

Johnny-jump-up (*Viola tricolor*) is an old-fashioned flower with a mind of its own. The small plants grow about a foot high, although they tend to sprawl and spread out along the ground, with five-petaled flowers that look like small pansies. Many are a combination of blue-violet, yellow, and white, but other combinations and solid colors also are available. Plants bloom in spring and early summer but self-sow with abandon, popping up all over the garden (and outside it, too) and delivering a new crop of flowers every several weeks throughout the summer. Sometimes the plants winter over, too. Johnny-jump-ups are fun to grow and quite captivating where you can let them have their way, but they're not for formal gardens.

Pansies (*Viola* x *wittrockiana*) are cherished for early color in spring. They are among the first plants to go on sale in garden centers, and they bloom happily in cool weather. They will continue all summer in a shady location where temperatures are not too hot and there's plenty of moisture. The compact plants grow no more

than 1 foot high—closer to 6 or 8 inches—and bear wide-petaled flowers in many shades of red, rose, pink, purple, lavender, blue, orange, salmon, yellow, and creamy white. There are varieties with and without the dark clown-face markings on the petals. Some are fragrant. Deadheading keeps the plants blooming longer; pull them when they get straggly in hot weather.

Plant johnny-jump-ups and pansies in light shade to full sun, in moist but well-drained soil of average to good fertility. Johnny-jump-ups can take drier, poorer soil than pansies.

Pansy (*Viola* x *wittrockiana*)

Set out in early spring when the danger of heavy frost is past. In warm climates, plant in fall for winter flowers. Space plants 6 to 12 inches apart. Gardeners in zones 6 to 8 also can plant in fall for early bloom the following spring.

Pansies and johnny-jump-ups are charming little plants for beds and borders or cottage gardens. Johnny-jump-ups also are at home in a wildflower garden, and pansies are terrific in containers.

Bulbs

Bulbs are a low-maintenance source of color for both sunny and shady gardens. Some bulbs, such as snowdrops and trout lilies, naturally tolerate shady conditions. Others that actually prefer sun, such as grape hyacinths and narcissus, will thrive in gardens that are shaded in summer by deciduous trees but are sunny in spring when the bulbs bloom. Many tender bulbs grow well in shade and are valuable because they have bright-colored flowers (tuberous begonia) or bold, colorful leaves (caladium) that are rare among shade plants. You can dig tender bulbs in fall and store them indoors over winter, or you can simply grow them as annuals where they are not hardy. You can choose spring-blooming bulbs for your garden, as well as bulbs that flower in summer.

Begonia

Tuberous begonias (*Begonia* x *tuberhybrida*) are made for the shade; they do not tolerate full sun. Plants grow to 1½ or 2 feet high, with large, flashy flowers in shades of red, pink, orange, salmon, yellow, and white. Flowers may be single, semidouble, or double, and some are classified as camellia, carnation, or rose forms. The leaves are dark green with irregular edges. A tender bulb, tuberous begonia must be grown as an annual everywhere except in frost-free climates.

You can either purchase plants or start tubers early indoors. Set plants in the garden after all danger of frost is past and the soil is warm. Tuberous begonias thrive in light, filtered shade, in rich, moist but well-drained soil. They grow best where summer weather tends to be mild and moist; hot, dry conditions are not for them. Set plants 2 feet apart. Dig the bulbs before the first frost and store them indoors over winter.

Tuberous begonias grow beautifully in containers and add a shot of brilliant color to a shady bed or border.

Caladium

Another tender bulb, **caladium** (*Caladium* x *hortulanum*) is valuable for its interesting foliage. Plants grow to 2 or 3 feet tall, with arrow-shaped leaves that are thin and delicate, almost translucent. They are splashed, mottled, spotted, and veined in various combinations of dark green, light green, red, rose, pink, and white. They are treated as annuals.

Plant caladiums in partial to full shade, in moist but well-drained soil of average to good fertility. The tubers can be started early indoors, and plants moved out to the garden after all danger of frost is past. Space them about 2 feet apart. Dig the bulbs before the first fall frost and store

Tuberous begonia
(*Begonia* x *tuberhybrida*)

Caladium (*Caladium* x *hortulanum*)

them indoors over winter.

Caladiums look good in shady beds and borders, or massed under a tree. They also grow well in containers and make interesting decorations for a porch or patio.

Cyclamen

Hardy cyclamens look much like the familiar florist plant. They grow from bulblike structures called corms and have lovely, graceful flowers with reflexed petals. The best-known species, *Cyclamen hederifolium*, is a

Hardy cyclamen
(*Cyclamen hederifolium*)

small plant that grows just 6 inches high or less. The pink or white flowers bloom in late summer and autumn; they have a deep red eye and the characteristic backswept petals. The heart-shaped leaves are light green mottled and veined with silver. The leaves grow to 5 inches long and die back to the ground in spring. Plants are hardy in zones 6 to 9.

Plant cyclamen in partial to light shade in well-drained soil rich in organic matter. Plant corms in summer while they are dormant, burying them just 1 to 2 inches deep. Space them about 6 inches apart. Water established plants during dry weather when they are actively growing. The corms need less water in summer while they are dormant. Plants will spread slowly.

Hardy cyclamen are lovely in beds and borders and massed under trees and shrubs.

Erythronium

Trout lilies are spring-blooming wildflowers. The genus also includes the dogtooth violet, fawn lily, and avalanche lily. Trout lilies got their nickname from their mottled leaves,

which reminded someone of the skin of the fish by the same name. There are several species suitable for gardens. Here are two of them.

Yellow trout lily (*Erythronium americanum*) grows to 10 inches tall and has yellow flowers with reflexed petals and mottled leaves to 8 inches long. It is native to eastern North America and hardy in zones 3 to 8.

Coast fawn lily (*Erythronium revolutum*), a western species, grows to a foot tall, with pink flowers and mottled leaves to 8 inches long. Some varieties have yellow and white flowers. It is hardy in zones 5 to 8.

Plant trout lilies where they will receive sun in spring and medium to partial shade in summer. They prefer moist but well-drained soil rich in organic matter. Plant bulbs in summer or autumn while they are dormant.

Trout lilies are good plants for deciduous woodland gardens, in wildflower beds, or under deciduous trees.

Fritillaria

Fritillaria is a genus of spring-blooming bulbs that includes the stately crown imperial as well as some quieter species like those described here.

Checkered lily or **guinea-hen tulip** (*Fritillaria meleagris*) grows about a

Checkered lily/Guinea-hen tulip
(*Fritillaria meleagris*)

Yellow trout lily
(*Erythronium americanum*)

foot tall, with bell-shaped flowers in a checkered pattern of white and brownish purple to maroon. Narrow bluish-green leaves grow to 6 inches long. The plant is hardy in zones 4 to 8.

Bells of Persia (*Fritillaria persica*) grows to 3 feet high, with clusters of purplish-brown bell-shaped flowers atop the stems in spring. The narrow leaves grow to 5 inches long. Bells of Persia is hardy in zones 5 to 7.

Plant both species in partial shade to full sun, in fertile, light, moist but well-drained soil. Checkered lily tolerates moister soil in the southern parts of the growing range, but good drainage is critical for them when they are grown farther north.

Both species are suited to beds and borders or wildflower gardens.

Galanthus

Snowdrops (*Galanthus nivalis*) are among the earliest bulbs to bloom in spring. They bear delicate, nodding white flowers with a green spot inside, on 6- to 9-inch stems, sometimes while snow still covers the ground. Plants produce narrow, straplike leaves. They are hardy to Zone 4.

Snowdrops (*Galanthus nivalis*)

Wood hyacinth/Spanish bluebell
(*Hyacinthoides hispanica*)

Summer snowflake
(*Leucojum aestivum*)

Plant snowdrops in light shade to full sun, in well-drained soil of average fertility. They endure dry conditions in summer when dormant. Plant bulbs 3 inches deep and 3 inches apart. They will spread and form clumps.

Snowdrops are charming massed under deciduous trees or shrubs, in mixed beds and borders, or near the edge of a woodland garden.

Hyacinthoides

The **wood hyacinth** or **Spanish bluebell** (*Hyacinthoides hispanica*) has undergone several name changes. Originally *Scilla hispanica*, it also is classified as *Endymion hispanica*. By whatever name you call it, wood hyacinth is a delight in spring, when it produces 18-inch stems of dangling bell-shaped flowers of violet-blue. Plants also have strap-shaped leaves that can be removed when they turn yellow. There are varieties with blue, pink, and white flowers. Wood hyacinth is hardy in zones 4 to 8.

Plant wood hyacinth in partial shade or full sun, in well-drained soil of average fertility. It prefers dry conditions during the summer dormant period. Space bulbs about 1 foot apart.

Wood hyacinths are lovely in a bright woodland garden, in beds and borders, and massed under deciduous trees or shrubs. Plant them with a ground cover or summer perennials to help camouflage maturing foliage.

Leucojum

Summer snowflake (*Leucojum aestivum*) is actually a late-spring bloomer that bears nodding, bell-shaped white flowers on 1-foot stems. It has glossy green, straplike leaves and is hardy in zones 4 to 9.

Plant summer snowflakes in partial shade to full sun, in moist but well-drained, fertile soil rich in organic

matter. Set bulbs about 5 inches deep and 4 inches apart.

Summer snowflake is pretty planted in drifts or masses under deciduous trees or between shrubs, or near the edge of a woodland garden. They make good companions for ferns.

Lilium

Several species of lilies grow well in shady conditions.

Meadow lily or **Canada lily** (*Lilium canadense*) grows to 5 feet tall, with lance-shaped leaves and clusters of drooping, narrow-petaled yellow, orange, or red flowers in summer. It is hardy in zones 3 to 7.

Lily (*Lilium*)

Wood lily (*Lilium philadelphicum*) grows to 4 feet high, with upward-facing cup-shaped flowers of red-orange. It is hardy in zones 3 to 8.

Turk's cap lily (*Lilium superbum*) reaches a height of up to 7 feet, with clusters of bright orange flowers with reflexed petals and dark spots. It is hardy in zones 4 to 9.

Plant these lilies in light shade to full sun, in moist but well-drained, fertile soil with a neutral to mildly acid pH. Meadow lily likes a moister location. Plant the bulbs two to three times as deep as the height of the bulb and 1 to 1½ feet apart.

These lilies are pretty in beds and borders or near the edge of a woodland garden. Meadow lily also can be grown near a stream or pond.

Muscari

Grape hyacinths (*Muscari* species) are small plants, growing 6 to 8 inches high, with dense, upright clusters of little round bell-shaped flowers along the tips of the stems in spring. The flowers are sweetly fragrant and blue to violet in color. There also is a white-flowered form. The leaves are slender and grassy. Hardy in zones 4 to

Grape hyacinth (*Muscari* species)

8, grape hyacinths are easy to grow and long-lived. Plants spread over time to form colonies.

Plant grape hyacinths in partial shade to full sun, in well-drained soil of average fertility that contains organic matter. Set bulbs 4 inches deep and 3 to 4 inches apart. Divide when they become crowded.

Grape hyacinths are good companions for small narcissus and tulips, and are delightful when they're allowed to naturalize in a bright location under deciduous trees.

Narcissus (*Narcissus* hybrid)

Narcissus

Daffodils and **narcissus** (*Narcissus* species and hybrids) are among the most widely grown of the hardy spring bulbs. In addition to the traditional bright yellow flowers with the long central cup backed by a perianth of flat petals, breeders have developed all-white flowers; narcissus with small or large cups of orange, cream, or salmon-pink; double-flowered hybrids; and split-corona flowers. There also are small cyclamineus varieties with reflexed petals, small jonquil types, and varieties such as 'Paperwhite,' which bear flowers in clusters. Many narcissus are fragrant.

Daffodils and narcissus run a gamut of sizes from 4 or 5 inches to 2 feet in height, with a corresponding range of flower sizes. Hardiness varies, but many are hardy in zones 4 to 7.

Plant daffodils and narcissus in full sun to partial or light shade, in well-drained soil of average fertility that is rich in organic matter. Depth and spacing varies, but a good rule is to plant bulbs twice as deep as the height of the bulbs. When in doubt, it is better to plant a bit too deep rather than not deep enough. Divide clumps of bulbs when they become crowded and bloom less lavishly.

Daffodils are spring classics with a multitude of uses. You can include them in beds and borders, mass them under trees and shrubs, or let them naturalize in an open area. The smaller species and varieties are charming growing at the edge of a woodland garden, in a wildflower bed, or in a rock garden.

Scilla

Siberian squill (*Scilla siberica*) are diminutive, early spring bloomers with star-shaped flowers of a celestial true blue. They grow to about 6 inches high, with each plant producing a few slender stems, each containing two or three flowers, and narrow, grassy leaves. They are hardy in zones 3 to 8.

Plant Siberian squill in partial to light shade; a location under deciduous trees, where it is sunny in spring and shady in summer, is ideal. Scillas are not fussy about soil, asking only decent drainage and average fertility. Periodic additions of organic matter are helpful. Set bulbs 3 inches deep and 3 inches apart.

Siberian squill is a plant to fall in love with; its heavenly blue flowers are a welcome sight in spring and a good companion for early daffodils. Plant them in masses under trees and shrubs, along the edge of a woodland, along a path, or in a rock garden.

Siberian squill (*Scilla siberica*)

Ferns

With their delicate, beautifully textured foliage, ferns bring a cool, lush feeling to the garden. No woodland garden is complete without ferns. They are lovely companions for wildflowers and shrubs and provide an elegant backdrop for more traditional garden flowers. There are ferns for both cool and warm climates and for wet and dry locations. They come in a range of sizes and a variety of foliage textures. Ferns are a low-maintenance way to add interest to the garden. They are tough, versatile plants. In nature, ferns grow on the forest floor, and they like similar conditions in the garden. Filtered sunlight and humusy soil are ideal for many ferns.

Adiantum

Maidenhair ferns are widely distributed in nature and suited to a broad range of locations in the garden.

Southern maidenhair (*Adiantum capillus-veneris*) has arching, triangular fronds up to 2 feet long with distinctive fan-shaped leaflets. It is native to the Southeast and also is found in the Rocky Mountains and California. Hardy in zones 6 to 9, the southern maidenhair fern prefers partial to full shade, and moist, alkaline soil that contains lime. It is often grown as a houseplant.

The **northern maidenhair fern** (*Adiantum pedatum*) has triangular fronds composed of wing-shaped leaflets with cut edges. The fronds are light green when young and deepen to rich blue-green. Plants spread by means of rhizomes to form clumps. The northern maidenhair fern is found in the eastern U.S. from Canada to the Gulf of Mexico and is hardy in zones 3 to 9. It grows to 3 feet tall.

Give the northern maidenhair fern a location in partial to full shade, in moist, humusy soil with a pH near neutral. The plants can tolerate some drought after they are established.

Maidenhair ferns are good choices for a woodland garden, to mass under trees and shrubs, or to use in foundation plantings.

Asplenium

This varied genus includes two excellent garden ferns that look quite different from one another.

European **hart's tongue fern** (*Asplenium scolopendrium* var. *scolopendrium*) has long, leathery, evergreen fronds that are undivided and indeed look like long tongues. They grow to 2 feet long and stand upright. Cultivars are available with ruffled, wavy, and unevenly jagged edges. Hart's tongue fern is hardy in zones 6 to 8.

Maidenhair fern
(*Adiantum capillus-veneris*)

Maidenhair spleenwort
(*Asplenium trichomanes*)

Maidenhair spleenwort (*Asplenium trichomanes*) somewhat resembles the southern maidenhair fern. Its slender, evergreen, grayish fronds are composed of small, rounded leaflets. The plants are small, growing just 6 inches tall. Maidenhair spleenwort is hardy in zones 3 to 9.

Plant hart's tongue fern in medium shade to full sun, in moist, humusy soil with a neutral to alkaline pH.

Add lime to mildly acid soils to raise the pH. Plant maidenhair spleenwort in similar soil in partial to medium shade. It likes to grow among rocks.

Both ferns are good choices for rock gardens. You also can plant them in pockets of soil in a dry stone wall.

Athyrium

Lady fern (*Athyrium filix-femina*) is among the most delicate-textured of ferns. Its lacy fronds are made up of many slender, finely cut leaflets of a light, fresh shade of green. Plants grow to 2 to 3 feet tall and are hardy in zones 3 to 8.

Japanese painted fern (*Athyrium nipponicum* 'Pictum') is one of the loveliest ferns. Its 1- to 2-foot fronds are not as finely cut as those of lady fern, but they are a shiny, silvery greenish-gray color with reddish veins. Japanese painted fern is hardy in zones 4 to 8.

Plant lady fern in partial to full shade, in moist to wet soil rich in organic matter, with a moderately acidic to neutral pH. Japanese painted fern likes partial to light shade (full shade in the warmer parts of the growing range) and similar soil but with better drainage. Both plants are deciduous, dying back to the ground in winter.

Lady fern and Japanese painted fern are beautiful additions to beds and borders. They mix well with other ferns and with flowering perennials.

Cyrtomium

Holly fern (*Cyrtomium falcatum*) has leathery, glossy, evergreen fronds and leaflets with toothed edges that are somewhat reminiscent of holly leaves. The stiff, arching fronds grow to about 2 feet tall. Plants are hardy in zones 8 to 11.

Holly fern will grow in partial to full shade, in evenly moist, humusy soil of average fertility with an acid

pH. It tolerates hot weather better than many ferns, but in the northern parts of the growing range cold, dry winter winds can damage the foliage. Cut any winter-damaged fronds back to the ground in spring. Gardeners in cold climates can grow holly fern in containers and bring the plants indoors for the winter.

Holly fern is lovely massed under shrubs and trees, where the shiny foliage reflects light. Or plant it in beds and borders with perennial flowers or in mixed plantings with flowering shrubs and small trees.

Dennstaedtia

Hay-scented fern (*Dennstaedtia punctilobula*) grows 1 to 1½ feet high, with finely cut, bright green fronds that smell like new-mown hay when they are crushed. Plants spread rapidly by means of rhizomes and are hardy in zones 4 to 7.

Plant hay-scented fern in partial to full shade, in moist, humusy soil with an acid to neutral pH. Plants also will grow in full sun if the soil is not allowed to dry out. Hay-scented fern will grow in rocky or sandy soil and can even tolerate salt air. Divide plants in autumn when they become crowded.

Hay-scented fern is an excellent ground cover and looks good planted in masses under trees and shrubs. It is tough enough to survive in seashore gardens and will grow around boulders and rocky outcrops.

Dryopteris

Male fern (*Dryopteris filix-mas*) is native to northern parts of North America, although it is hardy over a broad range: zones 3 to 9. The 2- to 3-foot-tall plant is upright and vase shaped, with lance-shaped, leathery, glossy, dark green fronds that are evergreen or semievergreen. Many cultivars have ruffled or crested fronds.

Japanese painted fern
(*Athyrium nipponicum* 'Pictum')

Holly fern (*Cyrtomium falcatum*)

Hay-scented fern
(*Dennstaedtia punctilobula*)

Marginal wood fern or **marginal shield fern** (*Dryopteris marginalis*) is durable, easy to grow, and hardy in zones 3 to 8. Its stiff, graceful, grayish-green fronds stand 1½ to 2 feet high.

Plant male fern in medium shade to full sun; shade is essential in the southern part of the growing range. Give it moist but well-drained soil rich in organic matter with an acid pH. Marginal wood fern is best in partial to full shade, in the same kind of soil male fern likes. Marginal wood fern will tolerate drought when it is well established. When planting either species, set the crown right at ground level; if the crown is underground, the plant is likely to rot.

You can include male fern in mixed beds and borders, grow it under shrubs or in foundation plantings, or use it in a woodland garden or a naturalistic planting along a stream. Use marginal wood fern in woodland gardens or beds and borders. It is especially attractive with wildflowers.

Matteuccia

The handsome **ostrich fern** (*Matteuccia struthiopteris*) is tall, growing up to 5 feet. Its tapered, upright fronds grow in a vase form. Ostrich fern is hardy in zones 2 to 8 and spreads by rhizomes to form clumps.

Plant ostrich fern in partial to full shade, in moist, humusy soil that never dries out and that has a pH near neutral. When planting, position the crown at ground level. Ostrich fern is easy to grow as long as it receives enough moisture.

Ostrich fern is wonderful in woodland gardens and provides a vertical accent in flower beds and borders. It makes a good companion for spring bulbs, perennials, and wildflowers. Ostrich fern also is a good choice for a moist location near the edge of a pond or stream.

Osmunda

This sturdy genus of American natives contains three well-known garden ferns.

Cinnamon fern (*Osmunda cinnamomea*) grows to a height of 4 feet, with tall, deciduous, upright fronds that form a vase shape. Fertile fronds appear in the center of the plant and turn a rich cinnamon-brown color as they mature, giving rise to the plant's common name. Cinnamon fern is hardy in zones 3 to 10.

Marginal wood fern/Marginal shield fern (*Dryopteris marginalis*)

Ostrich fern (*Matteuccia struthiopteris*)

Interrupted fern (*Osmunda claytonia*) grows to 4 feet high. The fronds are similar to those of the cinnamon fern, but with broader leaflets. On fronds that bear both fertile (spore-carrying) and sterile leaflets, the spore-bearing leaflets drop off in summer, leaving an empty space—an interruption—in the frond. Interrupted fern is hardy in zones 3 to 8.

Cinnamon fern (*Osmunda cinnamomea*)

Royal fern (*Osmunda regalis*) is sometimes called flowering fern, because it produces its spores in clusters near the tips of the fronds, a structure somewhat similar to a cluster of flowers. In fact, the spore clusters resemble brown astilbe plumes. Royal fern grows to 5 feet or more, with thickly set, ruffled leaflets crowding its light green fronds. It is deciduous and is hardy in zones 3 to 10.

Plant all three species in part to medium shade, in moist, humusy soil. Cinnamon fern and royal fern tolerate wetter soil than interrupted fern, but none of the three likes dry conditions. Prolonged drought will send them into dormancy. Cinnamon and royal ferns prefer an acid pH; interrupted fern thrives in acidic to neutral soil.

All three ferns are good choices for woodland gardens or beds and borders. They are lovely with wildflowers, perennials, and shrubs and can be used as accent plants. Royal fern is a good plant for a bog garden or a damp location near a stream, pool, or pond.

Polypodium

Two similar polypody ferns are widely grown in American gardens.

Rock fern or **rock polypody** (*Polypodium virginianum*) is an American native, and **common polypody** (*Polypodium vulgare*) is its European counterpart. Both grow about 10 inches tall, with narrowly triangular fronds composed of narrow, smooth-edged leaflets. Rock fern is hardy in zones 2 to 8. Common polypody is hardy in zones 4 to 8.

Plant polypodys in partial to full shade, in humusy, well-drained soil with an acid to neutral pH. Good drainage is important. Once they're established, these ferns are drought-tolerant. They are slow growing but easy to cultivate.

Common polypody (*Polypodium vulgare*)

Rock fern and common polypody are excellent rock garden plants and are at home in rocky soil, under trees, or in beds and borders with wildflowers. You also can plant them in pockets of soil in a dry stone wall or along the edge of a path.

Polystichum

Christmas fern (*Polystichum acrostichoides*) is a native of eastern North America and is hardy in zones 3 to 9. It grows to 3 feet high and has stiff, leathery, evergreen fronds with sharply toothed leaflets. Easy to grow and adaptable, Christmas fern spreads by means of rhizomes.

A similar but larger western species, the **western sword fern** (*Polystichum munitum*) grows 3 to 5 feet tall. It has clumps of upright, leathery, sword-shaped evergreen fronds and is hardy in zones 5 to 9. Western sword fern also is easy to grow.

Plant Christmas fern or western sword fern in partial to full shade, in moist but well-drained soil rich in organic matter with an acid pH. Once established, western sword fern will tolerate dry soil. Christmas fern needs constant, even moisture.

Plant both species in woodland gardens, with wildflowers and ground covers, in a shady perennial bed or border, along a path or sidewalk, or in a foundation planting.

Christmas fern
(*Polystichum acrostichoides*)

Ground Covers

Ground covers have many uses. Visually, they anchor trees, shrubs, and other tall plants to the ground. They create continuity among gardens on different parts of a large property when the same ground cover is repeated in each garden. Ground covers can create a visual link between trees and shrubs, uniting them into islands in a lawn. They can soften the hard edges of stone steps, sidewalks, or paths. Ground covers are useful in stony soil and around boulders—and around fences and walls where lawn grass would be difficult to mow. Well-planned areas of ground cover offer their own kind of visual interest—thoughtful compositions of color and texture create living carpets. And in woodland gardens, ground covers are an integral part of the plant community.

Ajuga

Bugleweed or **carpet bugleweed** (*Ajuga reptans*) is a creeping perennial suitable for both sunny and shady locations. Its small, dark green leaves grow just 4 inches high. In spring or early summer 6-inch spikes of little violet flowers are borne above the foliage. Some cultivars have pink or white flowers, bronze to bronzy-purple leaves, variegated green and white leaves, and foliage that's a blend of green, pink, and cream. Bugleweed is hardy in zones 4 to 9.

Plant bugleweed in light shade to full sun. It's not fussy about soil and will grow in average garden conditions. Bugleweed spreads quickly and can become a nuisance in a flower bed or lawn. The cultivars are usually less aggressive than the species. Space species and small-leaved cultivars 6 to 8 inches apart and larger-leaved varieties 1 to 1½ feet apart. Ajuga will not thrive in intensely hot, humid weather, but is otherwise very easy to grow.

Plant bugleweed in mixed beds and borders, under trees and shrubs, or alongside a path or sidewalk. Or use it as an alternative to lawn grass on a bank or other nontraffic area.

Arctostaphylos

This genus of low-growing evergreen shrubs offers plants for both cool and warm climates.

'Emerald Carpet' is a hybrid shrub that grows just 9 to 12 inches high, with a spread of 4 to 5 feet. It has small, glossy, evergreen leaves and attractive reddish-brown bark. There are pink flowers, too, but they are largely hidden by the foliage. This low, spreading shrub makes an excellent ground cover in zones 8 to 11.

Bearberry (*Arctostaphylos uva-ursi*) grows in zones 3 to 7, reaching a height of just 6 inches to 1 foot. Its spreading woody stems bear round,

Bugleweed/Carpet bugleweed
(*Ajuga reptans*)

Bearberry (*Arctostaphylos uva-ursi*)

glossy, evergreen leaves that turn bronzy in winter. In spring there are clusters of small, urn-shaped white flowers with pink tips, and these are followed in late summer and fall by bright red, berrylike fruits. Bearberry is about as maintenance-free as any plant gets.

'Emerald Carpet' grows best in partial shade to full sun but will not do well under blazing sun. Bearberry grows best in light shade to full sun. Both species need well-drained, preferably sandy soil with a mildly acid pH. Once established, the plants can tolerate drought. 'Emerald Carpet,' especially, is a good choice where summers are dry. Bearberry can tolerate strong wind and salt spray, but it will not hold up under foot traffic. Space 'Emerald Carpet' about 2 to 3 feet apart and bearberry 2 feet apart.

Both plants are good ground covers for dry locations, on slopes and banks and in rocky areas. Bearberry is a good choice for seashore gardens.

European wild ginger
(*Asarum europaeum*)

Asarum

Wild ginger acquired its nickname from its roots, which have the scent and flavor of ginger. The most desirable species is **European wild ginger** (*Asarum europaeum*), although there is a similar native species, **eastern wild ginger** (*Asarum canadense*), that also is a good garden plant. European wild ginger grows 6 to 9 inches tall, a low mound of glossy green, heart-shaped, evergreen leaves. In spring plants bear maroon or brownish flowers that are mostly hidden by the leaves. Euro-

pean wild ginger is hardy in zones 5 to 9. Eastern wild ginger is hardy to Zone 2.

Plant wild ginger in partial to full shade, in moist but well-drained soil of average fertility. It does not grow well in very dry soil. Space plants 6 to 12 inches apart. The plants spread rather slowly.

Wild ginger is lovely in a bright woodland garden, with wildflowers, in the front of a shady bed or border, or along a path. European wild ginger is so pretty it deserves a spot near a deck, patio, or sidewalk where you will see it often.

Ceratostigma

Plumbago or **leadwort** (*Ceratostigma plumbaginoides*) is an herbaceous perennial that spreads quietly through the garden in spring and summer, then bursts into bloom in late summer and fall when most other perennials have quit for the year. It produces a loose mat of rather oval, smooth, green leaves on reddish stems. The late-season flowers come in clusters and are an intense electric blue. The leaves turn reddish in fall. Plants grow to about 1 foot high and are hardy in zones 5 to 9.

Plumbago thrives in light shade to full sun, in well-drained soil of average fertility. Space plants 8 to 12 inches apart. In winter the plants die back in cold climates and go dormant where the weather is milder. To keep the plants vigorous, cut the old stems back to the ground in early spring to encourage new growth.

A fine addition to a mixed border, plumbago also is a good companion for spring bulbs—its foliage will fill the holes left by the departing bulb foliage. In late summer and fall the blue flowers provide a rich counterpart to the pinks, whites, and lavenders of asters growing in sunnier parts of the garden.

Plumbago/Leadwort
(*Ceratostigma plumbaginoides*)

Lily-of-the-valley (*Convallaria majalis*)

Convallaria

Lily-of-the-valley (*Convallaria majalis*) is a plant that manages to be both charming and aggravating at the same time. Hardy and vigorous, lily-of-the-valley is an easy-to-grow ground cover that can take difficult conditions. It produces flat, pointed, spear-shaped leaves and in spring, slender stems of little white nodding bell-shaped flowers with an intoxicating fragrance. The plants are hardy in zones 3 to 8 and spread quickly. The problem is that lily-of-the-valley can spread too far too fast, and it forms a dense mat of roots that crowds out other less vigorous plants. In light soil you will have to dig up and thin out some of the plants every year if you want to grow lily-of-the-valley in a garden with other plants. Still, if you love the flowers, it's worth the effort.

You can grow lily-of-the-valley in partial to full shade. The ideal soil is moist but well drained and rich in organic matter, but this sturdy plant will tolerate less-than-ideal conditions. Space plants 6 to 8 inches apart. Divide them as necessary to keep them vigorous but under control. The plants are less invasive in warm, dry conditions, and the leaves tend to turn brown and ragged in hot, dry summers.

Lily-of-the-valley is a good groundcover plant under trees, in woodlands, and in odd neglected corners where grass will not grow.

Barrenwort/Bishop's hat (*Epimedium grandiflorum*)

Bunchberry (*Cornus canadensis*)

Cornus

Bunchberry (*Cornus canadensis*) belongs to the same genus as the magnificent flowering dogwoods. A woodland native, it grows wild across the northern part of the country and is hardy in gardens from zones 2 to 7. Plants creep along the ground, growing just 6 inches tall. They have deeply veined, oval leaves and in spring, small clusters of greenish flowers surrounded by petallike white bracts—similar in structure to the flowers of tree dogwoods. The flowers are followed by bright orangy-red berries in late summer.

Plant bunchberry in partial to medium shade, in cool, moist soil rich in organic matter, with an acid pH. Do not let the soil dry out. Bunchberry takes a while to become established, but once it takes hold, it spreads quickly.

Bunchberry is attractive under shrubs—especially broad-leaved evergreens—and it is an excellent choice for a woodland garden.

Epimedium

Barrenwort or **bishop's hat** (*Epimedium*) is a group of very similar plants that make lovely ground covers in shady gardens.

Epimedium grandiflorum grows to 1 foot high. It has heart-shaped leaves to 3 inches long that are bronzy when young and turn a light shade of green. In warm climates the plants are evergreen. In spring the plant produces clusters of spurred white, pink, red, or violet flowers.

Epimedium x *rubrum* grows to 1 foot tall, with pink flowers. *Epimedium* x *youngianum* is smaller, growing just 8 inches tall with white flowers.

All three species are hardy in zones 4 to 8.

Plant barrenwort in partial to full shade, in moist but well-drained soil that is rich and humusy. Space plants 6 inches to 1 foot apart. Although the plants take some time to become established, once they do they form a wonderful ground cover that will exclude weeds.

Barrenwort is an attractive plant for flower beds and borders or under deciduous trees and shrubs.

Galium

Sweet woodruff (*Galium odoratum*) is easy to grow and attractive. Reaching a height of about 6 to 10 inches, the plants bear small, slender leaves clustered in whorls around the stems. They have a fresh scent like freshly mown hay when crushed; the fragrance sweetens and mellows when the foliage dries. In spring there are clusters of small white flowers. Sweet woodruff is hardy in zones 4 to 8.

Sweet woodruff grows best in partial to light shade in moist but well-drained soil of average fertility. In richer, more humusy soils, sweet woodruff can get out of control. Space plants 6 inches to 1 foot apart. They spread by means of runners.

Plant sweet woodruff beneath trees and shrubs and as a carpet under tall, vigorous perennials in flower beds and borders.

Sweet woodruff (*Galium odoratum*)

Gaultheria

Wintergreen (*Gaultheria procumbens*), which also is called **teaberry** or **checkerberry,** is native to the forests of eastern North America. A trailing, woody evergreen plant, wintergreen seldom grows more than 4 inches high. The glossy, oval leaves grow 1 to 2 inches long and have toothed edges. Small white to pinkish flowers bloom in late spring and early summer, and are followed in late summer by bright red berries that last into winter. Oil made from the leaves and berries is used as a flavoring and has a number of herbal healing uses as well. Plants are hardy in zones 4 to 9.

Plant wintergreen in partial to medium shade, in humusy, moist but well-drained soil with an acid pH.

Wintergreen makes an attractive ground cover in woodland gardens.

Wintergreen/Teaberry/Checkerberry (*Gaultheria procumbens*)

English ivy (*Hedera helix*)

Hedera

Ivy is among the most widely grown vines. It will either climb if planted next to a wall, or it will trail across the ground.

English ivy (*Hedera helix*) has been cultivated for hundreds of years, and makes a tough, durable ground cover. Its lustrous, dark green, lobed, evergreen leaves grow on stems that can be 20 to 30 feet long. There are many cultivars, some with smaller leaves, some with variegated leaves that mix dark green with white, gold, or light green, and some with greater hardiness than the species form. English ivy is hardy in zones 5 to 9.

Algerian ivy or **Canary Island ivy** (*Hedera canariensis*) has heart-shaped, oval, or lobed leaves to 6 inches long. Numerous variegated and small-leaved cultivars are available. Canary Island ivy is a warm-climate plant, hardy in zones 8 or 9 to 11.

Plant ivy in partial to full shade. English ivy will grow in almost any reasonable garden soil, while Canary Island ivy prefers soil that is moist, fertile, and rich in organic matter.

Trim the plants as needed to keep them in bounds; they tolerate shearing well. You can take cuttings of young stems to start new plants.

Ivy is an excellent ground cover for a slope or bank. It tolerates heavy shade and difficult city conditions better than most other plants. You also can grow ivy under a tree and let it climb the trunk. Small-leaved and variegated varieties of ivy look best in this situation.

Houttuynia

Chameleon plant (*Houttuynia cordata* 'Variegata' or 'Chameleon') is a low-growing ground cover with decorative, heart-shaped, ivylike leaves variegated in green, bronze, yellow, and pinkish red. It grows 6 to 9 inches high and spreads vigorously by creeping underground runners. Plants are hardy in zones 3 or 4 to 8.

Grow chameleon plant in light shade to full sun, in moist to wet soil of average fertility. Be warned that plants spread rapidly where moisture is abundant, and they can become invasive. Once established they can be difficult to eliminate. Still, the colorful leaves are appealing. Space plants 1½ to 2 feet apart.

Chameleon plant is best grown where it has plenty of room to ramble; it is not a good choice for a neat, formal garden.

Lamium

Spotted dead nettle (*Lamium maculatum*) is a handsome ground cover, especially in the more ornamental cultivar forms. Plants grow about 8 inches tall; oval leaves grow to 2 inches long, with toothed edges, on stems that trail or stand upright. The leaves are evergreen in warm climates. In spring and summer plants produce compact vertical clusters of little tubular flowers. The cultivar 'Beacon Silver' has pink flowers and leaves

edged in green and overlaid with silver. 'White Nancy' has silvery leaves and white flowers. Spotted dead nettle is hardy in zones 4 to 8.

Plant dead nettle in partial to light shade, in moist, fertile soil. It will not tolerate drought or intense heat. Space plants 6 to 12 inches apart. Shear them back in midsummer, if necessary, to keep them looking neat.

Dead nettle is easy to grow in the right conditions. Plant it in the front of beds and borders, or use it as an edging plant if you're willing to trim it regularly to keep it under control.

Chameleon plant (*Houttuynia cordata*)

Spotted dead nettle
(*Lamium maculatum*)

Liriope

Lilyturf is a clump-forming perennial that can be grown in the flower garden or as a ground cover.

The best-known species, **big blue lilyturf** (*Liriope muscari*), has clumps of narrow, grassy leaves that are evergreen in mild climates. In mid- to late summer, plants send up slender spikes of tiny violet or white flowers that

Lilyturf (*Liriope muscari*)

resemble those of grape hyacinth, only larger. Variegated cultivars with white-striped leaves also are available. This lilyturf grows 1 to 2 feet high and is hardy in zones 6 to 10.

Creeping lilyturf (*Lirope spicata*) makes an even better ground cover. The foot-high plants spread by means of underground runners to carpet an area with its grassy leaves. It produces small spikes of lavender flowers in summer, but they are less decorative than those of big blue lilyturf. The cultivar 'Silver Dragon' grows just 8 inches tall and has white-striped leaves. Creeping lilyturf is hardy in zones 6 to 10.

Plant lilyturf in partial to full shade. Big blue lilyturf blooms best, and variegated cultivars develop the best foliage color, in partial to light shade. Plants thrive in moist but well-drained soil of average to good fertility. Once established they can tolerate brief periods of drought. Space plants 1 to 1½ feet apart. Trim back the old, dishevelled foliage in late winter or early spring. Plants spread quickly and should be divided when they become crowded. Unfortunately, slugs love lilyturf, so take appropriate measures if slugs are a problem in your garden.

Creeping mahonia (*Mahonia repens*)

Lilyturf makes a good edging in a shady bed or border, or along a driveway, path, or sidewalk. It also is attractive planted under trees or in a city courtyard. You also can use it with other ground covers to create interesting compositions of foliage texture in an area that does not receive foot traffic.

Mahonia

Creeping mahonia (*Mahonia repens*) is a low, spreading evergreen shrub native to the western U.S. that grows 2 to 3 feet tall. Its three-part leaves are composed of three leathery, oval leaflets with spiny edges. The bluish-green leaves turn bronzy purple in winter. Plants produce small clusters of little yellow flowers in late spring to early summer, followed by clusters of oval fruits that ripen to deep blue-black in autumn. Creeping mahonia is hardy to Zone 5.

Plant creeping mahonia in partial to medium shade, in well-drained soil of average fertility. When established, the plants are fairly drought tolerant. Drying winter winds may damage the leaves, so give the plants a windbreak or other winter protection in exposed locations. Space plants 1½ to 2 feet apart in the garden.

Creeping mahonia makes a good ground cover in western woodland gardens or under trees.

Mentha

A diminutive member of the mint family, **Corsican mint** (*Mentha requienii*) makes a delicate-textured ground cover. The plants grow low to the ground, with small, round, bright green leaves just ¼ inch across on creeping stems. When stepped on, the foliage releases a refreshing, pepper-minty fragrance. Corsican mint is hardy only in warm climates, but the plants often self-sow in colder climates to return the following year.

Corsican mint (*Mentha requienii*)

Plant Corsican mint in partial to light shade, in moist but well-drained soil of average fertility. It is ideal for planting between flagstones or bricks in a path or patio.

Mitchella

Partridgeberry (*Mitchella repens*) hails from the woodlands of eastern North America. It forms a low, trailing mat of oval to round leaves and in spring, small, tubular, fragrant white flowers. These are followed by red berries. Partridgebery is hardy in zones 3 to 9.

Plant partridgeberry in partial to medium shade, in moist soil with an acid pH. Partridgeberry is most at home in a woodland garden, planted in patches under trees or along a path.

Partridgeberry (*Mitchella repens*)

Pachysandra

Probably the most widely planted of all ground covers, pachysandra is useful in dense shade where tolerant plants are hard to come by. The most common species is an oriental import, **Japanese spurge** (*Pachysandra terminalis*), although there also is a native species, **Allegheny pachysandra** (*Pachysandra procumbens*). Plants grow 6 to 10 inches tall, with whorls of glossy evergreen leaves with toothed edges clustered around the stems. Plants spread by means of underground runners to form a dense mat. Plants produce small clusters of white flowers in spring. Allegheny pachysandra spreads less vigorously than Japanese spurge, as does the variegated form of *Pachysandra terminalis*. Pachysandra is hardy in zones 3 to 8.

You can plant pachysandra in dense shade to full sun, although plants grow best in partial to light shade. The preferred soil is moist but well drained, fertile, and rich in organic matter, but plants will adapt to a range of soils. Space plants 6 to 12 inches apart.

Pachysandra is a good ground cover for a bank, slope, or other location that's difficult to get to to maintain plants. You also can grow it under trees or in tough city locations. Don't plant pachysandra in a bed or border with bulbs or perennials; it would overwhelm them.

Pulmonaria

Lungwort (*Pulmonaria* species) got its name back in the days of the Doctrine of Signatures, when herbalists believed that the shape of the spotted leaves indicated that the plant could be used to treat lung ailments. The leaves are somewhat irregularly oval and covered with silvery spots. The upright plants grow 8 inches to 1½ feet tall. **Jerusalem sage** (*Pulmonaria*

Japanese spurge
(*Pachysandra terminalis*)

officinalis) has clusters of five-petaled red, purple, or white flowers in spring. **Bethlehem sage** (*Pulmonaria saccharata*) has flowers that open blue and turn pink as they age. Both species are hardy in zones 3 to 8.

Plant lungwort in partial to full shade, in moist but well-drained soil rich in organic matter. Space plants 6 to 12 inches apart. They will spread to form clumps and will need to be divided when plants become crowded and bloom less abundantly. Slugs find lungwort tasty, so avoid planting them or be prepared to take appropriate measures if slugs are a problem in your garden.

Lungwort is attractive in informal beds and borders, as a companion to spring bulbs, or planted along a path in a woodland garden.

Soleirolia

Baby's tears (*Soleirolia soleirolii*) is a charming small ground cover for zones 9 to 11. It's a ground-hugging plant that grows no more than 6 inches high, with tiny round leaves. The

Bethlehem sage
(*Pulmonaria saccharata*)

Baby's tears (*Soleirolia soleirolii*)

plants create a delicate-textured carpet that looks good year-round.

Plant baby's tears in partial to full shade, in moist soil of average to good fertility. As long as it receives adequate moisture, the plant is not fussy about soil. It cannot tolerate drought or strong sun.

Baby's tears is pretty planted among flagstones or bricks in a path or patio. Use it also around boulders, in a rock garden, or as a carpet under trees, shrubs, bulbs, and perennials.

Vancouveria

American barrenwort (*Vancouveria hexandra*), native to northwestern woodlands, is a good ground cover that deserves to be more widely grown. Plants produce glossy compound leaves on thin, wiry stems, and may be 8 inches to 1½ feet high. In early summer it bears sprays of little white flowers. American barrenwort is hardy in zones 5 to 9, but grow best in the Northwest, where summers are not too hot. It spreads to form a delicate-textured but dense carpet.

Plant barrenwort in partial to medium shade, in moist but well-drained soil rich in organic matter.

Barrenwort is a good ground cover to plant under trees and shrubs, in woodland gardens, or in flower beds and borders.

Vinca

Periwinkle is handsome and easy to grow. There are two species suitable for gardens.

The larger of the two, *Vinca major*, has pairs of broadly oval leaves on slender stems. The most widely grown cultivar, 'Variegata,' has leaves variegated with cream. In spring plants bear five-petaled flowers of blue-violet. Plants trail along the ground. They are hardy in zones 7 to 9. This cultivar is grown as an annual farther north and is very popular in window

American barrenwort
(*Vancouveria hexandra*)

boxes and tub plantings as a companion to upright flowers.

Common periwinkle (*Vinca minor*) is smaller, growing about 6 inches high. Its glossy, deep green, evergreen oval leaves are about 1 inch long and are carried on thin, wiry stems. In early spring plants produce five-petaled flowers of violet-blue. White-

flowered cultivars also are available. This periwinkle adapts to a wide range of growing conditions and is hardy in zones 4 to 9.

Plant common periwinkle in medium shade to full sun and *Vinca major* in light shade to sun. Both species appreciate afternoon shade in warm climates. They are not fussy about soil and will thrive in any moist but well-drained soil of reasonable fertility. Plants growing in full sun need regular moisture. In the shade they can tolerate some drought. Space plants about 6 inches apart, and prune the long, trailing stems to encourage more branching and denser growth.

Periwinkle is an excellent ground cover for a bank or slope and makes a good companion for spring bulbs. You also can plant it under deep-rooted trees and shrubs. The foliage stays attractive year-round where plants are hardy. Gardeners north of Zone 7 can grow *Vinca major* as an annual. The plant is especially pretty trailing over the sides of a container on a deck, porch, or patio.

Common periwinkle (*Vinca minor*)

Ornamental Grasses

Ornamental grasses are easy to grow and versatile. Some spread and can be used as ground covers; others form tall, majestic clumps that draw the eye when planted by themselves. Some grasses can be planted in groups as hedges or screens; others combine beautifully with perennials and annuals in informal beds and borders. Although they don't possess the bright colors of flowering annuals, bulbs, and perennials, ornamental grasses possess subtleties of form, color, and texture that make them beautiful in their own right. Throughout the growing season they rustle and sigh in the breeze, and their plumy, delicate flowers and seed heads add interest through autumn and much of winter. Best of all, grasses are easy to grow and demand little in the way of maintenance.

Arrhenatherum

Bulbous oat grass (*Arrhenatherum elatius* var. *bulbosum* 'Variegatum') is clump forming and perennial, with flat leaves striped in green and white. Its flower heads are bristly and shiny green. The swollen, bulbous rootstocks gave rise to the plant's common name. Bulbous oat grass grows to 2 feet high and may spread up to 12 feet across. It is hardy in zones 4 to 9.

The best site for this grass is a location in partial shade to full sun, in moist but well-drained, fertile soil. It grows best in cool weather and will suffer in extreme heat and dry conditions. If the foliage looks ratty in midsummer, cut back the plants to encourage fresh new growth in cooler autumn weather.

Plant bulbous oat grass in beds and borders and meadow or rock gardens.

Carex

Sedges (*Carex* species) are small, grasslike plants that generally do well in moist, shady conditions. Most of them grow 1 to 2 feet high, although some species reach 3 or 4 feet. Sedges tend to be clump forming or tufted in habit, with narrow, arching leaves. Some cultivars have variegated, golden, or bronze leaves. Most sedges are hardy in zones 4 or 5 to 9.

Plant sedges in light shade to full sun, in moist, fertile soil. Never let the soil dry out.

Sedges are interesting planted in masses alongside a stream or pool. The more compact varieties are good for edging, rock gardens, or container planting. You also can plant them as ground covers in nontraffic areas. The larger sedges make handsome accent plants in beds and borders.

Bulbous oat grass (*Arrhenatherum elatius* var. *bulbosum* 'Variegatum')

Sedge (*Carex* species)

Tufted hair grass
(*Deschampsia caespitosa*)

Deschampsia

Tufted hair grass (*Deschampsia caespitosa*) forms a delicate-looking tuft for slender, arching leaves whose clusters of small flowers have thin, hairlike structures projecting from the tips. The flowers appear to float above the foliage like a soft cloud in spring and early summer. There are cultivars with golden-bronze leaves and yellow flowers and one, 'Fairy's Joke,' that has unusual small plantlets carried along with the flowers at the top of the plant. Tufted hair grass grows 1 to 4 feet tall, with a spread of up to 3 feet. It is hardy in zones 4 to 9.

Plant tufted hair grass in partial to full shade, in moist but well-drained soil rich in organic matter with a mildly acid pH. Plants cannot tolerate intense sun or dry conditions and grow best in cool weather. They prefer partial shade but will tolerate shadier conditions as well. Tufted hair grass tends to self-sow and spread.

Grow tufted hair grass in informal beds and borders, or allow it to naturalize in a partly shaded open area.

Festuca

Fescues (*Festuca* species) are included in lawn grass mixtures for shady locations, and many of them are grown as unmowed ornamental grasses. Best known is **blue fescue** (*Festuca ovina* var. *glauca*), which has thin, wiry leaves of silvery blue-green and a tufted form. In summer plants bear short clusters of beige to brownish flowers. The plants retain their compact form and do not spread. Blue fescue grows about 1 to 1½ feet tall and 8 inches across. It is hardy in zones 4 to 9.

Plant blue fescue—and most other fescues—in partial shade to full sun, in moist but well-drained soil of average fertility. In warm climates shade is essential. Once it becomes established, blue fescue will tolerate some dryness in the northern parts of the growing range. It needs regular watering in hotter locations.

Fescues can be planted as edgings along a path or sidewalk, in beds and borders, or in rock gardens. You also can plant them in masses as a ground cover where they will not get foot traffic. The tufted habit of the plants also allows for planting in geometric patterns in beds of their own for an unusual and futuristic effect.

Hakonechloa

Hakone grass (*Hakonechloa macra*) is a perennial that grows to 1½ feet tall and 3 feet across, with bright green 6-inch-long leaves similar to those of bamboo. The edges of the leaves turn rosy pink in fall. Hakone grass grows in a soft mound and is hardy in zones 7 to 9. The cultivar 'Aureola' has leaves variegated with golden yellow.

Plant hakone grass in partial to full shade, in moist but well-drained soil rich in organic matter. It does not thrive in dry conditions or in heavy clay soils. Hakone grass grows best in

Blue fescue (*Festuca ovina* var. *glauca*)

Hakone grass (*Hakonechloa macra*)

mild climates where summer weather is not too hot and humid.

Use hakone grass to edge a path, or plant it in masses as a ground cover.

Hystrix

Bottlebrush grass (*Hystrix patula*) is named for its upright flower clusters, which have horizontal bristles and, from a distance, resemble the brushes used to clean bottles. The plant grows to 4 feet high and 2 feet across and has flat, narrow, grayish-green leaves. Plants self-sow and will naturalize over time. Bottlebrush grass is hardy in zones 5 to 9.

Plant bottlebrush grass in light shade to full sun, in moist but well-drained soil. It needs plenty of moisture to thrive in full sun. It grows best in cool weather and does not do well in hot, dry locations.

Bottlebrush grass is good for naturalizing as a tall ground cover. You also can plant it in flower beds and borders, and pull up unwanted volunteer seedlings.

Golden wood millet
(*Milium effusum* 'Aureum')

Milium

Golden wood millet (*Milium effusum* 'Aureum') is a lovely plant with slender, 12-inch, light yellow-green leaves. In mid-spring to early summer it has fine-textured flower clusters of golden yellow. Golden wood millet grows up to 15 inches high, with a spread of up to 1½ feet. It is hardy in zones 5 to 9. The plants spread by means of runners.

The best spot for golden wood millet is in light to partial shade and moist but well-drained soil rich in organic matter. It grows best in cool weather and areas where summer weather is relatively mild.

Golden wood millet is attractive in a woodland garden, in a rock garden, or as a ground cover.

Bottlebrush grass (*Hystrix patula*)

Ophiopogon

Mondo grass or **dwarf lilyturf** (*Ophiopogon japonicus*) is actually a member of the lily family and similar to true lilyturf (*Liriope* species). The grasslike plants grow in a low mound, reaching a height of just 6 inches and a spread of about 8 inches. The cultivar 'Minor' grows just 3 inches tall. In midsummer there are clusters of small lavender or white flowers. The plants spread to form a dense mat of foliage. Mondo grass is hardy in zones 7 to 11.

Plant mondo grass in partial to full shade, in moist but well-drained or wet soil. Although it can take sun in Zone 7, mondo grass requires shade farther south.

Mondo grass is an excellent ground cover to mass in shady locations.

Phalaris

Ribbon grass or **gardener's garters** (*Phalaris arundinacea* var. *picta*) has flat green leaves with white edges and can be anywhere from 2 to 5 feet tall. In late spring to early summer plants bear slender spikes of soft white to pinkish flowers. It is hardy in zones 4 to 9.

Plant ribbon grass in light to partial shade; it needs shade in warmer parts of the growing range. Ribbon grass prefers moist, even wet, soil.

Ribbon grass is a good grass to plant alongside a stream or at the edge of a pool or pond. Give the plant a location where it has room to spread.

Typha

Narrow-leaved cattail (*Typha angustifolia*) has slender leaves 3 to 6 feet long that form erect clumps. In early summer stout stems rise above leaves and bear yellow male flowers on top of the densely clustered brown female blooms that form the cattail. Fuzzy brown seed heads persist into late autumn. *Typha angustifolia* 'Variegata' has striped leaves.

Plant narrow-leaved cattails in full sun to partial shade, in moist or wet, humus-rich soil. They can grow in standing water up to 1 foot deep. This wetland plant usually is not overly aggressive, but you can keep it from spreading with root barriers.

Ribbon grass/Gardener's garters
(*Phalaris arundinacea* var. *picta*)

Narrow-leaved cattail
(*Typha angustifolia*)

Mondo grass/Dwarf lilyturf (*Ophiopogon japonicus*)

CHAPTER FIVE

Starting the Garden

Planting is a favorite activity for many gardeners. There is something satisfying about planting a seed and watching the fragile shoots grow into sturdy plants, or tucking a young plant into the ground and watching it mature. All gardeners are care-givers at heart. To give plants a good home, choose the site carefully and prepare the soil well. Soil preparation is where the real work of gardening begins.

Preparing the Soil

Few of us are blessed with perfect soil, but almost any soil can be improved. The first step is to understand the kind of soil already present on your garden site.

The ideal soil for most shade plants is fertile, moist but well drained, and rich in organic matter. Woodland plants, especially, need lots of humus in order to thrive. A light, loose texture is important, too, because many shade plants have a special need for oxygen around their

Sandy soil

Clay soil

Loamy soil

roots; a well-aerated soil allows for optimum growth. Woodland plants such as ferns and azaleas grow best in light, spongy, humusy soil like the dark black-brown soil found in undisturbed woodlands.

For most annuals, perennials, ground covers, and small bulbs, soil that is of good quality to a depth of 6 to 8 inches will serve nicely. Shrubs and trees need good soil to a greater depth—1 to 2 feet in many cases.

In gauging the quality of your soil, begin with the topsoil. Is it sandy, clay, or loamy?

Sandy soils are light colored, porous, and loose textured, containing a high proportion of sand particles, which are relatively large as soil particles go. Sandy soils usually are well drained and easy to dig. Water passes through them quickly, with the result that the soil tends to be dry and also low in nutrients, because they are carried away by the fast-draining water before roots can absorb them.

At the other end of the soil scale, **clay soil** is dark colored and dense, containing a large proportion of tiny clay particles. The clay particles pack tightly together, resulting in soil that is dense and poorly drained. Clay soil does, however, usually contain a reasonable amount of nutrients.

Loamy soil, the ideal soil for gardening in general, contains a more or less balanced mixture of sand and clay, along with silt particles and organic matter. Loam soils are crumbly, naturally fertile, and drain well while still holding enough moisture for plants.

You can learn a great deal about your soil by examining it carefully, and by observing the kinds of plants that grow wild on your property and researching the kind of soil in which

Soil is critical to growing healthy plants, so test it every few years for soil type, nutrient and organic matter content, and pH.

such plants thrive. The best information, however, comes from having the soil tested. A good soil test will reveal soil type, nutrient and organic matter content, and pH. You can buy a home test kit or have soil samples tested through your USDA county Cooperative Extension Service office or by a private laboratory.

If you will be planting trees and/or shrubs, you'll need to examine the subsoil as well as the topsoil on your garden site. If the subsoil is in reasonably good condition, you can amend it to bring it up to garden quality. One simple test you can perform is to see if you can dig the soil. When the soil is evenly moist in spring (winter in warm climates), see if you can push a shovel into it without jumping up and down on the shovel. If you can, get a soil test done. If you're going to be amending the subsoil, first remove the topsoil and pile it to one side. Loosen the subsoil with a heavy-duty tiller, a small tractor with a plow attachment, or, if the area is small, a spading fork. Spread 2 to 4 inches of compost or other organic matter over the subsoil and till it in. Then replace the topsoil. You can go on to improve the topsoil, if necessary, as described on the next page.

If the subsoil is in poor condition, so compacted that you can't force a spade into it, the easiest course of action is to build raised beds 1 to 2 feet high on top of the subsoil and fill them with a good soil mix.

Improving Sandy and Clay Soils

To improve sandy soils, spread a 2- to 4-inch layer of compost, aged livestock manure, leaf mold, or other organic matter over the soil, and till or dig it into the top 6 to 8 inches of soil.

For heavy clay soil, spread a 2-inch layer of sharp builder's sand and work it in. Then work in 2 to 4 inches of organic matter.

Improving Wet Soils

To make a garden of moisture-loving plants in a poorly drained or boggy location, you must first get rid of the existing vegetation. Cut weeds, reeds, and other unwanted plants to the ground. Then apply an herbicide that degrades quickly and won't linger in the environment, such as a glyphosphate product. An alternative approach, if you're not in a hurry, is to cover the ground with black plastic and wait a year for the old plant roots to die before planting the garden.

Build raised paths or boardwalks through the wetland to provide easy access to the garden. It's best to make the paths before you put in any plants.

Improving Dry Prairie and Desert Soils

Arid soils tend to contain high levels of mineral salts because not enough rain falls to leach them out of the soil. As a result, such soils may be too alkaline for many plants to tolerate. You may need to saturate the soil with demineralized water to flush out the

A stone path meanders through a wetland garden planted with yellow flag iris (*Iris pseudocorus*), hostas (*Hosta* species), and lady's mantle (*Alchemilla mollis*).

salts. Then till in copious amounts of good compost, aged manure, leaf mold, cottonseed meal, and other organic matter to open up the soil structure and improve water retention at the same time. Organic matter will help to lower the pH, too. You also can add sulfur, sulfate fertilizers, and chelated minerals to lower pH to some extent.

Add enough organic material so the garden area contains roughly equal parts of existing soil and soil amendments.

Alternatives to the organic route would be to spread 6 to 8 inches of high-quality topsoil (which can be expensive and difficult to obtain), or to use native plants and wildflowers that will grow in the existing soil.

Mixing Your Own Soil

If you will be gardening in raised beds or containers, you can custom-blend a soil mix. A good all-purpose soil mix for shady gardens consists of 2 parts organic matter (compost or leaf mold, ideally), 1 part sharp builder's sand, and 1 part good, loamy soil. Screen the mixture to remove stones, roots, chunks of wood, and other debris before filling beds or containers.

Removing Grass

If you're carving a bed or border out of a lawn, field, or other grassy area, you must first move the grass. Begin by mowing the grass close to the ground.

If the garden will be small, lift the sod by hand. Cut it into strips by punching down into the soil with the edge of a sharp spade. Then push the blade of the spade horizontally under the turf and dig it up in patches. Pile the turf in an out-of-the-way corner, upside down, and let it decompose into the soil.

If the grass is thin, simply dig it into the soil. Thick grass, though, will grow back.

In a larger area, the fastest way to remove grass is to apply a biodegradable herbicide. Alternatively, you could cover the garden-to-be with sheets of black plastic, or 10 thicknesses of newspaper followed by a few inches of soil, and wait. It will take several months for the grass to die.

Planting Under Trees

To create planting areas under trees, first make sure enough light is present to support the garden plants. As explained in Chapter 1, the best trees for shady gardens have high, open canopies and deep roots. Prune off low branches to let in more light and to allow easy access to the garden without bending and stooping.

If the soil is full of tree roots and you're unable to dig in it, there are two ways to prepare for planting. One is to build a raised bed around the tree and spread a layer of good soil mix over the area. A 4-inch layer is deep enough for ground covers like vinca, pachysandra, or ivy. To grow flowers and foliage plants, make the soil 6 to 8 inches deep. The other approach is to carve out planting holes for individual plants. Chop out sections of the root with an ax, then dig them out of the ground. Fill the hole with good soil to create a planting area that should remain free of roots long enough for the plants you put in to become established. As long as you dig out only a few roots, you're not likely to harm the tree. Only tough, drought-tolerant shade-lovers are likely to survive for long surrounded by tree roots. The roots will compete fiercely for water and nutrients. You will need to water and fertilize your garden plants regularly, but this method can work if you're willing to put in the effort.

Although barely visible through the lush growth of hostas (*Hosta plantaginea*), anemones (*Anemone* x *hybrida* 'Queen Charlotte'), and white impatiens (*Impatiens* species), the raised bed made planting easier. It required new soil on top of existing soil that was full of tree roots and hard to dig.

A thick, loose layer of mulch creates a congenial environment for foxglove (*Digitalis ambigua*). Mulch such as shredded leaves simulates leaf litter found in natural forests.

Planting in the Woods

Turning an established woodland into a garden is a lot of work, but the results are rewarding. The biggest job is clearing out the tangled, dense undergrowth. You may need to take down some trees that are damaged, diseased, or otherwise in poor condition. Do that first. Then dig out the weedy shrubs growing beneath the trees, roots and all. Hire someone with a small tractor or earth-moving equipment to clear brush unless you have a small area or a real love of hard work. Woodland soil often is easily compacted, so don't work soil when it's wet.

When the undergrowth is cleared, lay out paths and do any necessary excavation. Finally, amend the soil in the planting areas if you need to. A thick layer of shredded leaves or other loose mulch can mimic the layer of leaf litter found in natural forests and can help create a hospitable environment for woodland wildflowers and ferns. Fill planting areas with pockets of good soil mix (as described above) and spread a 4- to 5-inch layer of mulch on top. Pull aside the mulch to plant and replace it when plants are large enough to project above it.

Starting Seeds

Growing plants from seed affords you a greater choice of plants—many more varieties are available in seed form than you can find at local garden centers or in the pages of mail-order nursery catalogs. Many gardeners grow annuals and perennials from seed. Trees and shrubs—and even bulb plants—can be grown from seed as well. Seeds of hardy trees and shrubs may need a cold period or other pretreatment to break their dormancy before they will germinate. If you purchase seeds from a seed or nursery company, you'll receive instructions on any necessary pretreatments (most seeds are pretreated before they're shipped to you). If you obtain seeds of woody plants from friends, neighbors, or the seed exchange of a horticultural group, consult a book on propagation to see if any pretreatment is needed.

Nursery Care

If you plan to start perennials, shrubs, and other plants that take more than a year to mature, you'll want to set aside an area in the garden to serve as a nursery, where you can give the young plants special care until they're ready to move to the main garden.

What You'll Need

Before you start any seeds, assemble the necessary tools and, if you're sowing indoors, containers and potting mix. Be sure tools and containers are clean and the potting mix is moist. Using a sterile growing medium reduces the risk of exposure to disease-causing organisms—young seedlings are especially susceptible. You can purchase a commercial seed-starting mix or make your own. One good recipe is 1 part peat moss, 1 part perlite or vermiculite, and 1 part sterilized or pasteurized soil. If you prefer a soilless mix, mix equal parts of perlite or vermiculite and peat moss.

Fill containers with the moist potting mix to about $\frac{1}{2}$ inch from the top. Follow instructions on seed packets for how deep and how far apart to plant. Generally, sow seeds two to three times as deep as their diameter. To make tiny seeds easier to handle, you may want to mix them with an equal volume of sand, then sprinkle them as evenly as you can over the surface of the potting mix. Press the seeds lightly into the soil and mist

Growing plants from seed expands your plant options and is less expensive than buying bedding plants.

thoroughly or set the container in a pan of water until the soil surface feels moist. Plant larger seeds in drills (shallow furrows) or individual holes.

Germinating Conditions

Optimum germination temperature varies from plant to plant. The origin of a plant offers a clue to the kinds of conditions it needs to germinate and grow well. Plants native to tropical parts of the world, which include many summer-blooming annuals and tender perennials that gardeners in the northern United States grow as annuals, often need warm temperatures of 70° F or higher to germinate. Many hardy annuals, perennials, trees, and shrubs need cooler temperatures of 55° F to 60° F to sprout.

Keep the potting mix evenly moist but not soggy until germination occurs. When shoots appear, give the seedlings plenty of bright light. The light can come from fluorescent fixtures kept 6 to 12 inches above the tops of the plants, or from an unobstructed east- or west-facing window, or a south window shaded by sheer curtains to keep temperatures moderate. Turn plants on windowsills every day so the stems grow straight. Water seedlings when the potting mix dries slightly, but never let it dry out completely. Water stress can permanently damage delicate young seedlings. The soil should not be soggy, either, or the seedlings could rot.

Thinning Seedlings

When the seedlings develop their first true leaves (the first leaves that have the shape characteristic of that plant, usually the second set of leaves to appear), it's time to thin them and to begin fertilizing. Thin crowded plants by snipping the stems of unwanted

Techniques for Sowing Small Seeds

♦ Put the seeds in an old salt shaker with a small amount of sand and sprinkle them on the soil mix.

♦ Mix the seeds thoroughly with white table sugar, distributing the seeds evenly throughout. Using a spoon, spread the mixture over the planting medium.

♦ Fold a seed packet in half lengthwise, and align the seeds in the crease. Tap the packet to drop one seed at a time.

♦ Run a strip of toilet paper down the furrow and plant the seeds on top. (The buried paper quickly breaks down into the soil.)

seedlings at the base with a manicure scissors, to avoid damaging the roots of the seedlings you want to keep. Seedlings should be far enough apart so the leaves of adjoining plants do not touch, and so air can circulate freely among them.

Fertilize seedlings with an all-purpose liquid fertilizer diluted to half the recommended strength. Overfeeding causes weak, rapid growth that makes seedlings more susceptible to disease.

When the seedlings have grown enough that their leaves touch again, transplant them to individual containers, or, if weather permits, to the outdoor garden or nursery bed. Lift plants carefully when transplanting, supporting under the roots with a teaspoon, wooden plant label, or your hand. Pick up small plants by a leaf rather than by the stem, to avoid

inadvertently breaking the stem or damaging the growing tip.

Seedlings going into the garden should be hardened-off as described opposite, under Planting Transplants.

Thin crowded seedlings after they develop their first true leaves, spacing the seedlings so leaves of adjoining plants don't touch.

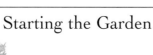

Sowing Outdoors

Some plants don't take transplanting well and are best sown directly in the garden where they are to grow. Prepare the soil for planting by tilling or digging by hand to loosen it, then rake to break up clods and clumps and create a smooth, level planting area. If you will be planting in a row, make a furrow of the correct depth with the edge of a hoe. Drop in the seeds as close to the correct spacing as possible, cover with soil, firm the soil over them, and water well with a fine spray.

To broadcast seeds over a large area, as when seeding a meadow, prepare the soil as directed above. Scatter seeds in handfuls over the soil surface as evenly as you can, making broad, sweeping motions with your arm as you release the seeds. Rake first in one direction, then again at a 90-degree angle, to cover the seeds. Roll with a lawn roller to firm the soil. Water well with a fine spray.

Planting Transplants

Plants raised indoors (at your house or in a greenhouse at the nursery) need to gradually become accustomed to harsher outdoor conditions to avoid suffering shock when they're transplanted in the garden. Harden-off plants over a period of a week to 10 days by stopping fertilization and by exposing them to outdoor conditions for gradually increasing lengths of time. The first day, set the plants outdoors in a protected location out of the wind for a couple of hours. Then bring them back indoors. Repeat the procedure each day, leaving the plants outdoors a bit longer each day. After a week to 10 days, leave the

To prevent shock to plants started indoors, harden-off the plants by setting them outdoors for gradually increasing amounts of time.

plants out overnight. After that you can plant them in the garden. If you have a cold frame, you can use it to harden-off plants by opening the lid a bit farther each day, finally opening it all the way or removing it for the last two or three days.

If you will be transplanting seedlings from undivided nursery flats, you will first need to "block" the plants to separate their root systems. A few days before you plan to transplant, take a sharp knife and cut down into the soil between plants. Cut the soil into blocks, with a plant in the center of each block. The cut roots will heal in a few days, and the plants will make an easier transition into the garden.

Try to transplant on a mild, calm, cloudy day. On a sunny, windy day plants can dry out more easily. Dig the planting hole before removing the plant from its container. Make the hole large enough to comfortably accommodate the root ball and deep enough so the plant sits at the same depth as it did in its container. If the soil is dry, fill the hole with water and let it drain. Press on the sides or bottom of the container, or tap on it with the handle of your trowel to loosen the plant. Turn the container upside

down, supporting the topgrowth with your other hand, and slide the plant out of the container.

Set the plant in the hole and fill in around the roots with soil. If the plant was pot bound, with a dense, tangled mass of roots, make several vertical cuts about one-third of the way up into the root ball with a sharp knife, and spread the root ball gently with your hands before setting the plant in the hole. Firm the soil gently after planting; do not pack it hard. Water well.

When setting out plants, don't put them closer together than the spacing distance recommended on the plant label or in Chapter 4 of this book. You can sometimes get away with setting plants closer together than the recommended distance when you're planting in a sunny location in rich soil. In the shade, however, plants tend to sprawl and spread out more as they reach for the light, and they won't thrive if packed too close together. Adequate space also is important for good air circulation among plants, which helps prevent the spread of mildew and fungal diseases.

Dig the planting hole before you remove a plant from its container. Set the plant in the hole at the same depth it was in the container.

Shopping for Shade Plants

Keep the following suggestions in mind when you're shopping for plants. Inspect plants carefully to make sure they're healthy. Purchase them on the day you plan to plant them in your garden. Look for plants that are still in bud rather than in bloom. They'll adapt more quickly after transplanting. Purchase plants that appear sturdy and stocky and have foliage that is healthy, with good color.

When you purchase plants from a local nursery or garden center, you can personally inspect the plants to make sure they're healthy

To reduce the possibility of transplant stress, set shade-garden plants in the ground the same day you purchase them.

Check the roots of a transplant before you buy it to make sure the white roots at the edge hold the soil ball together.

Plants to Avoid

◆ Plants with yellow or wilted leaves. This often is a sign of disease or lack of water.

◆ Plants with weeds in the container. Weeds are a sign the plant is being robbed of nutrients.

◆ Plants with spindly stems. This indicates the plant has been growing in the pot too long.

◆ Roots crawling out of the bottom of the pot. This is a sign the plant has outgrown its container and is in a stressed condition.

◆ Plants with many flowers. This is a sign that the plant has put most of its energy into blossoms and may easily succumb to transplant shock.

Planting Nursery Stock

Large plants that you purchase from a local or mail-order nursery come in one of three forms: container-grown, balled-and-burlapped, or bare-root. You will need an assistant to help you handle large shrubs and trees with heavy root balls and tall topgrowth.

Container-Grown Plants

When you buy a container-grown plant, make sure it was actually grown in the container. Some plants are sold in containers and called "container-ized," but they may have been dug from a nursery field while dormant and put into their containers with potting mix in which they didn't actually grow. These plants should be treated like bare-root plants, as described on page 159.

True container-grown plants can go into the ground at any time during the growing season when the weather is mild and not stressful. The planting procedure is basically the same as that described on page 159 for transplants. Prepare the planting hole before removing the plant from its container. Loosen the soil in and around the spot where you'll dig the planting hole. Make the hole a little bigger than the root ball and deep enough so the plant will sit at the same depth it was growing in the container.

To loosen a large plant or shrub from a container, lay the pot on its side. Roll the pot on the ground and tap or press with your hand on the sides to loosen the root ball. If you buy a plant in a metal can, you can ask the nursery to cut the can for you before you take the plant home, so it will be easier to remove.

Popular container-grown plants include astilbe and hosta. You can set container-grown plants in the ground almost any time during the growing season.

Examine the root ball before you set the plant in the hole. If the plant is pot bound, gently untangle and spread out some of the larger roots if you can. If the root ball is too tight, cut up into it vertically from the bottom in two or three places, and pull on the root ball to spread it apart; don't break it into pieces. If the plant has a long taproot, dig the hole deep enough to accommodate it, and straighten it as much as you can when planting. Cut off any roots you find growing on top of the soil ball, especially if they are coiled around the main stem.

If any soil falls out of a dense root ball, replace it before you set the plant in the hole so there won't be air pock-

Planting Container-Grown Plants

To remove a plant from its container, roll the container on the ground or tap the sides of the pot with your hand to loosen the root ball.

After you've set the plant in the hole, fill in around the roots with soil. Use your fingers to work the soil around the roots to fill any gaps.

ets left in the root ball. Roots in an air pocket can dry out and die, even when the plant is in the ground.

Set the plant in the hole, check the depth, and fill in around the roots with soil. If the root ball is loose, work the soil around the roots with your fingers to fill any gaps. When the planting hole is filled halfway with soil, water well, then fill the hole to the top with soil, firm the soil, and water again.

If you live in a dry climate or where summer dry spells are a common occurrence, or if your soil is light and sandy, make a depression in the soil to catch water for roots. Instead of making a saucerlike depression around the base of the trunk or stem, experts now recommend making a ringlike depression (like a doughnut) several inches out from the trunk and just inside the circumference of the planting hole.

Balled-and-Burlapped Stock

Many trees and shrubs are sold in balled-and-burlapped form, with the root ball wrapped in burlap (which may be real or imitation) and tied with ropes. Like container-grown plants, balled-and-burlapped stock can be planted whenever weather conditions are not too stressful, although spring and fall are generally the preferred times.

Examine a balled-and-burlapped plant carefully before planting, to see if it is truly balled-and-burlapped. Real burlap is made of cotton fibers or jute and will decompose in the soil; you can plant it along with the plant. Some nurseries now use imitation burlap made with plastic fibers; this material is not biodegradable and must be removed at planting time or

Planting Balled-and-Burlapped Stock

♦ To plant balled-and-burlapped stock dig a hole as deep as the root ball and twice as wide.
♦ Look for a soil line on the trunk or main stem (you should be able to discern a color change; the underground part is lighter in color) to see if the plant is sitting at the same depth it was when growing in the nursery field.

it will constrict root growth. Look over the soil ball as well. Plants are sometimes sold in artificial soil balls that are actually compressed peat moss. This kind of plant didn't really grow in the peat surrounding its roots, and it should be treated as a bare-root plant during planting.

Loosen the soil in the planting area and dig a hole as deep as the root ball and twice as wide. Remove any nails holding the burlap or ropes in place. Set the plant in the hole, and remove the ropes tying the burlap together. Roll back the burlap to partially uncover the soil ball. Remove imitation burlap completely and set it aside. Look for a soil line on the trunk

Planting Trees and Shrubs

Be sure to allow enough room for trees and shrubs to grow to their full height and spread. The International Society of Arboriculture suggests the following general guidelines:

♦ Plant small trees that will grow 10 to 15 feet tall 15 to 20 feet apart and at least 8 feet from buildings.
♦ Plant medium-size trees about 35 feet apart.
♦ Plant large trees 50 feet apart.
♦ Plant shrubs a distance equal to half their mature spread away from other plants or buildings.

or main stem (you should be able to discern a color change, with the underground part being lighter in color) to see if the plant is sitting at the same depth it was when growing in the nursery field. If the soil line is above the level of the surrounding soil, take the plant out of the hole and remove more soil to lower the level. If the plant is sitting too deep, take it out of the hole and add some soil to correct the depth. When the depth is right, fill in around the root ball with soil. Make sure you have rolled back the burlap far enough so it's not visible when the hole is filled. Firm the soil around the base of the plant and water thoroughly.

Bare-Root Plants

Deciduous trees and shrubs, small evergreens, and other plants are sometimes sold in bare-root form. Bare-root plants are shipped and planted while they are dormant, with the roots wrapped in damp sphagnum moss or other loose packing material, or wrapped in plastic, so they don't dry out during shipping. The best time to plant bare-root plants is in early spring as soon as the soil can be worked in Zone 5 and north, in early spring or fall in zones 6 and 7, in fall in zones 8 and 9, and in winter in zones 10 and 11.

When you receive a shipment of bare-root plants, unpack and examine them immediately. The roots and crowns should be firm, with no soft or moldy spots. Branches should be firm, not dry or shriveled. The plant should have no new shoots longer than a couple of inches. If the plants aren't in good condition, return them. Otherwise, set the roots in a bucket of water and let them soak overnight or for several hours before planting in the garden.

Loosen the soil in the planting area, extending out into the entire area likely to be covered by the roots of the mature plant.

Dig a planting hole as deep as the root ball and twice as wide. Make a mound of soil in the bottom of the hole. Remove the plant from the bucket of water, and clip off any broken or damaged roots with pruning shears. Set the plant on the soil mound in the bottom of the hole and spread the roots over and down the sides of the mound. Check the depth; the soil line on the stem should be even with the level of the soil surrounding the hole.

Fill in around the roots with soil, working the soil in with your fingers. When the hole is half full of soil, fill to the top with water. Let the water drain through, then fill the rest of the hole with soil and water again. Make a depression to catch water as described earlier in this chapter, under Container-Grown Plants, if you live in a dry climate or in an area where summer dry spells are common. Mulch to conserve soil moisture.

If the tree is too tall or weak-rooted to stand securely by itself, especially if you live in a windy location, staking is probably necessary. Don't stake trees unless it's necessary, however; they're believed to grow stronger without staking.

Drive three stakes into the ground outside the planting hole, spacing them evenly around the tree. Fasten a strong wire to each stake and wrap it around a low branch of the tree. Pass the wire through a piece of old garden hose to pad it where it contacts the tree. Allow some play in the wires so the tree can flex a bit in the wind and strengthen its wood. Remove the stakes after a year.

Planting Bare-Root Plants

◆ Dig a planting hole for bare-root plants as deep as the root ball and twice as wide. Make a mound of soil in the bottom of the hole.

◆ Set the plant on the soil mound in the bottom of the hole and spread the roots over and down the sides of the mound. Check the depth; the soil line on the stem should be even with the level of the soil surrounding the hole.

When planting trees and shrubs, allow enough space for them to grow to their mature height and spread, as was done here with azalea bushes, a Japanese maple, and hosta 'Francis Williams.'

163

For a natural look in a woodland or other naturalistic or informal garden, avoid setting out plants in neat rows or geometric patterns. Always plant in groups of at least three of the same plant, even in the smallest garden, for visual impact. Clumps and drifts of a dozen or more plants are even better. Odd-numbered groups of plants—7, 11, or 15—usually look more natural than even-numbered groups. When gardeners plant even numbers, they tend to make neat, symmetrical groupings. One way to devise a natural-looking random placement for plants is to toss a handful of stones into the planting area and put a plant where each stone lands.

Planting in groups can become expensive in a large garden, but it's worth it. If your funds are limited, start with just a few plants and propagate more as the initial plantings become mature. Concentrate the few plants in one small area of the garden and gradually expand outward. Don't dot plants over the entire area you eventually want them to fill. A smaller, more concentrated planting will look better than a scattered, spread-out approach.

Asiatic lilies, astilbe, and verbascum (top right) and ligularia (bottom right) are planted in clumps and drifts and in odd-numbered groupings in these gardens to create a natural, informal look.

If You Can't Plant Right Away

It is best to purchase plants when you're ready to put them into the garden. Events—and the weather—don't always cooperate, however, and it sometimes is necessary to postpone planting. Seedlings in cell packs and individual pots are most at risk from delayed planting, because the small amount of soil in the containers dries out quickly, especially on hot, windy days.

If you must postpone planting, set the containers in a shady spot, out of the sun and wind. Check the plants often to make sure they're not drying out.

If you keep the plants watered, they should be fine for a week or two. Plants in larger containers can be held even longer if they are not severely pot bound.

To hold balled-and-burlapped plants, place them in a shady location and pile loose mulch over the root balls. Water as needed to keep the root balls moist but not soggy. In very hot weather, mist the foliage to cool it.

You can hold bare-root plants for a few days by opening the wrapping, moistening the roots, reclosing the wrapping, and setting the plants in a cool, dark place.

To hold them for a longer period, heel them into the ground. Dig a shallow trench with angled sides. Lay the plants in the trench, roots down, and cover the roots loosely with moist soil. Don't firm the soil or the plants may root into it, and don't let the soil dry out.

Care After Planting

To help ease the transition to the garden, give new plants some special care. Keep the soil evenly moist, but not soggy, during the first couple of weeks after transplanting annuals and perennials, to make it easier for them to develop new roots. Don't fertilize until the plants show new growth, or you could overstimulate the plants and weaken them.

If a serious storm threatens, stake new plants of any appreciable height. Cover the plants with securely anchored floating row covers or "garden blankets" of spunbonded polyester or with baskets or boxes weighted down with stones. If left unprotected, the plants could be toppled by strong gusts of wind because they haven't yet had a chance to send roots deep enough into the soil to provide a firm anchor.

Trees, shrubs, and ground covers generally need less water than herbaceous plants, but they, too, need a chance to adapt to their new home. As a rule, water once every week or two during the first

year a woody plant is in the garden, while it is establishing a sturdy root system. Even drought-tolerant plants need to be watered until they become established.

The bark of young trees is not very tough. Drying winter winds and cold temperatures can cause damage during a tree's first year or two in the garden. Protect the trunk by wrapping it with tree wrap in the form of tape or a protective sleeve. The tree wrap also will help keep mice and deer from gnawing on the bark. Check the wrap regularly to make sure it's not becoming tight and constricting the tree's growth.

To make a sturdier animal guard, wrap the trunk loosely with hardware cloth or chicken wire.

CHAPTER SIX

Maintaining the Garden

Shady gardens often require less maintenance time than gardens in sunny locations. You won't have to water as often in the shade, especially if you mulch the garden, and your garden probably will have fewer weeds than gardens in full sun. Pest and disease problems, too, seem to be less frequent overall in shady gardens. Shade gardens are not entirely care-free, however. Some maintenance is necessary to keep the garden flourishing.

Keep soil healthy to promote the growth of vigorous, healthy plants, such as these tulips, ferns, and phlox, with minimal effort.

Soil Maintenance

Healthy soil is the basis of a healthy garden. Chapter 5 described how to prepare good soil for your shade garden. Once you've established a good growing medium, a little effort each year will ensure that the soil stays in good condition.

In established gardens, it's important to add fresh sources of organic matter to the garden each year, to maintain the structure and overall health of the soil. Organic matter improves the aeration, drainage, and water retention of the soil, and supports the underground community of earthworms, helpful insects, and microorganisms that keep soil healthy. Living soil is healthy soil, which supports the growth of sturdy, vigorous plants with a minimum of effort from the gardener. Adding organic matter to the soil annually is the single best thing you can do for your garden.

Once a year, in spring or fall (winter in warm climates), spread a 1-inch layer of compost, leaf mold, or other organic material over the entire garden. In areas where you grow annuals and the soil is bare at this time of year, dig or till the organic matter into the upper 6 inches of the soil.

In areas where perennials, bulbs, and woody plants are growing, begin by loosening the soil with a hand cultivator. Work carefully to avoid disturbing roots. Spread handfuls of organic matter around and between plants, and over the surface of the soil where bulbs are planted. Scratch the

Loosen soil with a hand cultivator before you add mulch to a garden containing perennials, bulbs, and woody plants.

material lightly into the soil with your cultivator, or work it into the loosened soil with your fingers. Where ground covers are planted, pull the trailing stems aside and work the compost into the soil as best you can.

If your soil is naturally fertile, or if you're growing native plants, you may find that these yearly additions of organic matter are all the fertilizer your soil needs. To provide a variety of nutrients for plants, make compost from a variety of ingredients and include some of the nutrient-rich materials used as organic fertilizers, which are described below.

Fertilizing

Although plants growing in the shade have a slower rate of photosynthesis than plants growing in full sun, they still need a continuous supply of nutrients in order to flourish. Plants growing among tree roots will need more frequent infusions of nutrients in order to compete with the more vigorous roots of the trees. Annuals, too, benefit especially from fertile soil.

You can use either organic or synthetic fertilizers to feed your plants. Acid-loving plants such as rhododendrons need specially formulated fertilizers that make nutrients available in a form these plants can use. Package

Spread a layer of leaf mold, compost, or other organic matter over your garden once a year to keep the soil healthy.

labels clearly identify which fertilizers are made for acid-loving plants.

Foliage plants prefer plenty of nitrogen, and flowering plants need larger amounts of phosphorus and potassium, but there are many all-purpose fertilizers that will nourish a wide variety of plants. For all-purpose use, look for a formula with relatively balanced amounts of the three major nutrients—nitrogen, phosphorus, and potassium—such as a 5-10-5, 10-10-10, or 5-3-3.

Fertilizers are available in powdered, granular, or liquid form. Many gardeners find that liquid formulas, which are diluted in water for use, are the most convenient kind to use for plants growing in containers. Organic gardeners rely on fish emulsion or fish-seaweed concentrates as all-purpose liquid fertilizers. As a rule of thumb, feed container plants monthly with liquid fertilizer while they are actively growing. Fertilize plants in smaller pots every couple of weeks. You can use some fertilizers more frequently, especially if they're diluted to half-strength. The best advice is to follow the directions on the label of the product you buy.

Application rates for dry fertilizers vary, depending on whether the product is organic or synthetic. Again, read package directions carefully.

Organic fertilizers must be applied before they're needed—something the labels don't always tell you. It takes time for the nutrients in organic materials to become available to plants in the soil. In a new garden, you can prepare the soil a season before you plant, or you can apply synthetic fertilizer along with the organic product when you do the initial planting to provide for both the short- and long-term nutrient needs of the plants. When the garden is established, if you get into a regular routine of adding organic fertilizer in spring before planting and in fall when you clean up the garden for the winter, there always will be plenty of nutrients available for plants.

Many gardeners like to add trace elements to the soil in addition to the three major nutrients. A soil test will show you if your soil is deficient in trace minerals. Organic materials that supply trace elements include kelp and other seaweed (which contain a variety of minerals), eggshells (calcium), dolomitic limestone (calcium and magnesium), Epsom salts (magnesium), and household borax (boron).

Synthetic fertilizers are more concentrated than organic materials, and their nutrients are available to plants quickly. Many of these fertilizers are meant to be applied monthly or several times during the growing season. If you inadvertently get some powdered fertilizer on plant foliage, rinse it off promptly with a hose, or the fertilizer could burn the leaves. Too much fertilizer also can damage roots.

Organic Fertilizers

If you garden organically, you can use one of the preblended organic fertilizers that are now widely available, or you can add individual nutrient sources to the soil. When buying preblended fertilizers, read the label to make sure the product is truly organic. Look for ingredients like the following:

Organic nitrogen. Sources include livestock manure, blood meal or dried blood, bonemeal (which contains a small amount), cottonseed meal, fish emulsion and fish products, guano, and soybean meal.

Organic phosphorus. Sources include bonemeal (although most of the bonemeal sold today is so highly processed that its nutrient content is questionable), colloidal phosphate, rock phosphate, guano, blood meal or dried blood (small amount), and fish products (also containing just a small amount).

Organic potassium. Sources include greensand, granite dust, seaweed, wood ashes, and fish products (small amount).

If you grow acid-lovers such as rhododendrons, you'll need to apply specially formulated fertilizers that make nutrients available in a form the plants can use.

Whatever kind of fertilizer you use, never use more than the package instructions direct. In addition to the potential for plant damage caused by overfertilizing, runoff can occur. Excess fertilizer that is not absorbed by plant roots is leached through the soil by rain and watering, and can eventually end up polluting the water table.

Mulching

Mulches can be an enormous work saver in the garden. They slow the rate at which moisture evaporates from the soil, so you have to water less frequently during dry spells. Mulches also help keep the soil cooler, which is beneficial to many plants in hot weather. A good layer of mulch will discourage weeds, too, preventing light from reaching their seeds and stimulating them to germinate. In winter, mulch can help prevent roots of dormant perennials from being heaved out of the soil during periods of thawing and freezing.

Mulches are not for every garden, however. Slugs and earwigs love to hide under loose mulches of shredded leaves, wood chips, or cocoa-bean hulls. If these pests are already a problem in your garden, mulching could encourage even more of them to take up residence. If your soil tends to be poorly drained and a bit on the soggy side, mulch could make it even soggier and eventually contribute to root rot. You would do better to work organic matter into the soil instead of spreading it on top.

Organic mulches are the most versatile and attractive in the garden, and are generally most appropriate for shady locations. They add organic matter to the soil as they decompose, which is especially valuable for shade plants because so many of them prefer humusy soil. Organic materials to use for mulch include cocoa-bean hulls, shredded leaves, compost, straw, shredded bark, pine needles, and wood chips. Add extra nitrogen fertilizer to the soil if you mulch with wood or bark chips, because wood draws nitrogen from the soil as it decomposes. Hay also makes good mulch, but it

ABOVE: Mulch around hostas, such as these 'Golden Tiara,' to help conserve moisture and discourage weeds. The large leaves of many hostas act as a mulch, producing similar results.

is likely to contain seeds that could lead to weed problems in the garden. Salt marsh hay is especially valuable as mulch, but there is growing concern that overharvesting may remove too much of the natural grass population from wetlands.

Most mulches are effective when spread 2 inches deep. Coarse materials such as straw are more effective at a depth of 4 inches, and fine materials such as cocoa-bean hulls are best at a depth of 1 inch. Lay summer mulches when the soil has warmed in spring and plants are several inches high. If you spread the mulch while the soil is still cold, it will keep the soil cold longer, delaying the growth of perennials and the planting of annuals.

Apply winter mulches after the ground freezes in early winter. The

ABOVE: Be wary about applying certain types of mulches in your garden if slugs or earwigs are a problem or the soil is poorly drained.

Mulches
- Cocoa-bean hulls
- Straw
- Pine needles
- Shredded bark
- Wood chips
- Compost
- Shredded leaves
- Dried grass clippings
- Buckwheat hulls
- Marble chips
- Pecan hulls
- Black plastic

purpose of a winter mulch is to keep the soil frozen during winter warm spells. When soil thaws and then refreezes repeatedly, it tends to buckle and heave, and dormant roots can be pushed out of the ground. Once exposed to frigid temperatures and drying winter winds, the roots are likely to die. A winter mulch prevents the soil from thawing during midwinter mild spells, lessening the chance that heaving will occur. In spring, when temperatures begin to moderate, pull aside or rake away the mulch to let the soil warm.

Watering

All plants need water to grow. The amount and frequency of moisture needed varies from plant to plant, but unless you're growing drought-tolerant plants or have special conditions such as a bog garden, you probably will have to water the garden occasionally to supplement rainfall.

Some generalizations can be made about watering, although they should not be followed literally. Generally, gardeners living in dry climates will need to water more often than gardeners in regions with higher rainfall. Shallow-rooted plants and plants growing in fast-draining, sandy soils need moisture from natural or artificial sources more often than plants that are deep-rooted or growing in heavy clay soils or soils rich in organic matter.

As a rule, plants growing in the shade don't need to be watered as often as those in sunny locations. Plants growing amid tree roots, however, will need regular watering to help them compete with the greedy tree roots surrounding them. Plants growing under trees with large leaves also may need watering because rain falling from overhead has difficulty penetrating the foliage canopy to reach the soil. Check garden areas after it rains to see if any of them are still dry because of thick overhead foliage.

Water shortages are expected to become more frequent and widespread across the United States in years to come, and as good gardeners you should strive to use water as efficiently as you can to avoid squandering this precious resource.

ABOVE: Rainfall alone provides sufficient moisture to sustain the primroses and phlox in this bog garden.

Water your plants faithfully if they must compete with nearby thirsty tree roots.

Moisture and Water Conservation

Most plants—even drought-tolerant ones—need soil that is evenly moist, but not soggy, as they become established in the garden. Moist soil enables seeds to germinate and new roots to develop. The period of establishment varies from plant to plant. Annual and perennial transplants and bulbs become established in a few weeks. Trees, shrubs, and woody ground covers may take as long as a year to fully settle into their new homes. Every garden is different, and you will have to judge for yourself when your plants need water.

As a basic guide, you can begin by assuming that annuals and perennials will need watering once a week if no rain falls. Trees and shrubs will need to be watered every

ABOVE: Water annuals and perennials about once a week if there's no rainfall.
BELOW: Water trees and shrubs every week to 10 days the first year, less often once they become established.

week to 10 days during their first year in the garden. Once established, they should need watering less often. Hot, dry weather, sandy soil, and above-average needs for moisture in particular plants call for more frequent watering.

If you have gardens in both sunny and shady areas, the shady gardens usually will need watering less often that the sunny gardens. In gardens receiving little or no direct sun, moisture evaporates more slowly than it does in bright, sunny gardens. It's important not to overwater the shady garden. Soil that is constantly wet can lead to root rot.

You can conserve water and still give your plants the moisture they need to grow well. First, water only when it's necessary. The old rule of giving the garden an inch of water a week doesn't hold true for all plants in all soils and climates, although

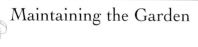

it's a reasonable average. A garden in a cool, shady location in heavy clay soil will need less than an inch of water a week, while a seashore or desert garden in light, sandy soil will need more. Don't blindly follow someone else's rules for watering, or set the timer on an automatic watering system and leave it the same all summer. Water your plants when they need it.

The best way to tell when your garden needs water is to poke a finger into the soil. When the ground feels dry more than an inch or two below the surface, it's time to water. Don't wait to water until your plants wilt or appear limp; wilting indicates severe water stress. Your goal should be to get water to plants before they become stressed, and checking the soil regularly will let you do so.

Second, water deeply and less often. When it's time to water the plants, water deeply so the moisture soaks far down into the soil. Deep watering encourages plants to send roots downward into the soil, where they'll be able to find more water during dry weather. You'll save water, because you won't have to water as often. The plants will be less dependent on you to supply all the moisture they need. If you water lightly and often—say a quick sprinkling from the hose every day—the plants will concentrate their roots near the soil surface, where they'll be vulnerable to dry weather and hot sun.

Third, reduce watering by mulching the garden as described above.

Overhead watering is less efficient than applying water directly to the soil.

To use the least amount of water, it's important to get the water to plants in the most efficient way possible. It's best to apply the water directly to the soil, where roots can use it. Soaker hoses and drip irrigation systems are two ways to water at ground level. Both are preferable to the traditional method of watering from overhead with a hose or automatic sprinkler. Overhead watering wastes water, because the water must filter down through the leaves to get to the soil and because water is lost to evaporation on hot days before it can reach the ground.

If you must water from overhead, do it in the morning or late afternoon, avoiding the hottest part of the day. If you water late in the day, be sure several hours of daylight remain so plant leaves can dry before dark. Wet leaves at night invite mildew and other diseases.

A better approach to watering the garden is to install a drip irrigation system or soaker hoses. Soaker hoses are made of canvas, fiber, or recycled tires, and allow water to trickle slowly through pores

in their walls. The hoses connect to one another and to an outdoor faucet that you turn on only partway. Lay the hoses through the garden early in the season when plants are still small, and cover them with mulch to hide them.

You can put together a drip irrigation system from a kit, or buy the component parts individually. Drip systems use lengths of narrow plastic tubing with small perforations along the sides. The tubing is connected with couplings and can be hooked up to a timer to run automatically. Drip systems usually are installed under the surface of the soil.

Efficient Watering Systems

Soaker hose

Drip irrigation system

Watering Plants in Containers

Viola cornuta 'Princess Blue' and 'Princess Yellow' decorate a large ceramic basket.

Because the volume of soil in a container—even a large tub—is so much smaller than that in even a minuscule garden in the ground, it dries out rapidly outdoors. Plants growing in containers need to be watered much more often than plants growing in the ground. In hot weather, especially on clear, windy days, you'll need to water potted plants in all but large tubs and barrels daily and small pots often twice a day, to give the plants the moisture they need. The smaller the container, the faster it will dry out. Plastic pots don't allow moisture to evaporate as quickly as porous clay pots, and grouping potted plants together also helps. You also might want to add a water-retentive polymer to your potting mix, to decrease watering frequency. These products are now widely available in garden centers. They get mixed reviews from gardeners. You'll need to water container plants often in summer even if you use these new products. Check container plants every day, or twice a day, and water whenever the soil feels dry below the surface.

If you're watering pots set inside decorative cachepots that don't have drainage holes, it's important to remove any excess water not absorbed by plant roots. Letting plants sit in water for extended lengths of time leads to root rot. If any water remains in the bottom of the cachepot 15 minutes after watering, pour it off.

This is the quickest way to saturate dry soil, but it's only practical for plants of modest size. If a plant or plants in a large, heavy container become wilted, remoisten the soil with conventional watering methods, using a watering can or hose. Just make sure you water thoroughly. When water begins leaking from the drainage holes in the bottom of the container, you can be reasonably sure that the soil is wet.

Water plants in tubs and barrels often during hot weather.

CPR for Dried-Out Container Plants

If a small to medium-size plant in a pot starts to wilt, you can probably save it if the wilting isn't too severe. Fill a bucket with water. The bucket should be large enough to comfortably hold the pot and deeper than the pot is high. Grasp the pot by

its upper rim with both hands, and plunge it into the bucket until the pot is submerged. You may want to first cover the soil surface with a paper towel or piece of cloth so soil doesn't float out of the pot. You'll see bubbles rising to the surface as air is forced from the dry potting mix and replaced with water. When the bubbling stops, the soil is saturated. Remove the pot from the bucket and let it drain. Mist the plant's leaves with tepid water, and set the pot in a shady location for a few hours until the plant recovers.

Pests and Diseases

Shady gardens tend to be less afflicted by pests than sunny gardens, but pests and diseases still can cause problems. In the garden, as in life, prevention is often the best cure. Healthy plants are less likely to suffer damage from pests and diseases than weak, sickly plants.

When choosing plants for your garden, select those that are well-suited to the growing conditions you have available. Be realistic in assessing your site. If you have full shade, a plant that likes partial shade is not going to thrive. It will be weak and spindly, and a likely target for pests and disease organisms. If you want to grow plants that need more light than your garden offers, try to modify the shade as described in Chapter 1 to let in more light.

Be equally prudent in assessing available moisture and soil type. You can modify conditions somewhat to create a better environment for plants, but you can only do so much. If you live in the Southwest and have dry, alkaline soil, don't try to grow mountain laurel, wintergreen, or other plants from the forests of the Northeast, where the soil is acid.

In addition to selecting plants that are compatible with your growing conditions, you can help reduce the threat of pests and disease by following the cultural practices outlined earlier in this chapter to keep plants strong and vigorous. Supply your soil with organic matter and nutrients, but avoid overfertilizing. Water when plants need it, but don't overwater.

Keeping the garden clean also helps prevent problems. If you don't mulch the garden, keep it weeded. Pick up dead leaves and flowers, fallen twigs and branches, and other debris. Plant trash lying about on the ground provides an excellent hiding place for pests to overwinter and lay their eggs, as well as a site for disease organisms to move in. Prune dead and damaged growth from trees and shrubs at least once a year, as described later in this chapter. Proper pruning helps keep woody plants healthy and vigorous.

Mulch can be a mixed blessing in a shady garden. Although it's wonderful

Thin plants such as phlox to improve air circulation. It will discourage growth of mildew, mold, and fungal diseases.

for conserving moisture, it offers a perfect hiding place for the slugs, snails, and earwigs that often afflict plants in the shade. It also can harbor disease organisms, especially in moist, humid climates or unusually wet conditions. If your garden has problems with mildew, molds, blights, or other fungal diseases, try removing the mulch every fall and spreading fresh mulch the following season. It also may help to plant disease-resistant varieties when possible.

When you plant the garden, allow adequate space between plants so air can circulate freely among them. Poor air circulation encourages the growth of mildew, mold, and fungal diseases.

Mixing many kinds of plants in the garden rather than planting a collection of one type of plant—all azaleas, or all hostas, for example—also can reduce the risk of pests and diseases.

Monitor the garden closely throughout the growing season so you can catch problems quickly when they occur. Examine your plants frequently for signs of pests and diseases. Check the growing tips, leaf axils, undersides of leaves, and buds. Look for chewing, holes, or discoloration of leaves and flowers.

Reduce the risk of pests and diseases in your garden by mixing different types of plants rather than growing a single type of plant.

Ousting Insects

If you spot a problem, act immediately. Delaying action will only worsen the problem. The safest approach is to use natural and plant-based controls that break down quickly after they're applied and don't linger in the environment.

Insecticidal soap is effective against small insects such as **aphids** and **whiteflies**, and it's gentle to beneficial wildlife. Lures and traps that employ pheromone baits, sticky substances, or insect-attracting colors also can be useful.

As a last resort, use plant-based insecticides, such as rotenone, pyrethrum, ryania, and neem. These insecticides are effective and break down quickly in the environment but kill beneficial insects as well as pests.

If **slugs** and **snails** plague your garden, you can trap them in saucers of beer sunk into the ground, and they'll drown. Beer traps, however, may draw slugs from your neighbor's garden as well, so you may want to locate the traps outside the garden. If you're ambitious, you can go out at night with a flashlight, a pair of gloves, and a shaker of salt, and sprinkle slugs with salt to kill them. Salt causes a slow and gruesome death, however, and you're left with unpleasant heaps of slug mush to clean up.

A better solution is to drop the slugs into a bucket of soapy water. Commercial slug and snail baits are effective, but they're not recommended where curious pets or small children could ingest them.

Barriers also can keep slugs and snails out of the garden. Sprinkle wood ashes or diatomaceous earth around the garden perimeter, and slugs and snails will avoid it because

Slug Deterrents

Trap slugs and snails by sinking saucers of beer in the ground. They'll drown. You're likely to attract even more slugs, however, so place the beer traps outside the garden.

Slugs are a relentless bunch. If other strategies fail, try poison bait in infested areas. You'll need to reapply the poison after rainfalls.

the abrasive material damages their soft bodies. Use diatomaceous earth intended for horticultural use, not the type used in swimming pool filters.

The tannin in fresh wood chips also is reputed to repel slugs and snails. Copper strips are another effective barrier.

Earwigs are a troublesome pest in many shady gardens. You can trap them by providing cozy daytime hiding places. One method is to place rolled-up newspapers in various parts of the garden. Another technique is to crumple a sheet of paper and put it in a tin can. Lay the can on the ground on its side, or place it upside down on a short stick, close to the plants that seem to be suffering the worst damage. The earwigs will crawl inside the paper during the day. In the morning, collect the paper traps (either kind) and burn them, dump the contents into a small jar of kerosene, or seal them inside plastic bags and put them in the garbage.

Root weevils can be a problem in West Coast gardens. The larvae of these beetles do the worst damage, chewing on roots and underground stems, and eventually killing the plants. Unfortunately, some of the choicest shade plants rank near the top of the root weevil menu. They seem especially fond of pieris, azaleas, rhododendrons, and viburnums, as well as perennials such as astilbe, bergenia, corydalis, and hardy cyclamen. If you notice a plant suddenly going limp despite receiving plenty of

Root weevils have a distinct preference for many shade plants, including pieris.

moisture, then turning brown and drying up, root weevils are a likely cause. Watch, too, for leaves that are chewed around the edges—that's a sign of the adult beetles.

You can kill weevil larvae with repeated applications of soil-drench insecticides, but there's no guarantee they won't come back. Probably the best defense is a healthy soil, rich in organic matter, and a thriving community of beneficial insects. The balance of nature will do more than insecticides to keep the weevil population in check.

Discouraging Deer

There is, unfortunately, no foolproof way to keep deer from eating your plants, short of enclosing the entire garden with netting or fencing. When deer are hungry enough, they will eat almost anything. To exclude deer, a fence must be at least 8 feet tall—they can jump surprisingly high. The most effective fence is a double-walled con-struction with a second fence 3 to 4 feet high placed inside the taller fence. Angle the top of the outer fence outward.

You can enclose special trees, plants, or beds of plants in cages made of wire or plastic mesh stapled to a wood frame. Use plastic tree guards or tree wrap to protect the trunks of trees. Cover small plants with floating covers of spunbonded polyester securely anchored at the edges. The covers are available at most garden centers.

Because covers and cages are unattractive solutions, some gardeners use repellents to discourage deer—with varying degrees of success.

Wrap wire or plastic mesh around plants to deter deer, one of the most common pests in shade gardens.

Deer Repellents

Although no deer repellents are foolproof, try these if deer are ravaging your garden:
◆ Blood meal or dried blood sprinkled around the garden (reapply after rainfall)
◆ Bars of soap hung from trees near the garden
◆ Hot pepper solution sprayed on plants (reapply after rainfall)
◆ Mesh bags of human hair hung from trees
◆ Strips of aluminum foil, mylar, or cloth hung from a wire or string running around the perimeter of the garden
◆ Commercial repellents

Shade Plants and Deer

Plants Deer Love
Don't grow these shade plants that are deer favorites:

Azaleas
Cardinal flower
English ivy
Euonymus
Firs
Hardy geraniums
Hollies
Hostas
Impatiens
Irises
Meadow-rue
Phlox
Rhododendrons
Tulips
Wood hyacinth
Yews

Plants Deer Avoid
Grow these shade plants that deer are less likely to eat:

Anemone
Baneberry
Bee-balm
Bishop's weed
Boxwood
Bugleweed
Calendula
Daffodils and narcissus
Ferns
Forget-me-nots
Foxglove
Inkberry
Joe-Pye weed
Leucothoe
Lily-of-the-valley
Monkshood
Mountain laurel
Periwinkle
Pines
Spruces

Bee-balm

Baneberry

Combating Disease

If you notice signs of disease when you inspect your plants, immediately remove the infected part of the plant. If more symptoms develop, pull up the entire plant and put it in the trash. Never put diseased plant material on the compost pile; even a hot pile is unlikely to get hot enough to destroy all pathogens.

Sulfur sprays can help control fungus and mildew before they take hold in the garden. Chemical fungicides also are effective. Use all such products with care. Check with your county extension agent or a reliable local nursery about the best time to apply fungicides and the correct kind to use for diseases common in your area.

Whatever pesticide or fungicide products you use, handle them with extreme caution and follow the directions on the package to the letter. Even organic, plant-based products that degrade quickly are poisonous when you apply them, and they should never be treated casually. Follow instructions for mixing, applying, and storing all of these products. Always wear gloves to handle them, and don't spray or dust on a windy day when you might inhale them or get them on your skin. Keep them out of the reach of children and pets. If you wish to dispose of unused material, check with local authorities about proper procedures for disposing of hazardous household wastes. Many towns have special collection sites and times for these materials. Never pour leftover pesticides or fungicides on the ground or down the drain. Don't flush them down the toilet.

Tools you may find helpful for pruning chores include various types of pruning saws, long-handled loppers, short-handled loppers, anvil-type hand pruning shears, scissors-type hand pruning shears, and hedge shears.

Pruning

If your garden includes trees and shrubs, you'll need to do at least some pruning. To keep pruning chores to a minimum, allow plants to assume their natural form as much as possible. When choosing a location for a new tree or shrub, make sure there is enough space for the plant to grow to its mature size. Select plants that are in scale with the size of your garden; if space is limited, choose compact plants and dwarf varieties. Don't try to train a plant to grow in an unnat-ural form. If a plant naturally grows to a rounded, bushy shape, don't try to prune it to a narrow upright. A formal garden with neat topiaries and espaliers requires frequent, painstaking pruning and clipping to maintain.

Another don't in relation to pruning involves the all-too-common practice of topping trees. It's never a good idea to simply hack off the ends of all the branches to leave a bunch of short, stumpy limbs. It looks terrible, and the new growth that is produced often comes in dense, twiggy, and crowded—an unhealthy situation.

Tools for Pruning

Buy good, sturdy tools for pruning, and keep them sharp.

Hand pruning shears will cut stems and branches up to about 1 inch in diameter. This is one of the most useful gardening tools you'll own.

Long-handled loppers will cut branches with a diameter slightly larger than 1 inch. Use them to cut branches overhead and in hard-to-reach places, to cut stems back to the ground, and to thin or rejuvenate overgrown shrubs.

Pruning saws allow you to remove branches up to 4 or 5 inches in diameter. Larger branches call for a chain saw.

Hedge shears are best for neatly trimming hedges. You also can use them to keep some ground covers in bounds.

Maintaining the Garden

Prune trees and shrubs to keep them healthy, improve their appearance, and ensure a safe environment.

14 Reasons to Prune Trees and Shrubs—and When to Do It

Generally, you should prune trees and shrubs to maintain their health, improve their form, and ensure convenience and safety. Specific reasons for pruning include:

♦ To remove dead and broken branches
♦ To remove branches that are diseased or infested with insects
♦ To remove weak, V-shaped crotches
♦ To remove girdling roots
♦ To reduce wind resistance and possible storm damage
♦ To improve light penetration and air circulation
♦ To shape for aesthetic or other reasons
♦ To direct new growth
♦ To renew an old tree or shrub
♦ To eliminate suckers and wild growth
♦ To hold a tree or shrub within bounds
♦ To produce new fall growth for winter color
♦ To encourage growth of larger fruits and flowers
♦ To keep paths clear and accessible

Most pruning is done in winter or very early spring, when plants are dormant. There are a few exceptions to the standard practice. Shrubs and vines that bloom on old wood, such as mock orange, set their flower buds for the following year before the end of the current growing season. Prune these plants shortly after they finish blooming, or you'll run the risk of pruning away some of next year's flower buds. Remove suckers that grow around the base of some trees and shrubs and water sprouts that grow vertically from the branches of some trees in summer—whenever you notice them. Remove diseased wood promptly to prevent the spread of infection. Prompt pruning may save a tree.

Pruning Trees and Shrubs

Maintenance Pruning

As part of normal maintenance, remove crossed branches, branches growing into utility wires or against the house, and weak branches overhanging your roof. You also may want to remove large branches with a weak crotch—branches that leave the trunk at a very sharp angle and would be likely to snap in an ice storm or in strong winds.

Removing Damaged and Diseased Growth

When a tree or shrub is damaged by a storm or exhibits signs of disease, remove the affected branches immediately. Cut branches back to the collar, the swollen ridge of bark that is visible where the branch joins the trunk. Don't cut into the collar itself, and don't leave a stub extending beyond the collar. Either practice increases the possibility of disease or insect invasion.

To remove part of a branch, cut back to a bud or a smaller branch to avoid leaving a bare stub.

When removing diseased wood, cut back to healthy tissue at least several inches away from the diseased portion. After each cut, dip your pruning tool into rubbing alcohol or a solution of chlorine bleach and water to sterilize it.

After you remove a branch, don't cover the cut with wound dressing or tree paint. These sealants can actually hinder the healing process.

Pruning for Shape

To improve a tree's shape, prune selectively to thin out dense, twiggy

Prune trees and shrubs to improve their shape, thinning out dense, twiggy growth and branches that are crowded together.

Remove lower tree branches to let in more light, to make it easier to walk underneath, or to expose decorative bark on the trunk.

Removing Large Limbs

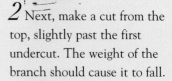

1 First, cut halfway through the limb from underneath, several inches from the trunk.

2 Next, make a cut from the top, slightly past the first undercut. The weight of the branch should cause it to fall.

3 Finally, cut off the remaining stub close to the trunk. Cut outside the branch bark ridge and collar.

growth that looks cluttered and branches that are crowded too closely together. This type of pruning is the most difficult, because it's based largely on aesthetic judgments that take practice and skill to develop. When you attempt this kind of pruning, start by removing twigs and small branches, and gradually work up to larger limbs. Step back and look at your work often, perhaps even after each cut, until you gain experience. When in doubt, be conservative; prune less rather than more.

Directing Growth

You also can prune to direct a plant's growth. When you cut back to a bud, the new growth will develop in the direction the bud is facing. To encourage bushier, denser growth on a tree or shrub that looks sparse, prune back to the buds on the inside of the branches. To promote a more open habit, prune to outward-facing buds.

When you prune back to a bud, make the cut ¼ to ½ inch above the bud. Don't cut closer to the bud than ¼ inch, or farther away from the bud than ½ inch.

Limiting Growth

Pruning can limit a plant's growth. Hedges are sheared regularly to keep them at the desired height. When you clip a hedge, angle the sides so they're slightly wider at the bottom than at the top. The angled shape allows all the foliage to receive light and prevents development of bare lower stems as the plants age.

Pruning Shrubs

Heading back
Heading back a shrub reduces its size, improves its shape, and promotes vigor.

Thinning out
Thinning out a shrub lets in more light and improves air circulation around the plant.

Severe heading back
Severe heading back stimulates production of a few strong stems and showier flowers.

Regular pruning also can keep trees and shrubs growing in containers happier longer in their limited space.

Flowering shrubs often are pruned in a similar way, in a process called heading back. Heading back means, simply, removing part of a branch. Heading back keeps plants smaller, and on flowering shrubs that bloom on new wood (the current season's growth), it improves the shape and encourages fresh, vigorous growth.

To head back a plant, cut the ends of the branches at ¼ to ½ inch above a bud. Make the cut on an angle, with the bottom of the cut just about even with the top of the bud. Step back often and look at your work, to make sure you like the shape you're creating.

Thinning and Rejuvenating

In many cases, you can restore dense, overgrown shrubs to vigor with severe pruning. Shrubs that tend to form clumps or thickets are particularly good candidates for this treatment. To rejuvenate an old shrub, cut one-third of the oldest stems back to a few inches from the ground. Repeat the process annually for the next two years. After the third year, the shrub should be renewed, with fresh, healthy new growth. Keep the shrub well watered and fertilized during the growing season to nourish the new growth.

Rejuvenate an overgrown shrub by removing about a third of the oldest, inner canes to improve air circulation and let in more light.

Deadheading and Pinching

Removing faded flowers and pinching back the tips of nonwoody plants also are forms of pruning.

Deadheading

Deadheading, the term used for removing old flower heads, prevents a plant from producing seeds. It may induce repeat bloom in perennials, and it encourages annuals to continue producing more flowers. On any plant, deadheading helps the plant remain vigorous because none of its energy will be channeled into seed production. When you deadhead a plant with a branched, bushy habit, cut back the flower stem to the near-est set of leaves; don't just clip off the flower and leave a bare stem. To dead-head a plant that produces its flowers on a tall stem above a low clump of leaves, such as astilbe or columbine, cut off the flower stem at its base.

Pinching Back

Annuals and perennials with a branched form, such as coleus, becomes bushier if you pinch back the tips of the stems when the plants are young. Pinching encour-ages more side shoots to grow. Pinch off the tip of the young stem back to the next set of leaves. New shoots will form in the leaf axils. To make the plant even bushier, pinch back the tips of the new shoots when they're long enough.

Deadheading Plants

To encourage increased flowering, deadhead plants by cutting back flower stems to the nearest set of leaves.

Shade Plants to Deadhead

- ◆ Calendula
- ◆ Coleus
- ◆ Collinsia
- ◆ Nicotiana
- ◆ Salvia
- ◆ Viola

Pinching Back Plants

To promote bushier growth on plants, pinch back stems to the set of leaves below the uppermost set.

Shade Plants to Pinch Back

- ◆ Coleus
- ◆ Foxglove
- ◆ Fuchsia
- ◆ Hypoestes
- ◆ Lobelia
- ◆ Nicotiana

Deadheading and pinching back shade plants such as coleus (above) and nicotiana (inset) can result in bushier growth, increased flower production, and a longer bloom period.

Maintaining the Garden

Garden Cleanup

When the garden winds down for the season in fall, or the pace at least slows in winter in warm climates, it's a good time to clean up the garden in preparation for the next growing season. Pull up spent annuals and put them on the compost pile. Pull weeds, and gather material for winter mulch, if you plan to use one. Don't spread the mulch over the garden until the ground freezes. In warm-climate gardens, renew mulches that have worn thin on gardens still actively growing.

Clean up dropped flowers, twigs, and other plant debris. Dispose of any diseased or insect-infested plant material in the trash—don't add it to the compost pile. Rake and shred fallen autumn leaves to use for mulch or to make leaf mold or compost.

Before the first frost, dig any tender bulbs you want to save. Spread out the bulbs in a cool, airy place and let them dry for a couple of weeks. Brush

Autumn is the ideal time of year to clean up the garden. When raking leaves and cutting back dead stems, remove any weeds or diseased plants you find.

Clean up dropped flowers, twigs, and other plant debris. Compost healthy plant cuttings, but discard diseased material.

off any loose soil clinging to them, and inspect them for soft spots, mold, and rot. If the bulbs are sound, wrap them in newspaper or spread them on a shelf in a cool, dark, dry place where the temperature won't fall below 40° F over the winter.

When perennials begin to die, or after the first frost, cut them back to within a few inches of the ground. Don't cut all the way to ground level or you could inadvertently damage the crowns. Remove stakes and other temporary supports, and store them for next year.

Spread slow-working organic fertilizers such as rock powders over the garden in late fall so they can begin decomposing in the soil. Don't apply fast-release synthetic fertilizers now.

If winter weather brings heavy rains or snow to your garden, you may want to cover your compost pile with a tarp to protect it.

If you grew annuals in pots, tubs, window boxes, or hanging baskets, clean out the containers. Dump the soil mix into the garden unless the plants had diseases. Brush out the pots. Scrub the containers in warm water, without soap, to loosen any accumulated fertilizer salts. Then soak clay pots in a solution of 1 part liquid chlorine bleach to 9 parts water for an hour or so. If the containers are too big to soak, rinse them with the bleach solution. Allow the containers to dry completely, then store them for the winter.

In window boxes or other permanently mounted containers, remove annuals and at least half of the soil mix. In spring, add fresh soil mix before planting. Wait until spring to remove old soil from containers that hold plants all winter.

Gardeners in the North who grow tender perennials in containers should bring the containers indoors when the weather turns cool, before the first frost occurs. Check the plants carefully before you bring them indoors, to make sure they aren't harboring whiteflies or other pests. If insects are present, treat plants with insecticidal soap or another pesticide. Isolate the plants from the rest of your houseplants and monitor them closely when you do bring them back indoors.

Propagating

There are many ways to reproduce plants asexually, that is, without seeds. The process is known as vegetative, or asexual, propagation. Propagating plants in your garden is a good way to get more plants inexpensively and is a necessary part of maintaining perennials and bulbs that spread to form crowded clumps. Propagation techniques also make it possible to reproduce hybrids that can't be grown from seed and other plants that seldom produce seeds under normal garden conditions or are difficult to grow from seed. Three simple propagation methods are discussed below.

Propagation by Division

Dividing Perennials

Many perennials and bulbs spread by offsets or underground rhizomes to produce new plants. When the clump of plants becomes too crowded, flowering declines or ceases altogether, and the plants lose some of their vigor. When this happens, it's time to divide the plants to rejuvenate them.

Divide perennials when they aren't blooming. Early spring is the best time to divide plants that flower in summer and fall. Spring bloomers usually are divided in fall or, in Zone 5 and north, after they finish blooming. When dividing plants in autumn, do it four to six weeks before you expect the first frost, so the new divisions can develop new roots before they go into their winter dormant period.

Begin by cutting back all the stems to within a few inches of the ground. Brush away the topsoil from around the base of the plant to expose the crowns. Push a spade or shovel vertically into the soil in a ring around the plant, keeping well away from the crowns. Then push the shovel in at an angle under the roots, and lever it back and forth to loosen the plant. Lift the plant out of the ground, leaving intact as many of the roots as you can. If the plant has fibrous roots, pull apart the clump of crowns with your hands. For thicker, tougher roots, cut the clump apart with a sharp knife or a hatchet. Pull or cut the clump into sections to create several smaller crowns, each of which has both stems and roots, and several growth buds or eyes around the base, from which new growth will emerge.

Remove and discard the old, tough, woodier, central portion of the original plant, and replant the younger, outer portions. Work quickly, so the roots and crowns don't dry out.

Replant the divisions immediately, at the same depth they were growing when they were part of the original plant. Water well after replanting.

Divide summer- and fall-flowering plants such as hostas in early spring and spring-blooming plants such as tulips in fall.

Dividing Perennials

1 Dig around the outside of a clump. Use a shovel or fork under the root ball to loosen the roots. Remove the clump.

2 Gently shake or brush excess soil from the root ball. Pull or cut the clump apart, saving the outer sections.

3 Replant the divisions immediately, before they begin to dry out. Water them well.

Divide daffodils in late spring or early summer, after they've finished blooming but before they go dormant.

Dividing Bulbs

To divide a clump of bulbs, dig it up after the plants have bloomed, when the foliage turns yellow. For true bulbs, such as narcissus, simply separate the smaller offset bulbs from the parent. Replant the new bulbs and the original bulbs at the correct depth and spacing. (See Chapter 4 or a book on bulbs for this information.)

To divide a scaly bulb, such as a lily, carefully pull off the flat scales from around the outside of the parent bulb, as if you were separating cloves of garlic. Set the scales, with the pointed end facing upward, in containers of moist vermiculite or propagation mix. The scales will produce little bulblets, which you can plant in the garden to develop into new plants that will reach blooming size in a few years.

Plants that grow from corms, such as crocuses, are handled much

Dividing Bulbs

1 To divide a lily, dig up a bulb and pull off the scales from around the outside of the plant.

2 Insert the scales in a container of moist vermiculite or propagation mix, and water sparingly. Once roots appear, increase the amount of water.

the same as scaly bulbs, except the old corm is discarded instead of replanted after the young cormels are detached. Replant the cormels to grow into blooming-size plants.

To divide the tubers of tuberous begonias, cut a tuber into several pieces. Make sure each piece has at least one eye, or growth bud, from which new shoots can grow.

Propagation by Cuttings

Cuttings are pieces of a plant's top-growth that can be induced to form roots when severed from the parent plant. The most commonly used cuttings are taken from the ends of stems, but you also can take cuttings from other parts of stems, as well as from leaves and roots. Many annuals, perennials, shrubs, trees, and ground covers can be reproduced from cuttings.

Take cuttings to increase the number of coralbells in your garden.

Wax begonias are one of the easiest plants to propagate by cuttings.

Stem cuttings can be taken from soft (green) tissue, from harder wood, or at a stage in between known as semihardwood or semiripe.

Softwood or green cuttings come from the green stems of herbaceous perennials or annuals, or new growth of woody plants, and are taken when plants are growing actively. Take softwood cuttings about halfway through the plant's growing season. Generally, you take softwood cuttings of summer- and fall-blooming perennials in late spring, and from spring-blooming perennials, shrubs, and trees in summer. You also can take cuttings of annuals in fall to grow indoors for winter houseplants.

Use stems that are flexible but firm and can be bent without breaking or crushing. Young side shoots that are 2 to 6 inches long and of medium vigor are ideal. Cut the shoot at the base, where it joins the main stem. Don't remove a piece of the main stem (heel) along with the cutting. You also can take the cutting from the tip of a longer shoot, cutting right below a leaf or node (dormant bud).

Remove the leaves from the bottom half of each cutting, and insert the cutting in a container of moist rooting medium up to about one-third of its length. A good rooting medium is a mixture of equal parts of peat moss and perlite or vermiculite. Work quickly so the cuttings don't dry out. Keep the medium evenly moist until the cuttings root. Give the cuttings plenty of light.

Stem Cuttings

1 Cut a shoot at the base, where it joins the main stem, or cut from the tip of a longer shoot, right below a node or leaf joint.

2 Root the cutting in a moist mixture of peat moss and perlite or vermiculite, giving the cutting plenty of light.

Hardwood cuttings come from the current season's growth of trees and shrubs and are taken at the end of the growing season. The best time to take hardwood cuttings is in fall, when deciduous trees and shrubs drop their leaves. Use the ends of branches or canes, and cut the shoots into pieces 6 to 10 inches long. Try to make the bottom cut of each piece just below a node, and

Boxwood is propagated from hardwood cuttings taken in the fall.

Propagation by Layering

Layering is a way to root new plants before severing them from the parent. It's a good method of propagating ground covers, vines, and shrubs with low, flexible branches. Layering is easiest to accomplish if you're working in soil that is light, porous, and rich in organic matter. If your garden soil is not of this quality, carefully scoop out several inches of soil from around the base of the plant you want to layer and replace it with the soil mix described on page 186.

Healthy, 1-year-old shoots are best for layering. Layer in spring,

Hydrangeas are good shrubs to propagate by layering.

the top cut about ¼ inch above a bud. Cut the top on an angle and the bottom straight across so you remember which end is which.

Gather the cuttings into bundles if you have a lot of them, and store them over the winter in a cold frame or a 12-inch-deep trench in the ground. Stand the cuttings upright to store them, and cover them with sand. This winter cold storage is necessary to break the dormancy of hardy plants native to regions where winters are cold.

In spring, plant the cuttings as soon as you can work the soil, in a nursery bed where the soil is loose and well drained. Plant the cuttings about 8 inches apart, and bury them to the uppermost bud or pair of buds. Keep the soil evenly moist until the cuttings root, a process that takes about three months. When roots have formed, transplant the cuttings to individual containers.

Layering

1 Bend a section of stem into a shallow hole. Cover it with soil, leaving the tip of the shoot free.

2 Cut the new plant from the parent. Transplant it once you see new growth coming from the tip.

as soon as you can work the soil and before the plant begins its new season of active growth.

Insert the tip of a spade about 6 inches into the soil below the stem. Wiggle the blade back and forth to make a slit. Bend a stem to the ground and insert it into the slit. Hold the stem in place with U-shaped metal pins or clothespins. Bend the tip of the stem upward so 3 to 6 inches of it projects above the ground. Cover the buried part with more of the good soil mix, firm it well, and water.

Keep the soil moist until roots form. Roots can take from three months to three years to develop, depending on the plant. Pull gently on the stem occasionally or carefully remove some soil to see if roots have formed. When the stem has rooted, cut it from the parent plant and transplant it in a container or in a protected location where you can monitor it. Keep the soil evenly moist until the new plant becomes established and starts to grow.